SWEET JESUS,
I HATE
BILL O'REILLY

SWEET JESUS, *I HATE* BILL O'REILLY

JOSEPH MINTON AMANN & TOM BREUER

NATION BOOKS
NEW YORK

Sweet Jesus I Hate Bill O'Reilly
Copyright © Joseph Minton Amann and Tom Breuer 2006

Published by
Nation Books
An Imprint of Avalon Publishing Group, Inc.
245 West 17th St., 11th Floor
New York, NY 10011

AVALON

Nation Books is a co-publishing venture of the
Nation Institute and Avalon Publishing Group, Inc.

Library of Congress Cataloging-in-Publication Data

ISBN 1-56025-881-0

9 8 7 6 5 4 3 2 1

Book design by Pauline Neuwirth, Neuwirth & Associates, Inc.

Printed in the United States of America
Distributed by Publishers Group West

For Rupert Murdoch
The blind squirrel who found our favorite nut

Contents

▼

INTRODUCTION:
An Open Letter to Bill O'Reilly

▼

Dear Bill,

We've written this book because we care about you. We know it might not seem that way right now. We're sure as you read this you're angry and embarrassed and scared. But we feel at this point that an intervention is our only option.

You had so much promise, Bill. You could have done so much good but you're throwing it all away. We know you, Bill. We know how you hurt inside. We're worried you're losing your mind.

We know it's scary to be in your position. We know you're not the smartest guy in the world, and to suddenly have this much influence is frightening. The first step is to admit that. You need to admit that half the time you don't know what you're talking about. It's crucial to stopping the cycle. The second step is to admit you're not well. If you can't see it, if you can't admit it, you'll never get better.

You lie, Bill. You lie a lot. The scary thing is that you don't even realize you're doing it anymore. You deny you've said things that you said thirty minutes earlier. You constantly misrepresent the truth. You spin incessantly . . . usually right after shouting "no-spin zone." It's getting sad.

Now, a lot of what follows is going to be tough to hear. It's going to sound mean-spirited in parts. It's going to sound like we're mocking you. It's going to sound like we're attacking you. But we're only attacking the illness.

We know it may seem like this is all coming out of left field— like you're being blindsided. After all, your FOX News cable show is hugely successful. You've written several best-sellers, your radio show is heard nationwide, and your columns are printed in dozens of newspapers.

But more and more we see cracks developing in your fragile psyche. You're on top of the world, but your public comments simply do not mesh with your many real-world successes. We don't see the big, important man who's revolutionizing and remaking the news media; we see the brave little boy continually haunted—indeed terrified—by his past.

As a result, it appears you are losing your grip not only on reality but on your audience as well. You've lost millions of viewers in the last few years, and your audience is around half what it was at its height in March 2003.

But you—and your show—can be healthy again. We know the title of this book is harsh. It's meant to be. You know why? Because we love you, Bill. We just hate what you've become. The intervention won't work if we don't expose the truth about what's happening. We're hoping that if enough people read this, if enough people know the truth, the healing can begin. We know you don't like to hear this, but Hillary is right. It takes a village, Bill. With a little self-examination and hard work on your part, a year from now we could be halfway through *Sweet Jesus, I Love Bill O'Reilly*. It's your decision. Things can't go on the way they are. Change can start today. Change must start today. You can do it.

You ready, Bill? Okay, let's begin.

STUPIDITY, INSANITY, ARROGANCE, AND IMPOTENCE

▼

LIKE A RECORD BABY,
RIGHT ROUND ROUND ROUND

Everything we do here is based on fact. All right? . . . We tell you what reality is. For example, in the Red Cross situation, the United Way situation, we tell you what the facts are, all right? And then we say, here is the good guy. Here's the bad guy.

—Bill O'Reilly debunking former CNN commentator Bill Press's contention that O'Reilly spins

BILL O'REILLY IS a straight shooter. Bill O'Reilly is a fiercely independent freethinker who carefully weighs the merits of an argument before staking out a position. Because of this, he often finds it a challenge to fight through the fusillade of B.S. his sometimes-less-than-candid guests are ideologically encoded to send his way. But Bill O'Reilly is more than up to that challenge, and guests who are intent on spinning plain facts on *The O'Reilly Factor* will be vigorously confronted without exception.

This, we maintain, is how the world appears to Bill O'Reilly. It has to. The man is as self-aware as a legume.

Of course, the plain truth is that O'Reilly is a master spinner. And here's the weird part: We've observed him carefully and we're convinced he doesn't know he's doing it. Indeed, O'Reilly is to the unvarnished truth as Lennie from *Of Mice and Men* is to cute, furry animals. He can't help mangling it.

This is an odd thing to say, to be sure. After all, O'Reilly is a veritable media dreadnought. His television and radio shows influence millions, as do his books and newspaper column. To say, then, that the declared raison d'être of his journalistic efforts is not just a sham but the polar opposite of his intentions sounds pretty strange. Unfortunately, there's no other way to interpret the data.

Indeed, listening to O'Reilly talk about his distaste for spin is a little like hearing Michael Jackson discuss the thirteen-year-old boys he shares his bed with. He has no idea how it looks to the outside world. How could he possibly?

Consider the May 27, 2004, installment of *The O'Reilly Factor*. His guest that night was right-wing pundit, media darling, and frothing yellow-haired banshee Ann Coulter.[1] She was on the program to discuss conservative support for George W. Bush despite the president's falling poll numbers. Fair enough. At its noblest, television inspires, educates, and challenges us, and part and parcel of this role is promoting a bracing marketplace of ideas.

However, when Bill aired the teaser for the segment, up popped Coulter's face with the tagline "No Spin Ann." In case you missed that, it said "No Spin Ann."

Seriously. No. Spin. Ann.

Now, this woman is a wackadoodle, and everyone knows it. For instance, after O'Reilly's rather absurd teaser, she had this to say: "We have found weapons of mass destruction. That is something the media is repeatedly lying about. We have not found stockpiles. We found the plants for manufacturing, we found the experiments, we found the room for human experimentation labs. We found lots of weapons of mass destruction."

Um, not really, no.

But while that's a pretty distorted argument, Coulter's at her best when engaging in antiliberal polemics:

"We need to execute people like John Walker [Lindh] in order to physically intimidate liberals, by making them realize that they can be killed, too."

"Whether they are defending the Soviet Union or bleating for Saddam Hussein, liberals are always against America. They are either traitors or idiots, and on the matter of America's self-preservation, the difference is irrelevant."

"There are a lot of bad Republicans; there are no good Democrats."
And just for fun:

"My only regret with Timothy McVeigh is he did not go to the *New York Times* building."

Love her or hate her, agree or not, that's spin. It's not particularly good or subtle spin, but it's a form of spin nonetheless.

Now, just so we all know we're on the same page, here's one definition of spin, from the Random House Webster's College Dictionary: "To cause to have a particular bias; influence in a certain direction: *His assignment was to spin the reporters after the president's speech.*"

It's hard to imagine a clearer example of bias against a group than saying that they're wholly corrupt, traitorous morons who should be threatened with execution. But Bill is blind to it. He considers this the essence of a straight shooter.

Of course, most people who choose not to take Coulter at face value see her at worst as a sort of lightweight provocateur—a sticky Republican confection that's too rich even for those apt to agree with her. She's fun but at best she offers no nutrition and at worst she makes you want to vomit.

So we watched that night's *Factor* with special interest, eager for some mitigating morsel of evidence that somewhere in Bill's bag of tricks was a well-concealed sense of whimsical irony. Or maybe, we thought, he was launching a new segment in which normally rock-ribbed ideologues came on his show and dispassionately recited dry government statistics from the U.S. Department of Agriculture or the Centers for Disease Control. Perhaps the following night's teaser would be "No Spin Michael Moore," followed by a verbatim recitation of the Congressional Record.

Seriously, we didn't want Bill to be this crazy. He has a wife and two children, and a hopeful, gray-haired mother with weary ovaries.

No such luck. Coulter was as rabid as ever. Bill had topped himself again.

ON A CAROUSEL

AFTER OBSERVING O'REILLY for some time now, it is our considered opinion that Bill, despite calling his show a "no-spin zone," writing a book of the same name, and continually upbraiding his guests for supposedly spinning the truth, has no clue what spin is.

He thinks he does. In his head he does. Unfortunately, his lack of self-awareness remains a fatal handicap to his understanding of the world outside his skull.

A normal person looks at a character like James Carville and says, "Boy, what a slick guy. He's spinning up a storm." Indeed, O'Reilly often calls Carville on his B.S. That's fine. Carville's an unapologetic partisan, and a darn good one. Someone has to keep him honest.

But O'Reilly can also look at, say, Newt Gingrich, Dick Morris, or Ann Coulter and see nothing but unclouded envoys of truth.

But, you may ask, how can he hold such odd notions so comfortably in his head? The same way medieval astronomers could stare at the sky and think the sun orbited the earth. You see, O'Reilly believes he and his opinions are the center of the political universe, and so everything that departs from those opinions by definition spins around him. Of course, if you happen to be standing with him—on Planet Earth, as he sees it—you simply speak the truth. If you don't, you spin wildly like the stars in the firmament. You become, as he usually describes those with whom he disagrees, "an ideologue."

Of course, part of the reason we're writing this book is that we want to be Bill's Copernicus and Galileo. We fully expect the edict of Inquisition to come down from FOX News for our heresies, only to be lifted by William Spencer O'Reilly XXI, the duly anointed vicar of O'Reilly on earth, roundabout the year 2364 or so. But we're doing this for his own good. And we're not alone. Others have tried to pierce Bill's no-spin pretensions and failed miserably—though not through lack of effort.

For example, in November 2001, O'Reilly interviewed Bill Press of CNN's Crossfire. See if you can follow this:

PRESS: Okay, I'm going to give you an example of your conservative spin. Okay? Here's how you opened the show on March the third this year: "Tonight, violent demonstrations on the rise all over the world as capitalism comes under assault and America's college campuses are being besieged with socialistic messages. We'll have a report. The first hundred days of Hillary Clinton in the Senate. Did she actually do anything? We'll find out. And was Al Gore antagonistic toward some of his students at Columbia? That's the word. Caution. You're about to enter a no-spin zone."

O'REILLY: Right.

PRESS: Now, I just find that very funny. That's full of spin. That's nothing. . . .

O'REILLY: Those are teases with question marks on them. Those are teases with question marks on them.

PRESS: Bill, be honest.

O'REILLY: I am being honest.

PRESS: You spin each of those things to the right, the way you see them, and then you call it no-spin.

O'REILLY: All right, look.

PRESS: Come on, it doesn't lie.

O'REILLY: If we were that bad, if *The O'Reilly Factor* was all spin all the time, as you say, why are we crushing your program? I mean, we are absolutely crushing *Crossfire*. Last night, twenty-eight *O'Reilly Factor*, twelve *Crossfire*. We're wiping you off the map. If I was that dishonest, and that's spinful, why is that happening?

Um, yeah. How on earth can you argue with that?

The lesson here, of course (other than that the EPA should redouble its efforts to eradicate lead and mercury from Levittown's[2] drinking water) is that spin is evidently not spin as long as you present it in the form of teases with question marks on them.

By that standard, then, the following could be considered straightforward reportage and not in any way politically motivated:

> Tonight, worldwide protests against George W. Bush's foreign policy as democracy comes under assault and FOX News viewers are besieged by fascist messages. Is George W. Bush a dick? He's a dick. But is he? He very well could be. Oh, he is *so* totally a dick. But is he, seriously? We'll have a report. Bill O'Reilly celebrates his show's ninth year on the air. Does he ever make any fucking sense? We'll find out. And did Dick Cheney tell Senator Patrick Leahy to go fuck himself? That's the word. Caution. You're about to enter a no-spin zone.

Second, trying to counter O'Reilly's main defense for these spin-like teases—that *The Factor* is crushing *Crossfire*—is like trying to argue with the drunk asshole at the bar who says he should be dating your girlfriend because he has a Camaro and you only drive a Prius. Where do you start? It's idiotic on so many levels.

For one thing, why does O'Reilly have his and his competition's previous day's ratings information at his fingertips? Is this what all broadcasters do? If Stone Phillips runs into Jim Lehrer on the street, do you figure maybe he asks him for his take on the ongoing turmoil in the Middle East or do you think he says, "Hey, kicked your ass again last night, Lehrer. *Dateline NBC* twenty-eight, *NewsHour with Jim Lehrer* three! We're *crushing* you!"

Of course, we're almost embarrassed to point out the other big fallacy in O'Reilly's logic for fear of looking stupid ourselves. Seriously, does anyone outside of O'Reilly, his preschool-aged children, and the confused old woman in Ohio who tunes in to Bill every night because she thinks he's Merv Griffin *not* know the answer to this one?

We know, dear reader, that you know. We give you more credit than that. But to help out those poor, beleaguered *O'Reilly Factor* staffers who have been ordered to comb this book for actionable material, here's the answer: ratings don't have anything to do with how much truth you tell or how free of spin your reports are. If they did, the *National Enquirer* wouldn't outsell most major dailies by hundreds of thousands of copies, and all the networks would be scrambling to keep up with C-SPAN.

Come on, Rush Limbaugh is hugely successful. Does that mean he doesn't spin? O'Reilly claims that Al Franken spins everything, but according to that partisan rag *Publishers Weekly*, Franken's *Lies and the Lying Liars Who Tell Them*[3] outsold O'Reilly's *Who's Looking Out for You?*[4] by almost a hundred thousand copies in 2003. Ergo, he must have been telling more truth. Is there any other conclusion? Oh, that's right. Franken's from Mars.

FAIR AND CHEMICALLY IMBALANCED

ON MARCH 14, 2005, Bill O'Reilly proved two things on national television. One, he doesn't know how to read a chart. Two, he's so out of his mind that somewhere Richard Speck is saying, "Now that guy's a nut."

Here's what spilled from his speckled head:

> A new study from the Project for Excellence in Journalism at Columbia University examined the Iraq war coverage. On cable news it broke down like this:
>
> Thirty-eight percent of the stories FOX News ran were favorable to the war effort, 62 percent neutral, negative, or not able to be classified.
>
> Over at CNN, 20 percent of the stories were positive, 80 percent neutral, negative, or not classifiable.
>
> And at MSNBC, just 16 percent positive, 84 percent neutral, negative, or not classifiable.
>
> So once again, you can decide which network is fair and balanced.

Actually, from the information Bill just gave, you *can't* decide which network is fair and balanced. You see, he chose not to give all the results. He just isolated the "positive" category and lumped all the others together. Basically, all he proved is that FOX News did more positive stories on the war.

Here are the actual results from the study:

Tone of Iraq War Coverage on Cable News
Percent of Iraq War stories

	CNN	Fox	MSNBC	Total
Positive	20%	38%	16%	24%
Neutral	41	39	28	36
Negative	23	14	17	19
Multi-Subject	15	9	40	21

Totals may not equal 100 due to rounding.

As you can plainly see, CNN and MSNBC were far more balanced in their coverage of the war: They aired nearly equal numbers of positive and negative stories. The main conclusion of the study is painfully obvious. Were it a tumor, it would be one of those three-hundred-pounders that gets its own miniseries on the Discovery Channel.

But more important, this episode illustrates exactly *how* O'Reilly spins. He spins not like a pundit but like a sociopath. It's clear that when O'Reilly looks at a chart or reads a study, he simply sees what he wants to see. Indeed, if M. Night Shyamalan ever wanted to do a rough remake of *The Sixth Sense* about a guy who doesn't know he's an idiot, he'd have his man.

How, for example, do you miss this little bit of analysis from the authors of the study?

FOX journalists were even more prone to offer their own opinions in the channel's coverage of the war in Iraq. There 73 percent of the stories included such personal judgments. On CNN the figure was 2 percent, and on MSNBC, 29 percent.

The same was true in coverage of the presidential election, where 82 percent of FOX stories included journalistic opinions, compared to 7 percent on CNN and 27 percent on MSNBC.

Those findings seem to challenge FOX's promotional marketing, particularly its slogan, "We Report, You Decide."

Gee, O'Reilly seems to imply that the study showed FOX was fair and balanced, but the study's authors drew completely different—one might even say precisely opposite—conclusions.

This, of course, simply shows the lengths to which some researchers will go to spin their own studies.

DEFENDING THE FOLKS—O'REILLY SPINS THE ESTATE TAX

TAX DAY 2005. *The O'Reilly Factor*. FOX News. Bill O'Reilly is presenting fair and balanced commentary on the estate tax. He looks at both sides of the issue and comes to a conclusion based on plain facts.

Caution, you're about to enter a no-logic zone:

"The House has passed a law that would repeal the death tax, but the Senate might once again vote to keep that un-American tax in place."

You could not get more spin out of this sentence if you put it in a centrifuge.

"The liberals love the fact that the federal government can take half of your stuff when you die if you are wealthy. Now, since the death tax kicks in at $3 million, most Americans don't have to deal with it, which is why this example of socialism is allowed in this country."

Ah, it's no longer just un-American . . . it's socialist. Oh, and the only reason you're allowing it is because it doesn't affect you personally. Shame on you.

"Most of us simply ignore this gross violation of our private property rights."

Translation: *My* private property rights.

"[The left] wants income redistribution. That is, taking assets from the affluent and giving it to those less well off. Somewhere Karl Marx is glowing."

If he'd said "Harpo Marx" this would have made about as much sense. Karl Marx wanted workers to control the means of production and envisioned a collectivist utopia in which nearly all property was public. Even Ted Kennedy, one of the most liberal members of Congress, doesn't want this, as collectivist utopians as a rule don't get much tail. So Marx wouldn't be glowing, he'd wonder what's taking so long. John Pierpont Morgan on the other hand would love O'Reilly's plan.

"If you are poor because of addiction, laziness, or apathy, the government is apathetic. It doesn't care. You'll get the handout. But what liberals really want is more than a handout. They want subsidies that would lift the poor into the middle class. They want Americans who succeed to support those who fail, no matter what the circumstance."

Now he's all over the map. Is he saying the estate tax is wrong because it's un-American to tax inherited wealth as you would other income? Or is he now saying that the government is just giving it to lazy people anyway? Of course, in O'Reilly's world, inheritance money shouldn't be wasted on the lazy and irresponsible. It should be given to Paris Hilton.

"In addition to the federal government, nineteen states, and D.C. also have death taxes—more seizure of private property. This isn't in the Constitution, where private property is supposed to be protected from seizure."

And if government thugs were breaking into O'Reilly's home without search warrants and running off with cases of English Leather and limited-edition wildlife prints, this might mean something. Unfortunately, government seizure of private property is sorta the definition of taxation. You can't really have a society without it. The only rational area of disagreement is who we should tax: struggling middle-class people or dead rich ones.

Of course, if O'Reilly is talking about what he appears to be talking about—the Fourth Amendment, which prohibits unreasonable searches and seizures—he's a complete loon. But we'll give him the benefit of the doubt for now.

"It is time for Americans to decide just what kind of country we want. We should vote on the death tax. Let's have a referendum on capitalism."

Yeah, we can see it now: "Honey, does a yes on Prop. 231 mean I'm voting for robber-baron capitalism or Soviet-style communism?"

"And the next time these closet socialists scream about taxing the rich, point out that all Americans should be treated equally."

Especially the ones with huge offshore bank accounts, company cars, and corporate country-club memberships. The tax system was never set up to treat everyone "equally." If we were really all treated equally, the government would take the federal budget, just divide it by the population, and make everyone kick in their share. But we can't run the country like it's an office happy hour at Bennigan's. The tax system O'Reilly hates so much aspires to treat everyone fairly, not equally. The distinction is lost on Bill. But when O'Reilly says stuff like "the left wants income redistribution," he can only mean the left wants more income redistribution than the right does. After all, *all* taxation is income redistribution. If the government takes money from your check to buy a jet that protects O'Reilly's considerable assets, that's redistributive. You might even think it's unfair if you voted against capitalism in the referendum.

Now, one could reasonably argue that we should ditch the estate tax because it's a hardship on America's heirs and heiresses, but one can't say that it's wrong because it's redistribution and America doesn't do that. America's been doing that since the beginning. Indeed, the estate tax itself has been around since the early part of the twentieth century. Had it not been implemented, chances are you'd be paying higher taxes and working for a snappy chappy named Cornelius Astor Vanderbilt VII. Oh, and just to make it even more soul-crushing, he'd wear a top hat and tails to work and say things like "top drawer" and "capital idea." We don't think you want that. Neither does the federal government.

But this isn't about lofty principles and well-reasoned conclusions. And in this case, it's not mere spin. It's spin on behalf of O'Reilly's own narrow interests. Seriously, what multimillionaire goes on television night after night complaining about how he can't keep more of his money? What sort of journalist is O'Reilly to ask his viewers to back a campaign that keeps his son from paying estate taxes when the kid is finally big enough to shove his old man down the stairs?

"If you wanna live in Havana, go there."

According to United for a Fair Economy, nearly half of all estate taxes are paid by the richest 0.1 percent of the population. That's just a few thousand families each year. A permanent repeal of the estate tax would benefit a tiny sliver of the population, mostly billionaires and multimillionaires. Exempting more estates by raising the limit to reflect inflation might make sense, but watching pundits and politicians go to bat for the Gates and Walton families—and themselves—is just nauseating.

According to a fact sheet released in July 2005 by Representative Henry Waxman, the estate tax repeal would also save the families of President Bush, Vice President Cheney, and eleven Cabinet members as much as $344 million total.

And if you don't like it, O'Reilly will be the first to kick your Castro-kissin' ass to Cuba.

JESUS CHRIST, LOGICAL POSITIVIST

BEFORE YOU READ this next excerpt, ask yourself two questions: 1) Who was Jesus of Nazareth? and 2) What kind of holiday is Christmas?

If you said, 1) a religious figure and founder of one of the world's great religions; and 2) a religious holiday observed by the world's Christians that commemorates the birth of Jesus Christ, you're part of the large subset of cognizant humans in the developed or developing worlds that does not include Bill O'Reilly.

So we're agreed then, right? Chances are, anyone who gives anything other than those two answers, or something close to them, is spinning. Okay, just checking.

Here's our boy:

In 1870, President Grant made Christmas a public secular holiday, and the federal government gave workers the day off. The reason was a holiday . . . to honor a man, Jesus, whose philosophy that all men are created equal and that one should love your neighbor helped the Founding Fathers of the United States craft the Constitution.

By almost all accounts, our system of laws and justice is based on Judeo-Christian philosophy, which puts human rights ahead of government wants. Our system here was not developed according to Islamic law or Buddhist thought. It was modeled after the tenets of Judaism and Christianity, and that's the truth.

However, philosophy is different from religion, and our founders made sure that no religion could be imposed by the government, and all religions were to be tolerated unless they violated civil law.

Thus the secular holiday of Christmas honoring the birth of that great philosopher, Jesus in Bethlehem.

But according to the ACLU and some other misguided Americans, because some people believe the philosopher Jesus to be God, then all the people should be denying seeing his image displayed in a public setting.

Does that make any sense at all? (Talking Points Memo, December 2, 2002)

Well, O'Reilly might want to ask the Founding Fathers about this, because they think the philosopher they based their most important ideas on was John Locke, not Jesus. In fact, we entered Locke's name into our electronic World Book Encyclopedia, and it brought up such familiar terms as "democracy," "freedom of speech," "government of the United States," "Declaration of Independence," and "Bill of Rights." Punch in "Jesus" and you'll get "Christianity," "God," "religion," "faith healing," "Gospels," "Holy Grail," "messiah," "resurrection," "parable," "transfiguration," and "wandering Jew," which we actually thought was a plant but apparently has something to do with a Jew who offended Jesus on the way to the crucifixion (probably by shouting something like, "Hey, secular philosopher, where's your secular philosophy now?") and was cursed to wander the earth until the Second Coming.

You'll also get "Jesus Christ Superstar," but strangely enough, no "Declaration of Independence" or "Bill of Rights." So if common resource materials are to be believed, Jesus has more to do with Andrew Lloyd-Webber than he does with Thomas Jefferson.

But why are we telling you this? No one in his right mind thinks he's getting off for Christmas because it's a philosophical holiday. No one asks for time off work for Immanuel Kant's birthday. You don't see public displays honoring the virgin birth and resurrection of Friedrich Nietzsche.

And if you're a member of a church and you say enough times that Jesus was really a philosopher, they'll ask you to stop showing up. You might as well call him a master illusionist along the lines of a David Copperfield or a Doug Henning. So O'Reilly, a Catholic, isn't just spinning here, he's flirting with excommunication.

Of course, all the ACLU wants to do is honor the Constitution and protect the rights of minorities by keeping religion and public life in different spheres.

Seems pretty reasonable—unless you're one of the few (Okay, actually only one) who believes Jesus is as important to the foundations of the Constitution as he is to Christianity.

Does that make any sense at all?

MISSION ACCOMPLISHED, MISSION SHABOMBPLISHED (ONE LAST THING)

IN SEPTEMBER 2004, Bill O'Reilly interviewed George W. Bush. When he got to the subject of the war, O'Reilly asked Bush the following question, an obvious allusion to the giant, conspicuously placed "MISSION ACCOMPLISHED" banner that hung behind our commander-in-chief throughout his nationally televised speech from the *USS Abraham Lincoln*.

O'REILLY: The "mission accomplished" statement in May 2003, if you had to do it all over again, would you not have done it?

BUSH: Well, first of all, the statement said: "Thank you for serving in Afghanistan and Iraq. Thank you for being on one of the largest, longest cruises in our nation's history. Thank you for serving our country. And we've still got tough work in Iraq." Now, I'm going to go and thank our troops every chance I get.

O'REILLY: But the press spinned it, you know how they spinned it.

Your honor, we rest.

NOTES

1. This is an example of pure (but fair, considering what a dreadful, ghoul-faced, gonad-withering bitch she is) liberal spin.
2. While O'Reilly's hometown has been a bone of contention, with some claiming that he actually came from Westbury, we have chosen throughout this book to defer to Bill and reference Levittown, as it's a funnier-sounding name, and a little more sad.
3. Al Franken, *Lies and the Lying Liars Who Tell Them* (New York: Dutton, 2003).
4. Bill O'Reilly, *Who's Looking Out for You?* (New York: Broadway Books, 2003).

2

O'REILLY AND THE ART OF
THE IMPOTENT BOYCOTT

I think boycotting is un-American; I don't believe in it.

—Bill O'Reilly, from his book The No Spin Zone

IN **MARCH 2003,** Bill O'Reilly asked his fans to shun all French products to punish that country for its refusal to back the United States' campaign in Iraq. Imports from France in 2003 would eventually increase by almost $1 billion over the previous year.

On July 13, 2004, O'Reilly urged his viewers to dump Vivendi Corp. stock in retaliation for the provocative lyrics of Jadakiss, one of the media giant's signature stars. Vivendi stock soared 20 percent by year's end.

On April 15, 2005, O'Reilly ended a segment on Reebok's affiliation with rapper 50 Cent by saying, "Don't buy Reebok." In August, against O'Reilly's advice, Adidas announced plans to buy the company, driving the stock price up nearly 30 percent in one day.

Of course, one might look at such numbers and ask the obvious: Why does O'Reilly keep trying to boycott things? A better question, however, might be: Why has our country still not moved to convert to an entirely O'Reilly-boycott-based economy?

Now, it's been said that one definition of insanity is doing the same thing over and over and expecting different results. True enough. However, a better definition of insanity would be trying single-handedly to tear down our country's most stable and lucrative trading partnership because two guys escaped to Vancouver in a VW minibus. A good definition of stupidity might be not knowing what the word "boycott" means.

Mr. Webster, meet Mr. O'Reilly.

BOYCOTT FRANCE! DON'T LAUGH, CANADA, YOU'RE NEXT!

FIRST THINGS FIRST. On April 27, 2004, O'Reilly had the following exchange with Heather Mallick of the *Toronto Globe and Mail*. Bill was in a lather over two American war deserters who were seeking asylum in Canada:

> **O'REILLY:** Now, if the [Canadian] government—if your government harbors these two deserters—doesn't send them back . . . there will be a boycott of your country, which will hurt your country enormously. France is now feeling that sting. . . . Disagreement we respect, but if you start to undermine our war against terrorists, even if you disagree with it—again, we respect disagreement, if you start to undermine it, then Americans are going to take action. Are you willing to accept that boycott, which will hurt your economy drastically?

> **MALLICK:** I don't think for a moment such a boycott would take place because we are your biggest trading partners.

> **O'REILLY:** No, it will take place, Madam. In France. . . .

> **MALLICK:** I don't think that your French boycott has done too well. . . .

> **O'REILLY:** . . . they've lost billions of dollars in France, according to the *Paris Business Review*.

> **MALLICK:** I think that's nonsense.

Unfortunately, being Canadian, Ms. Mallick is woefully unfamiliar with how things work down here. Our countrymen have a long, hallowed tradition of wriggling out of tight spots by citing bogus statistics from nonexistent European economics journals. It got us through the American Revolution and two World Wars.[1]

And the only reason it may seem like France hasn't lost billions of dollars in trade with the United States since O'Reilly announced his boycott is because, in fact, it hasn't. But that's just the sort of nitpicking that makes regular folks hate arrogant foreign media like the insufferably fact-based *Toronto Globe and Mail*.

But that doesn't keep the elite media, as O'Reilly calls them (i.e., any newspaper or magazine that no longer runs regular Vince Foster updates), from trying to use misleading facts to paint a completely true yet uncomfortably embarrassing picture.

For instance, in a June 28, 2004 column, Jack Mathews of the *New York Daily News* called O'Reilly an ideological thug who plays loose with the facts. Mathews also noted O'Reilly's reference to the inconveniently nonexistent *Paris Business Review* and the fact that O'Reilly's France boycott didn't really work—at least not the way it was supposed to.

O'Reilly was having none of it. He fired off an indignant letter to Mathews's paper that appeared on July 6: "First, Mathews writes that an *O'Reilly Factor*-led boycott of France did no economic damage to that country. According to U.S. government figures, in the months following the boycott call, France did $138 million less business with the USA than it did the previous year."

Now, what O'Reilly writes here may or may not be true. (Actually, it's not.)[2] But claiming credit for a seasonal hiccup in French imports over a vaguely defined period of time is a little like putting Bob Hope in your celebrity death pool for five years running and then claiming psychic powers when he finally keels over.

As anyone not leading a megalomaniacal boycott knows, trade naturally fluctuates month to month and year to year, so a multi-million-dollar downturn in imports over the span of a short time, as impressive as it may sound to his viewers, proves exactly nothing. A more relevant figure, though not really slam-dunk proof of anything either, would be annual revenue from French exports to the United States. That went up in 2003. And while exports did drop slightly during the two months following O'Reilly's boycott, they dropped more, for example, in January and February 2002 compared to the same months in 2001 ($401 million). And as the far-left bomb-thrower Web site mediamatters.org noted, this was long before O'Reilly cast his mighty gypsy curse.

Of course, anyone can spin statistics—especially economic statistics—by referencing only a small window of time. And that's certainly what we would accuse O'Reilly of doing if we thought him clever enough to actually think of it. But alas, O'Reilly's not a slick spin doctor; he's more like an infant who thinks he can make things in his room disappear by closing his eyes.

Much as he conjured the *Paris Business Review* into existence and made Vivendi stockholders rue the day they took those first, fool-hardy steps down the path to financial windfall, O'Reilly apparently believes he's some sort of mighty fiscal sorcerer who can sway mul-titrillion-dollar economies to and fro with a wave of his wand.

Of course, it is odd that though Mathews challenged O'Reilly to address specifically the alleged lost billions and the phantom econ publication, O'Reilly's letter to the editor merely cited the vaguely sourced $138 million figure.

Now, a bigger man would apologize for his error. A lesser man would ignore the column entirely. But a delusional man would ignore the stuff he couldn't refute and try to hit back with irrelevant stats. An impotent man would fail miserably in this exercise.

Just in case you can't figure it out, O'Reilly's the impotent guy.

OY, CANADA

WHEN O'REILLY SAYS stuff like, "Hey, I know, let's boycott Canada!" one naturally wonders what sort of people he has on his staff.

The English language is going to have to come up with a more degrading term than "boot-licking lackey" because it just isn't capturing the extent to which his hangers-on have committed themselves to following him down whatever rabbit hole his head leads him to.

For instance, almost a year before Mallick slapped him down over the notion that we should get into economic fisticuffs with our best trading partner (because, you know, it's nuts), O'Reilly said the following in his Talking Points Memo:

> Canada is utterly dependent on the USA for its economic well-being, as we know. Nine million Americans cross into Canada more than 40 million times each year. We spend at least $10 billion up [there] annually and are taxed billions more by the socialistic government. So, if we stop going north, Canadians will fall into a depression, not a recession, a depression.[3]

Now there's a captivating bit of analysis. It's as if Bill had received an honorary degree in economics from Levittown Beauty Academy Online.

First of all, while $10 billion is a lot of money, it's a drop in the bucket compared to Canada's $1 trillion annual GDP. We don't know what you'd call that, but only a moron would call it "utterly dependent." But aside from asking himself how exactly a Canadian depression helps us, Bill might like to check his math and history. As every schoolkid knows, it took a devastating stock market crash to cause our last depression. Refusing to drive to Ontario to see Alan Thicke perform dinner theater is probably not going to get the job done.

Secondly, in 2004, Canada bought $190-billion-worth of our crap. In fact, Canada buys around 23 percent of our total exports, nearly ten times that of France. We also get a huge percentage of our oil from Canada, often importing more from our northern neighbors than from Saudi Arabia, and you know how difficult it is to swear off *that* crack pipe.

So let's not get into an economic pissing match with Canada just now, 'k, sport?

Of course, we can only imagine O'Reilly's staff meetings when he pipes up about his idea for a Canadian boycott about once every year or so. If one of his luckless minions were ever to challenge this little nugget of crazy, at best the scene might resemble the heartbreaking sight of some brave, beleaguered young woman gently guiding her escaped, pantless grandfather back to his room at the nursing home.

More likely, though, O'Reilly's greeted by a small, office-sized sea of dumbfounded looks and stony silence.

Yes, we're starting to realize that the "he's nuts" versus "he's stupid" argument may soon rival the "you've got your peanut butter on my chocolate" debate of the mid-seventies.

THE BOYCOTT OF A NEW GENERATION

So I'm calling for all responsible Americans to fight back and punish Pepsi for using a man who degrades women, who encourages substance abuse, and does all the things that hurt particularly the poor in our society. I'm calling for all Americans to say, "Hey, Pepsi, I'm not drinking your stuff. You want to hang around with Ludacris, you do that, I'm not hanging around with you."

—*Bill O'Reilly on* The O'Reilly Factor, *August 27, 2002*

First of all, I never do anything tacitly. I do things directly. I simply said I wasn't going to drink Pepsi while that guy was on their payroll. No boycott was ever mentioned by me.

—*Bill O'Reilly on* The O'Reilly Factor, *February 4, 2003*

FIRST OFF, O'REILLY appears to forget what he's said on the air so often that we may want to look into whether the government has resumed its fifties-era LSD mind-control experiments or the equally likely possibility that his mother was freebasing Ajax cleanser when she was pregnant with him.

But assuming O'Reilly retains at least some memory of things he does from one month to the next, it's safe to conclude that he's not quite clear on what a boycott is.

"Calling for all Americans to say, 'Hey, Pepsi, I'm not drinking your stuff,'" is pretty close to the precise definition of boycott. In fact, it may even be phrased that way in the off-brand corporate-sponsored dictionaries the dirt-poor Levittown school district is forced to distribute to stupid, impoverished Irish children in its underfunded schools, which would explain a lot.

Of course, as others, including hip-hop mogul Russell Simmons, would later point out, Pepsi seemed to be pressing a double standard, as it later tabbed legendary shock-rocker Ozzy Osbourne as a sponsor after dropping Ludacris. In fact, Simmons's group, the Hip-Hop Summit Action Network, ultimately threatened its own boycott over the move.

Now, as authors, we have no special interest in or knowledge of hip-hop culture. Culturally speaking, we're probably about as white as O'Reilly. Even whiter, if you count his liver spots.

But to our tender ears, one profanity-laced song seems as bad as any other. That Pepsi isn't trying to grab market share from people who listen to Pat Boone is understandable. That the lesson it would take from O'Reilly's threats is that the company shouldn't hire a *black* vulgarian is at best regrettable.

For the record, after O'Reilly moved to crush him, Ludacris went on to sell a few more million albums, appeared in some movies, and collaborated on Usher's Grammy-nominated "Yeah!," one of the biggest hits of 2004.

On the rapper's album *The Red Light District*, Ludacris gave a little shout-out to Bill: "Hi, Mr. O'Reilly. Hope all is well. Kiss the plaintiff and the wifey."

Maybe Ludacris should announce a boycott of *The Factor*—you know, on moral grounds.

BOYCOTT AMY GRANT! DON'T LAUGH, ANDREA BOCELLI, YOU'RE NEXT!

WHILE BILL'S ROILING, hair-trigger outrage may not spring to life over white metal singers—or for that matter, shit-kickin', whiskey-drinkin', spouse-cheatin' country artists—he's a regular Big Brotha with respect to hip-hop artists.

On July 13, 2004, O'Reilly read some lyrics by rapper Jadakiss. He was particularly piqued over these two lines: "Why did Bush knock down the towers" and "Why Halle have to let a white man pop her to get an Oscar."

The first lyric apparently alluded to conspiracy theories surrounding the 9/11 attacks. Whether Jadakiss literally believes or wants other to believe that George W. Bush had some sort of active role in the terrorist strikes is at best a matter of speculation. It seems equally likely that he was referring to the president's horrible Jenga skills.

The second lyric referred to the fact that the first African-American to win an Academy Award for Best Actress received it for a film in which she was banged by a white guy.

Taken as a whole, the song seems to question why people in the inner cities make a lot of the bad choices they do and how society keeps them in their place. For instance, Jadakiss also asks, "Why would niggas push pounds and powder" and "Why they stop lettin' niggas get degreez in jail?"

So the song is a powerful protest against poor choices and benighted government policy, and, sure, one line is pretty crazy.

However, Bill's whack-job conclusion is that both George Bush and Halle Berry should be able to sue. Seriously.

Since this is not possible and, more important, just plain stupid, Bill suggests one of his famous boycotts.

But who should he boycott? Jadakiss? Come on, what *Factor* viewer is buying hip-hop music anyway?

Well, what about boycotting his record label? Again, not ambitious enough.

Maybe he could get his fans to boycott the label's parent company, Universal Music Group (UMG). *That's* a pretty big target—and a suitably insane one to boot. According to the company's Web site, "Its global operations encompass the development, manufacture, marketing, sales and distribution of recorded music through a network of subsidiaries, joint ventures and licensees in 77 countries, representing approximately 98% of the music market." Included in its stable of artists are jazz crooner Diana Krall, renowned opera tenor Andrea Bocelli, and the foul-mouthed Amy Grant.

Ah, but O'Reilly isn't content simply to tilt at windmills. He sees a nuclear cooling tower on the horizon.

With a little research, Bill ultimately discovers that the colossal UMG is actually just one division of the enormous Vivendi Universal, which has tens of thousands of employees and annual sales in the billions.

Now, to boycott Vivendi you'd pretty much have to just stop buying music. Who would sign on to such a ridiculous crusade? Oh, but Bill knows his viewers well. He proudly announces that Vivendi is a *French* company. *Merde!*

So Bill has the link. The French are responsible for Jadakiss's lyrics and should be held accountable.

Here's how the mad boycotter sold it to his viewers: "The latest atrocity is a rap song by a guy named Jadakiss, who is just a pitiful pawn being run by the huge Vivendi Corporation, a French company that's distributing some of the most vile entertainment 'Talking Points' has ever seen."

Now, the notion that somehow Jadakiss is being manipulated into writing controversial lyrics by a multinational European conglomerate may just be the cherry on top of the hot fudge sundae with nuts that is O'Reilly's lunacy.

We can just imagine the interoffice memos:

FROM: Jean-Rene Fourtou, CEO Vivendi Corporation
TO: Jadakiss
cc: Jorgen Larsen, CEO Universal Music Group; Board of Directors, Vivendi Corporation; Board of Directors, Universal Music Group
RE: Lyrics from your album *Kiss of Death*

It has come to our attention that your latest rhymes, while most assuredly the shiznit, have relied on far too penurious use of the terms "niggaz," "bitchas," and "motherfuckas."
As you know, gratuitous vulgarity is the raison d'être of hip-hop culture, and upper management is united in the belief that your lyrics should more faithfully reflect that sensibility. To

stress, our corporate philosophy vis-à-vis said lyrics is that the niggaz must represent.

Sincerely,
Jean-Rene

P.S. If you could work something into your next album about George W. Bush's complicity in the 9/11 attacks, that would be sweet.

Unfortunately for O'Reilly and his redneck horde, Vivendi also distributes music from country artists such as Toby Keith, Reba McEntire, and Shania Twain. So boycotting the company is, well, just pants-wetting crazy. Ah, but it soon becomes apparent that this is less about not buying music anymore and more about grinding axes. Bill appears to still be teed off that his weird campaign to block distribution of Al Franken's book was laughed out of court: "It's impossible for famous people to sue and win defamation judgments, and the Vivendi Corporation knows it."

See, it's an evil French corporation that smears good people and spreads filth throughout the world. Mind you, he's talking about the parent of the largest music company in the world and saying his viewers should stop patronizing them because of a murkily understood set of lyrics from one song.

"Both President Bush and Halle Berry should be able to sue Vivendi and Jadakiss for millions."

We'd love to see those lawsuits, because the FOX News–Franken suit was quite awhile ago, and we haven't laughed that hard since.

Of course, all this is coming from a man who claims to support tort reform. Little Jimmy's mom can't sue because his wiener got ripped off by a vacuum cleaner, but Bush should be able to obtain a financial judgment against anyone who criticizes him.

Finally, the pièce de résistance: "*The Factor*, of course, is boycotting everything Vivendi produces, because it's a French corporation."

Um, yeah right, you moron. Hope you weren't planning on seeing the next *Bridget Jones* sequel or buying, um, music.

Of course, all of this is a little hard to square with O'Reilly's statement, which began this chapter, that boycotting is un-American, or with the following statement from August 2003, which was presumably made in reference to FOX's insane Franken lawsuit:

> The main point here is that trying to hurt a business or a person because you disagree with what they say is simply unacceptable in America. And that message has been sent by FOX. There's a principle in play. Vigorous debate is embraced by us, but smear campaigns will be confronted.

Yeah right, you loon. Unfortunately, by O'Reilly's admittedly hypocritical standard, we couldn't have had the Montgomery Bus Boycott, a signal event in American history that helped break the back of racism in the segregationist South. And the Boston Tea Party, which helped rally the colonies to the cause of independence? That was kind of boycottish, wasn't it? Let's chuck that one, too. But anything that hurts O'Reilly's feelings? That will be confronted.

We close with O'Reilly's take on what could be considered the bête noire of Levittown's favorite son and his followers: snooty French wine manufacturers. Here's O'Reilly in his March 2, 2005, Most Ridiculous Item of the Day:

> An update on *The Factor*'s boycott of France. According to an article in today's *Wall Street Journal*, French wine sales in the USA have dropped 21 percent over the last two years. *The Factor* has been boycotting French products during that time, and although we can't prove it, we believe we are a factor in the wine sales drop. Pardon the terrible pun.

Sadly, that was the cleverest thing he's said in five years.

You may also remember that some of those ridiculous far-left Web sites took issue with our boycott information. As usual, we were right, and they were wrong. Finally, "Boycott France" bumper stickers are available on billoreilly.com. Sales are way up, unlike French wine.

This is really quite sad. O'Reilly's boycott of all things French is failing miserably. French exports to the United States are up. So he picks one commodity, wine, and shows sales are down, thus implying the boycott is a resounding success.

Furthermore, he claims this is proof that those "far-left Web sites" are wrong and Bill is right. He might as well have come out and said, "sales of Renault LeCar are down 100 percent."

As for the success of *The Factor*'s boycott with respect to French wine, we have this interesting tidbit from that very same issue of the *Wall Street Journal*: "The dollar's weakness against the euro has hurt not only French wine sales but also all kinds of European imports to the U.S., from silk scarves to truffle oil."

And although we can't prove it, that probably has a little more to do with sales of French wine than O'Reilly's hex.

Of course, the idea that O'Reilly might have affected French wine sales is based on the theory that *Factor* viewers ever drank French wine to begin with. Indeed, it seems far more likely O'Reilly's *Factor*-led boycott inspired his viewers proudly to dump their Yoplait yogurt and French's mustard into the gutters of Levittown.

NOTES

1. Of course, as many observers have noted, there is no *Paris Business Review*. There never has been. Neither is there any publication that sounds remotely like "Paris Business Review." There's no *Paris Bidness Review*, no *Paris Business Revue*, no *Harris Business Review*. Nothing of the sort, in fact. It's just made up. In O'Reilly's head it's probably very prestigious and maybe even won a shitload of fake journalism awards. By now he's probably worked out a whole back story, down to the publication's sexy Parisian receptionist and its wine-besotted editor-in-chief, Pepe. To O'Reilly, that would be easier than just admitting he made a mistake.

2. www.census.gov gives figures on French exports to the United States on a month-by-month basis. O'Reilly called for his boycott in March 2003. Giving him the benefit of the doubt and including all of March (a month when

imports from France were down from the previous year), a quick back-of-the-envelope calculation shows that trade went down a total of $288 million for the months of March and April 2003 compared to the same period in 2002 ($136.2 million in March and $151.8 million in April). However, trade went up a total of $343.2 million in May and June 2003, eclipsing the losses of the previous two months.

From March through December 2003, French imports were up $877.2 million over the same months in 2002. Imports were up again in 2004, to $31.6 billion from $28.2 billion in 2002. And in June 2004, just before Bill wrote his letter "correcting" Mathews, French imports were up $368.3 million over June 2002.

So just about any way you slice it, O'Reilly's wrong. Furthermore, since O'Reilly doesn't bother to define what he means by "the months following the boycott call," no one could make an accurate calculation. We learned that back in third grade when we were doing story problems.

3. Incidentally, in the same Talking Points Memo, which centered on Bill's anger over Canada's plans to turn over wanted Iraqis to an international court instead of the United States, O'Reilly said this of Bill Clinton's plans to meet with the Canadian prime minister: "Don't schmooze around with Jean Chrétien at this point in time. If you do, a firestorm of bad will befall you." Now, if you heard a character in a straight-to-video Jean-Claude Van Damme movie say "a firestorm of bad will befall you," you'd probably say, "Gee, Van Damme's writers have really fallen off their game." But O'Reilly can *write it down* and millions of Americans still take him seriously.

3

BILL IS OUTRAGED
AND LOVIN' IT

WE'VE ALL KNOWN people who spend a little too much of their time in the pursuit of idle outrage. It could be your neighbor grousing about an increase in garbage pickup fees. Or your cousin and his Schlitz-leavened indignation over the sorry prospects of your local football team. Or the old lady on the bus ranting incomprehensibly about the satellite receiver the UN has planted in her living room.

Well, tune in to FOX News for a couple days and you'll soon realize the old lady on the bus is about a Starbucks grande latte and a LexisNexis account away from being a research assistant for *The O'Reilly Factor.*

Outrage is O'Reilly's drug of choice, and he's long since become addicted. And like any addict, if he can't get the good stuff he continually lowers his standards to secure his fix. Indeed, once he starts a binge, if no one stops to intervene on his behalf, it's only a matter of time before he's mainlining cheap Ann Coulter tracts in a seedy Manhattan office complex off the Avenue of the Americas.

And woe to the pinhead who won't shoot up with him. You're sure to be branded a narc and summarily banished from Lord Bill's opium den.

Indeed, O'Reilly has trolled some pretty deep gutters to find his high. So if you'll forgive the mixed metaphor, let's all take the brown acid, shall we?

CLOSE ENCOUNTERS OF THE MURDERING ALIEN KIND

IF THERE'S ONE thing that really gets Bill's hemorrhoidal tissues inflamed, it's illegal immigration. And guess what sort of illegal immigration most enrages O'Reilly? If you said Quebecois separatists pouring over the Vermont border or salty fisherfolk from the coasts of Nova Scotia rafting to Bangor, move to the back of the cramped, 120-degree hidden compartment with the other undocumented Mexicans.[1]

No, it's not the subtle swarthiness of Montreal that's the burr in Bill's britches but the ruddy chocolate-brown of our neighbor to the south.

This is one of O'Reilly's pet issues that—no matter how much he flogs it—never quite catches on the way he thinks it should. And boy does he flog it. He knows it hasn't gotten the traction he'd like, and make no mistake about it, this irritates him to no end.

Of course, many commentators believe passionately in certain pet issues and set out to build their case meticulously, appealing to the good sense and logic of their audience while relying from time to time on the emotional resonance of their cause. But that's not O'Reilly's style. O'Reilly's style is to lose all sense of perspective and, when this doesn't work, his feeble grip on reality.

Bill tried to resurrect the immigration issue in September 2004 during his heavily promoted interview with President Bush, remarking that "every year, 3.5 million illegals come over." But this startling fact was accompanied by no outrage from the masses—no public outcry. The issue was at a simmer, but Bill wanted a rolling boil.

On November 15, 2004, O'Reilly turned up the heat: "Terrorists have an open invitation to attack America from the south." Now the game was changing. O'Reilly was deemphasizing the grim specter of brown hordes spilling over the border and was playing the terrorist card. Surely the nation would throw a massive conniption fit. But nary a conniption was to be found.[2]

On May 4, 2005, O'Reilly trotted out his biggest guns to date: "A micro-9/11. Mary Nagle allegedly killed by an illegal alien. That is the subject of this evening's Talking Points Memo."

Yes, Bill had at last found his terrorist threat, and it was a micro-9/11. That's right. A micro-9/11.

Now everyone who was alive at the time remembers where he or she was when the Japanese attacked Pearl Harbor, when JFK was assassinated in Dealy Plaza, and when commercial airliners piloted by Muslim terrorists crashed into Manhattan's World Trade Center. But we'll wager that few of us can recall what we were doing when Mary Nagle of suburban New York was attacked by an undocumented Guatemalan worker from a power-washing company.

Of course, any incident like this is a tragedy. It's a terrible tragedy for Mary Nagle and her family. But it's not a micro-9/11. It's not a nano-9/11. It's not a pico-9/11. It has nothing to do with 9/11. It's another murder in a country that, sad to say, sees thousands of murders each year.

But Bill is a classic scaremonger. He has to know that in a country of 300 million people with millions of illegal aliens among us, eventually one of them is bound to murder a suburbanite. He also knows that a suburban mother of two kids getting killed by a brown person with an accent is worth barrels of ink—more so than if, say, one of those Nova Scotian scoundrels knifes a black guy in a bar.

Bill's solemn duty as a journalist, then, is to find the one-in-ten-million story and make it sound like a trend. He has no evidence that illegal aliens kill suburban mothers at a greater rate than do naturalized citizens or natural-born citizens or even at a greater rate than suburban mothers kill illegal immigrants. But he knows how the idea of Hispanic foreigners infiltrating homes with murder in mind plays to his audience.

Unfortunately, this is the same kind of subtle racism that makes people buy the argument that because brown, Middle Eastern Muslims attacked us on 9/11, we should invade a country full of unrelated brown, Middle Eastern Muslims. Indeed, not since the Frito Bandito has one media figure done more to advance Hispanic-white relations than Bill O'Reilly: "So Mary Nagle becomes yet another victim of illegal alien killers. She is no less a victim of our government's failure to protect us than all of those who died on 9/11."

Yes, and not since the killer bees scares of the seventies has there been a sillier campaign than this. To say that this murder is analogous to 9/11, you basically have to argue that there's a concerted effort on the part of illegal immigrants to kill U.S. citizens. Bill found one illegal-alien killer among millions of illegal aliens living in the country. Of course, as Bill has no solid numbers to back him up, the Mary Nagle murder is pretty much a worthless factoid. There's no evident trend here, much less anything remotely like the organized hostilities of al-Qaeda.

Whichever side you come down on on the illegal immigration issue, it's hard to deny that.

Indeed, if you pored through Mexico death records, chances are it wouldn't take long before you found an account of a drunk underaged Californian who plowed his SUV into a Mexican grandmother on his way back from Tijuana. That would hardly make it a micro-Mexican-American War—unless of course you're Bill Jorge O'Reilly-Gonzales of Mexico's fiercely patriotic Noticias del Zorro Network.

JUDGE NOT, LEST YE BE JUDGED BY O'REILLY

IN FEBRUARY 2005, nine-year-old Jessica Lunsford was abducted and murdered in Florida. A convicted sex offender, John Evander Couey, confessed to the murder. It was one of those tragic stories that gripped the nation and sickened the hearts of its citizens, and Couey may get the death penalty. There was a lot to be saddened by in this story, and a lot of grieving was done by all involved, most significantly the girl's family. Naturally, Bill saw it as an opportunity to pad his ratings and sell more *Factor* Gear.

O'Reilly seized on the fact that three of Couey's housemates, Dorothy Dixon (who is Couey's half-sister), Madie Secord, and Matthew Dittrich, were interrogated after failing to disclose that Couey was living at their mobile home when questioned by police.

The three were arrested, but charges were dropped when State Attorney Brad King decided the case could not be successfully prosecuted as there was no evidence that a crime had technically been committed. King personally explained this to Jessica Lunsford's father, his attorney, and the sheriff's department.

But that wasn't good enough for Bill, who apparently thinks there are so few winnable cases on court dockets in this country that we need to start fabricating hopeless ones:

> Initially, those three were charged with a crime, obstructing an officer without violence. But now those charges have been dropped by State Attorney Brad King. "Talking Points" believes that's outrageous and there is something very wrong going on in Citrus County. King will not talk to the media to explain himself. That's another outrage! Surely he owes the people who elected him a full explanation as to why he's not prosecuting those people. Surely he owes Jessica's family that. (Talking Points Memo, April 11, 2005)

And what sort of "full" explanation would have suited Bill? A red-faced, barely cogent diatribe liberally seasoned with baseless accusations of wrongdoing and ad hominems topped off by a crass plug for the latest in State Attorney Brad King Gear?

Of course, King had given the full explanation to Jessica's family. But as we know, public figures are accountable only to O'Reilly.

Still, King held his ground: "While we may believe what they did was wrong, legally it's not a crime," King was quoted as saying in an AP story. "To charge somebody just to make the public feel better, I'm not going to do that."

Sadly, Florida State Attorney Brad King lives in the real world and not O'Reilly's world, where up is down, black is white, and criminals are vigorously prosecuted to the fullest extent of the law they didn't break:

Can you believe this guy? There's no question these three obstructed justice and perhaps worse. You charge them to send a message. If they get off, they get off. Brad King is off-the-chart misguided, and Americans have to do something. (Talking Points Memo, April 14, 2005)

Of course, the only message a state attorney is likely to send by prosecuting unwinnable cases is that the justice system is confused, weak, ineffectual, and a huge waste of money.

Then, on April 15, 2005, Bill invited Mark Lunsford, Jessica's father, onto *The O'Reilly Factor*. Lunsford told O'Reilly that King had met with him and explained why they couldn't charge Couey's housemates. But Bill still wouldn't drop it:

O'REILLY: but there's another thing you can do here. And you know, you can go after them civilly in the death of Jessica. You can hold them civilly.

LUNSFORD: But what would we get?

O'REILLY: You'd get nothing, but you would get them in a court of law.

O'Reilly added that a lawsuit would "make their life really uncomfortable and send a message."

The message being that when Bill talks about tort reform, it means he supports eliminating only lawsuits that might accomplish something.

But once again, for Bill it's all about getting back at people. This is the leitmotiv of his life and a key to understanding his all too frequent trips down Crazy Lane.

When something sets him off, the light of reason is violently bent to the black-hole-dense whims of his rage. It's never about truth, justice, or fair play with Bill; it's always about retaliation.

But make no mistake about it. Outrage sells. He knows it sells. The more things Bill can find to get upset about, the longer a story stays alive. And while one might think a child molester who buried a nine-year-old girl alive would be villain enough, O'Reilly somehow felt the need to hound an innocent public official who was faithfully executing his office.

Eventually, King had had enough and released a letter in response to O'Reilly:

> I appreciate your frequent invitations to appear on your opinion program. I will continue to respectfully decline to do so. Most recently, however, your staff has upset my neighbors, followed my wife and children, and disrupted the business of my office apparently in an effort to record the "official" reason for my decision to not appear.

Yes, O'Reilly is the champion of truth and justice . . . and ratings. The state attorney explained himself not only to the Lunsford family but, through the Associated Press, to the world. Yet O'Reilly will do anything to get this guy on his show, including harassing his children. That pretty much sums him up.

But just when we thought Bill was nothing but a self-aggrandizing blowhard with a black, bloodless knot of a heart, this showed up in our mailbag. Be assured, this is not an attempt at satire. Following is a portion of an actual Bill O'Reilly e-mail newsletter from April of 2005:

The Spin Stops Here Newsletter

Straight to you from the desk of Bill O'Reilly . . .

> Hello. Well, they say nothing is certain except for death and taxes and it has been a week that proves the point. We've had death (The Pope, little Jessica Lunsford) and we've had taxes (our own) to think about. It seems only right for billoreilly.com to try to help divert your attention and help lighten the load.
>
> Last week I told you we were planning to offer something special for Mother's Day and we have come up with something really good. Check out our Mother's Day Factor Pack. It's our

Factor hooded sweatshirt, tote and keychain all bundled together at a great price. When you get it for her, Mom will love you more than ever, if that's possible.

You know, just once we wish O'Reilly could look out for "the folks" without trying to sell them something.

THOSE DAMN SOCCER-PLAYING', U.S.-HATIN', TERRORIST-LOVIN' MEXICANS

THERE ARE A lot of things to be outraged by in this world. Liberals can get infuriated by discrimination against gays, the destruction of the environment, and unnecessary wars, conservatives by declining values, rampant drug use, and high taxes. Everyone can rally against the corporate scandals of Enron and WorldCom that left so many victims in their wake.

O'Reilly likes to get outraged by a lack of outrage:

In the Back of the Book segment tonight. Yesterday in Guadalajara, Mexico, sixty thousand fans watched the USA soccer team lose to Mexico four to nothing. But what happened in the stands may be more important than what happened on the field. (*The O'Reilly Factor*, February 11, 2004)

Prepare to be outraged:

Our U.S. players were booed during the National Anthem, and some in the crowd also chanted—are you ready?—"Osama, Osama," according to the *New York Times*. And I talked to a reporter on the radio today, and he witnessed it. It happened in the twenty-sixth minute of the game. "Osama, Osama."

Now, to clarify, the AP reported that the Osama chants came from "a few dozen fans" who were obviously sitting within earshot of the reporter. The real story here is that a large number of fans booed during our national anthem, which is just one sad example of the anti-American sentiment currently in vogue throughout much of the world. But to O'Reilly, equally as important are a few drunk guys who acted like idiots.

O'Reilly continued:

> See, I said to the *New York Times* reporter, okay, you've got a bunch of drunken clowns chanting "Osama, Osama." What did the rest of the crowd do? Did they boo those people like they would at Yankee Stadium or somebody else going like that? No, they didn't, and that disturbs me.

All right, let's draw a parallel here. Imagine you're at Yankee Stadium for the big United States versus Indonesia cricket match. Okay, just bear with us. Indonesia has just swept up its last five wickets to seal an innings and 261-run walkover, and a couple of dozen drunk New Yorkers start yelling, "Prepare for a tsunami. . . . Tsunami! Tsunami!"

Now, that would be a stupid thing to yell, but there are few things as stupid as drunk Americans. Regardless, it's a fair comparison in terms of the maliciousness of the fans shouting it. The destruction and loss of life caused in the December 2004 Asian tsunami far exceeded that of 9/11.

Now, some of you may be thinking, "but no one would be so vile as to shout such a thing here in the United States." On the contrary, gallows humor reigns in the loutish backwaters of, say, New York, Philadelphia, or Oakland arenas. Were we panelists on the McLaughlin Group, we'd give it a 10, representing complete metaphysical certitude. It may not happen at Churchill Downs or at the annual Scripps National Spelling Bee in Washington, but then again it might.

So how do you think the fans at Yankee Stadium would react? Would they do as O'Reilly suggested, and turn on those oafs? Of course not. Some people would look on in disgust, others would join in, and the vast majority of the fifty thousand or so in attendance would know nothing about it. Why? Because it's a *huge stadium*.

But in O'Reilly's world, this was a clear-cut indicator of the lack of sympathy the world has for those who died on 9/11, when in reality it was a clear-cut indicator of what several Negra Modelos can do to a bunch of assholes.

Now, had the Mexican ambassador to the United States and some of his buddies from the diplomatic corps gotten together and spelled out "AL-QAEDA RULES" on their bare chests, O'Reilly might have a real gripe. But that didn't happen. You know it didn't happen, 'cause it would have been Bill's top story for sixteen straight days if it had.

OUTRAGED BY MISINFORMATION

O'REILLY WILL often take a story that's ninety-nine parts pathos and go out of his way to find the outrage.

Many readers will remember Audrey Seiler, the University of Wisconsin-Madison student who went missing for four days back in March of 2004. After a nationwide panic (fueled in large part by cable networks such as FOX, which apparently had nothing better to cover), Seiler was found walking out of a Madison wilderness area.

Seiler claimed she had been abducted, but soon we all discovered the truth—that she was a disturbed young woman who had walked off on her own and who had been suffering from depression since the death of her aunt. It was an embarrassing situation for the girl, marked by sadness and regret on the part of Seiler, her family, friends, and neighbors. But on April 2, O'Reilly was pissed: "Now for the top story tonight. Talk about dishonesty and deceit. That young woman supposedly kidnapped in Madison, Wisconsin, apparently fabricated the whole thing, costing the taxpayers millions."

Now, reams of clever media analysis could be written on why exactly a top cable news broadcaster thought that a previously unknown woman who ran off for a few days at a Midwestern college and then turned out to be depressed was the day's top story.

That aside, to characterize it as a story of "dishonesty and deceit" is harsh. It could just as easily be called a story of depression and despair. But that's subject to interpretation. What isn't subject to interpretation is how much the incident cost the city. While O'Reilly claimed it cost the city's taxpayers millions, the pinheads at the Madison mayor's office had a different story.

Here's what the incident actually cost, according to city officials:

- $54,000: overtime and benefits
- $41,000: estimated salary and benefits for regular time
- $1,000: miscellaneous expenses

At the time, city officials estimated that overtime pay for the incident would actually be less than $54,000 because some of it was counted toward compensatory time. The city also pointed out that the $41,000 for regular pay was already in the budget. Thus it didn't really make sense to attribute that cost to the search.

So realistically, the whole thing probably cost the taxpayers about fifty grand, if that. That's still a waste of money, but probably not quite as bad as bringing three people to trial who can't be convicted.

Anyway, the point is that to pull wildly overblown numbers out of one's ass to beat down horribly depressed college girls who find themselves not only at the lowest point of their lives but also stuck in the middle of an embarrassing media circus you helped create is not journalism. If anyone in the so-called liberal media did it, you'd worry they were off their lithium. Seriously. Which brings us to the richly ironic coda of this chapter.

LOOK AT THOSE OUTRAGE-PEDDLIN' BASTARDS AT THE *NEW YORK TIMES*

BILL IS OUTRAGED at the *New York Times*. He's outraged that they're peddling outrage. He's so outraged by this that he will not stop until each one of his viewers shares his outrage. It's outrageous!

On May 27, 2004, O'Reilly said the *New York Times* had run a "total of fifty front-page articles" about the Abu Ghraib scandal, and on June 21 said, "They got forty-seven stories on Abu Ghraib on the front page."

While those of us still using the Gregorian calendar might take issue with Bill's facts, his main point was that the *Times* was using the Abu Ghraib story as "a political hammer."

Brian Montopoli, writing for cjrdaily.org, noted that from June 2004 to May 2005, O'Reilly had criticized the *New York Times* for its coverage of Abu Ghraib on June 11, June 14, June 30, July 1, July 9, July 21, August 9, October 8, October 25, November 9, November 22, February 16, March 9, April 12, May 3, May 16, and May 17.

Montopoli's take on this? "The notion that the *Times* is allowing ideology to dictate its coverage has become a common refrain on the show."

Now, many of O'Reilly's viewers will recall his coverage of the controversial academic Ward Churchill, who called certain of the 9/11 World Trade Center victims "little Eichmanns." We'll go into O'Reilly's odd obsession with the obscure University of Colorado professor more extensively in Chapter 9.

However, one thing is certain: O'Reilly's coverage of Churchill, whom few had ever heard of before Bill basically agreed to be his publicist, is ideological in the extreme. If the *Times* is trying to give the Bush administration a black eye by pointing out military abuses in Iraq, O'Reilly is taking a machete to liberals' heads with his sorry attempts to hold up Churchill as somehow emblematic of the progressive movement.

Montopoli cited twenty-five instances of Churchill coverage on *The O'Reilly Factor* from January through May of 2005, including on nine straight shows from the end of January through the early part of February.

The only conceivable explanation other than that O'Reilly is twisted by ideology is that he actually thinks the unheralded and previously ignored ideas of an unknown college professor are worth twenty-five shows out of a possible eighty over the course of three and a half months on the nation's highest-rated cable news program.

Or else he's nuts. Come to think of it, that old lady on the bus is looking more lucid by the day.

NOTES

1. Or "wetbacks" as O'Reilly calls them (*The O'Reilly Factor*, February 6, 2003).
2. Of course, if terrorists wanted to enter the country secretly, there are no doubt easier ways to do it than hopping a crowded delivery truck to the border and swimming across the Rio Grande. The government has also done little to address the prospect of al-Qaeda operatives dressing as bears and drifting over the border from Saskatchewan. But you have to set your priorities, such as protecting nuclear and chemical plants, which we haven't done quite enough about either.

4

SEE BILL. SEE BILL JACK.
SEE BILL JACK AND CALL JILL

HERE'S A FUN little game. Following are two statements by embattled celebrities. See if you can guess who said each:

Celebrity 1: I have always maintained my innocence and vehemently denied that these events ever took place. I reluctantly chose to settle the false claims only to end the terrible publicity and to continue with my life and career.

I ask all of my neighbors . . . the people to whom I give my loyal trust and admiration, to keep an open mind and give me a chance to show that I am completely innocent of these charges. I will not let you down.

Celebrity 2: I have something very important to tell you. All litigation has ceased in that case that has made me the object of media scorn from coast to coast. Today, lawyers issued a statement saying there was no wrongdoing in the case whatsoever by anyone. Obviously, the words "no wrongdoing" are the key.

On a personal note, this matter has caused enormous pain,

but I had to protect my family and I did. Some of the media hammered me relentlessly because as you know, I'm a huge target . . . All I can say to you is please, do not believe everything you hear and read.

Here's another clue:

Celebrity 1: They served a search warrant on me which allowed them to view and photograph my body, including my penis, my buttocks, my lower torso, thighs and any other areas that they wanted. They were supposedly looking for any discoloration, spotting, blotches or other evidence of a skin color disorder called vitiligo.

Celebrity 2: I don't look like that. *This* is what I look like.[1]

Celebrity 1, of course, is Michael Jackson. Celebrity 2 is Bill O'Reilly. The first two quotes came following the settlement of civil cases that threatened to kill their careers and mortally embarrass them. The next two quotes were made in reference to their respective splotches.

What are we getting at? Or rather, what do these two celebrities have in common other than being spotty men who had to settle high-profile sex charges brought against them? Well, first off, Jackson is well-adjusted enough to admit his deformities.

But aside from Jackson's being marginally more healthy mentally, they both appear to view hefty payoffs to an accuser as some sort of vindication.

Now, some may think it unfair to compare Bill O'Reilly to Michael Jackson, who has twice been accused of pedophilia. O'Reilly masturbated *himself* while harassing an underling, so he's more like a cross between Paul Reubens and Clarence Thomas.

Further, some might take issue with our reference to detailed transcripts from a lawsuit filed by O'Reilly's accuser, which appear to be meticulously transcribed all the way down to inserted "ums" and "uhs" and the awkward transposition of bath items and Middle Eastern dishes.

After all, O'Reilly never had his day in court, because his accuser unfairly accepted a payoff before the whole truth could come out. Shouldn't we at least consider both sides of the story?

"All right, would you tell both sides of the story for Hitler?"—Bill O'Reilly commenting on new charges brought against Michael Jackson.

No, Bill, you wouldn't. But, to be fair, Hitler had lovely skin.

So let's get into it, shall we?

Bill, of course, was raised Catholic. As authors, we happen to be steeped in Catholic tradition. One of us spent eleven years in Catholic parochial schools, and the other was raised by an ex-nun.

But Bill's Catholic upbringing appears to have mixed with his innate sexuality like the militia movement with ammonium nitrate fertilizer.

Indeed, it seems to have a great deal to do with the way he views sex. In public, of course, Bill likes to project the image of a traditionalist. He sees himself as a moral man who bases his beliefs on Judeo-Christian philosophy. Yet there have always been signs of a dark and skanky underbelly to our redoubtable anchorman.

Now this is a complicated issue. To begin with, unlocking O'Reilly's psyche has never been a simple thing. But when you add his penis to the equation, it suddenly becomes the advanced calculus of psychological dysfunction. Amateur teen hackers on Commodore 64s would have a better shot at securing the Pentagon's missile launch codes than a workaday New York therapist would have at getting to the root of O'Reilly's problems vis-à-vis women. The level of repression evidenced in his books and television program is simply astounding.

O'Reilly forces himself into a public persona that drastically contradicts his more base urges. These urges seep out in public forums and gush out in private.

This is especially evident in O'Reilly's books, where he moves from Puritan to dirty old man with the agility of Gord the Rogue.

Indeed, there are times when O'Reilly can barely mask his tendencies.

For instance, in his book *The O'Reilly Factor*, Bill includes chapters on sex and dating that sound alternately like bad advice for lovers and a drunken dial from Pat O'Brien. From hackneyed observations about how men only want sex while women want relationships to a truly bizarre section about how once the kids are out of the house you can loosen up on sex, this book is a treasure trove of sexual weirdness that could have put Alfred Kinsey off his feed for a month.

Along with his vulgar ramblings about his sexual prowess, his libertine disco days, and the "hundreds" of women he's dated, we're treated to a creepy sojourn in a shadowy labyrinth of middle-aged whack-off fantasies: "For me, that means Tyra Banks in the Victoria's Secret catalogs. (Can you believe you get these things for free?)"

No, Bill, we can't. Can you believe that each time one arrives in the mail from now on, we'll be confronted with the realization that somewhere you're settling into your favorite easy chair with said catalog and a fresh tube of K-Y warming gel?

Of course, Bill doesn't stop here. He goes on to tell us about other objects of his desire, including "Sarah Michelle Gellar in a tight T-shirt," "Jacqueline Bisset in a very wet T-shirt," "Vanessa Williams doing anything anywhere," and "Melanie Griffith before the lip implants."

Okay, it's bizarre enough that Bill is ticking off the names of every woman who turns him on, but now he's critiquing the ways they've made themselves less desirable to him. No doubt Griffith is *really* regretting the collagen now.

But he's *still* not done: "Sharon Stone reacting with such openness to Michael Douglas."

What's the purpose of these chapters again? To give his viewers some fatherly advice and a few genteel observations about the fairer sex? Or to ensure that Gellar, Bisset, Griffith, and Stone, et al., are put on suicide watch after discovering that O'Reilly has been typing their names with one hand?

Sadly, Stone's infamous pantyless boogina[2] flash in *Basic Instinct*, which fourteen years later remains the talk of pathetic middle-aged broadcasters and twelve-year-old boys without broadband Internet, represents just the halfway point of O'Reilly's sick literary cul-de-sac of masturbatory daydreams.

But this is quite far enough, except to say that O'Reilly's list of turn-ons, part deux, includes the charming "Kim Basinger in no pants."

Imagine if Dan Rather had included this kind of thing in his book.

I JUST MET A GIRL NAMED ANDREA

BUT WHY BUST O'Reilly's balls over the kind of sexual musings most men admittedly engage in from time to time (though, to be fair, such musings are rarely put in books about the decline of American values)? Well, because O'Reilly's odd sexual pathologies are merely the ceiling of the Sistine Chapel on which he would ultimately paint his masterpiece—the Mackris sex scandal.

As many will remember, in October 2004 Bill was hit with a sexual harassment suit by Andrea Mackris, one of his associate producers. Among the allegations in Mackris's affidavit were that O'Reilly had subjected her to a monologue about sex over the phone while he masturbated, encouraged her to get a vibrator and name it, and launched into a Caribbean sex fantasy that clumsily juxtaposed the plaintiff's genitalia with Middle Eastern food staples.

The Mackris thing came as a shock to many of O'Reilly's viewers. But should it have? The distance between allusions in best-selling books about supermodel jerk-off sessions and the lurid revelations alleged in Mackris' affidavit is like an afternoon bus ride from Levittown to Greenwich Village, when it comes right down to it.

Indeed, the following accounts from the Mackris court documents are actually vintage O'Reilly.

To avoid stealing Larry Flynt's thunder, we offer only excerpts. (While we understand some of you have probably seen this stuff already, we're actually hoping to trick O'Reilly into suing us based on copyright infringement of his work.)

would be work-related, and returned the call. Instead, Defendant **BILL O'REILLY** once again launched into a lewd and lascivious, unsolicited and disturbing sexually-graphic talk.

➡ 77. Despite informing him that she was not at all interested in the conversation, and despite her adamant refusal to participate in such talk, Defendant **O'REILLY** informed Plaintiff **ANDREA MACKRIS** that he was watching a porn movie and babbled perversely regarding his fantasies concerning Carribean vacations because, purportedly: "Once people get into that hot weather they shed their inhibitions, you know they drink during the day, they lay there and lazy, they have dinner and then they come back and fool around... that's basically the modus operandi."

78. During the course of his monologue, Defendant **O'REILLY** further stated:

Well, if I took you down there then I'd want to take a shower with you right away, that would be the first thing I'd do... yeah, we'd check into the room, and we would order up some room service and uh and you'd definitely get two wines into you as quickly as I could get into you I would get 'em into you... maybe intravenously, get those glasses of wine into you....

You would basically be in the shower and then I would come in and I'd join you and you would have your back to me and I would take that little loofa thing and kinda' soap up your back... rub it all over you, get you to relax, hot water... and um... you know, you'd feel the tension drain out of you and uh you still would be with your back to me then I would kinda' put my arm - it's one of those mitts, those loofa mitts you know, so I got my hands in it... and I would put it around front, kinda' rub your tummy a little bit with it, and then with my other hand I would start to massage your boobs, get your nipples really hard... 'cuz I like that and you have really spectacular boobs....

So anyway I'd be rubbing your big boobs and getting your nipples really hard, kinda' kissing your neck from behind... and then I would take the other hand with the falafel (sic) thing and I'd put it on your pussy but you'd have to do it really light, just kind of a tease business....

Wow, if that doesn't make you feel like you've just eaten an entire bag of Circus Peanuts after getting trapped for three hours on the Tilt-A-Whirl, we don't know what does. But it arguably gets better:

two" and alluded to having a menage a trois with Plaintiff and her friend.

41.   On or about May 2003, Defendant BILL O'REILLY took Plaintiff ANDREA MACKRIS and her college friend to dinner at Da Silvano's. During the course of the dinner, O'REILLY repeatedly propositioned the women, singing the praises of telephone sex, offering to telephone them both, and suggesting that the three of them "go to a hotel together and have the time of [their] lives." O'REILLY further suggested that the women needed to be trained so they'd be equipped and ready to go when a "real man shows up in your lives," and offered "lessons." O'REILLY further suggested they use their sexuality to their advantage so they'd have power over men, otherwise men would have power over them. Plaintiff was extremely embarrassed and protested: "Bill, you're my boss!"

➡ 42.   During the course of this dinner, in approximately May 2003, Defendant BILL O'REILLY, without solicitation or invite, regaled Plaintiff and her friend with stories concerning the loss of his virginity to a girl in a car at JFK, two "really wild" Scandinavian airline stewardesses he had gotten together with, and a "girl" at a sex show in Thailand who had shown him things in a backroom that "blew [his] mind." Defendant then stated he was going to Italy to meet the Pope, that his pregnant wife was staying at home with his daughter, and implied he was looking forward to some extra-marital dalliances with the "hot" Italian women. Both Plaintiff and her friend were repulsed, but felt powerless to protest strongly since Defendant was Plaintiff's boss and a powerful man at FOX. Defendant finally stopped after noting: "MACKRIS can't handle it."

43.   On or about September 2003, Defendant BILL O'REILLY asked Plaintiff ANDREA MACKRIS to dinner at an Italian restaurant around the corner from FOX, purportedly to discuss business. During the course of dinner, Defendant once again raised the

See? That's our boy.

Now, as the lawyers involved in the lawsuit said—and O'Reilly took pains to point out—there was "no wrongdoing" in this case by anyone. Yeah, whatever you say, Jacko. Unfortunately, the public is not so kind a mistress. Or, more to the point, the public is not so accommodating as a girl at a sex show in Thailand.

While the scandal simmered, O'Reilly, true to form, without ever actually addressing the substance of the allegations, heaped

scorn on those who took issue with him. In essence, he was shouting "cut his mic!" to the world:

> Just about every famous person I know has been threatened
> by somebody. Fame makes you a target. It is something that has
> to be taken very seriously. As I've mentioned before, I've received
> many threats over the years. Everything from death letters to
> some guy running around the country offering people twenty-five
> thousand dollars to sign affidavits accusing me of whatever.
> (Talking Points Memo, October 13, 2004)

So Bill merely implies the lawsuit is frivolous without actually saying it's baseless:

> The lawyers here at FOX News have been great in dealing
> with these situations, but there comes a time when enough's
> enough. So this morning I had to file a lawsuit against some
> people who are demanding sixty million dollars or they will
> "punish" me and FOX News. *Sixty million dollars.*

What the amount the plaintiff was seeking has to do with the
price of hookers in Thailand is beyond us but, again, O'Reilly
wasn't exactly trying to deny the allegations here as much as
bluster through the crisis with righteous indignation about the
plaintiff's "extortion" attempt.

"I really can't say anything else. I don't want to waste your time
with this. The justice system has the case. We'll see what happens.
But in the end, you should know that this is all about hurting me and
the FOX News Channel." Again, Bill and Fox News are just victims
and this is about punishing them.

"It's a shame we have to live in a country where this happens, but
got to go through it. All right, that's it. End of story." Why is it a
shame? Bill doesn't really explain why. It just is. Again, no denial.
Just implied victim status.

After FOX and O'Reilly settled the suit to "protect his family,"
O'Reilly, skilled projectionist that he is, tried to turn the whole

thing into the rest of the world's problem, blaming the scoundrel's all-purpose scapegoat, the amorphous and all-powerful "media."

But "the folks," he said, stayed with him:

> The good news is that *Factor* viewers and listeners seemed to have given me the benefit of the doubt when some of the media did not. You guys looked out for me, and I will never forget it. This brutal ordeal is now officially over and I will never speak of it again. (*The O'Reilly Factor*, October 28, 2004)

Yeah, *Factor* viewers gave O'Reilly the benefit of the doubt. Then again, people still send money to Pat Robertson. It doesn't really prove anything.

Of course, in the court documents "family man" O'Reilly came off as anything but. Indeed, it could be that Bill O'Reilly is one of those people who leads two lives—not in the Lifetime Movie sense of the word, but close. So close, in fact, that Treat Williams and Ann Jillian will be vying for leads in the TV movie.

The most salient issue, however, is not that O'Reilly fancies himself a "traditionalist," rejects the secularization of America, extols the Judeo-Christian foundations of our nation, and bemoans the perfidious culture war being propagated by the liberal Hollywood elite while simultaneously threatening to massage an employee's tits. No, what's most disturbing is that that he completely sucks at phone sex.

Of course, true to form, he thinks he's awesome at it. He thinks he's the frickin' MacGyver of phone sex, making women who've never orgasmed gush with just a phone call. But as the court documents show, Bill's technique is really quite dreadful. The man has absolutely no game.

So, as we've written this book primarily to help Bill navigate his way past life's many obstacles, we figured we'd give him some pointers for future producer-harassing endeavors. Here goes:

1. Don't use unnecessarily complicated words. Okay, Bill, at times during phone sex you use complicated, almost clinical terms such as "intravenously" and "modus operandi."

Dude! The ladies like French and Italian. But Latin? Not so much. Use action words. Paint a picture in her mind. Talk about how you're strong enough to pick her up and just bounce her up and down on your cock while standing up in the shower.

Use construction words (e.g., nail, pound, hammer, drive, etc.). You gotta keep it hot. Don't tell her that you want to feed wine into her veins intravenously. That's just creepy, man. It sounds like something a guy would do to a girl he has trapped in his basement.

2. Avoid immature descriptions. This is key, Bill. You sound like a thirteen-year-old when you use phrases like "rubbing your big boobs."

   Okay, first and foremost, don't use the word "boobs." However, if you do, don't say "big boobs." You sound like Beavis and/or Butthead. If you continue, she's not going to breathlessly anticipate your next salvo; she's just going to expect an awkward "heh-heh, heh, boooooobs."

   Say breasts if you must, but the internationally accepted phone-sex term is "tits." Got it? It's not up for debate.

3. Avoid misspoken or mispronounced words. Now, a lot has been made about your falafel comment, and it was obviously a blunder, but come on. It's a big blunder. No one is cummin' after that one. No one!

   Now Bill, everyone has that uncle who says he loves to watch Seinfeld, or tries to engage your niece in a conversation about Justin Timberwolf, and you simply laugh it off and don't bother correcting him. But no one wants to have phone sex with him. Bill, when it comes to phone sex, you are that guy. You just need to stop.

   Okay? End of lesson.

O'Reilly actually makes a very astute comment about sex in *The O'Reilly Factor* book:[3]

"Control it, don't let it control you," he warns his readers.

Oh, Bill.

NOTES

1. Bill O'Reilly remarking on a splotchy picture of him, excerpted from Al Franken, *Lies and the Lying Liars Who Tell Them: A Fair and Balanced Look at the Right* (New York: Dutton, 2003).
2. Special thanks to Muffy's World of Vagina Euphemisms (www.starma.com/penis/muffy/muffy.html) for help in researching this chapter.
3. Bill O'Reilly, *The O'Reilly Factor: The Good, The Bad and the Completely Ridiculous in American Life* (New York: Broadway Books, 2000).

5

THREE-DOLLAR BILL:
O'REILLY AMONG THE QUEERS

ONE OF THE reasons Bill pops a vein whenever someone accuses him or FOX News of being conservative is that he believes he's actually liberal on several issues. For instance, he professes to support gay rights. Unfortunately, O'Reilly supports gays the way Strom Thurmond supported his Negro daughter.

In high school, when taking a trig or algebra test, they always made us show our work to make sure we weren't cheating. Now, O'Reilly could simply say, "I support the right of consenting adults to do what they want in the privacy of their bedrooms" and leave it at that. But, unfortunately, O'Reilly shows us his work. He gets the answer right but he's obviously copying off someone else's paper.

Indeed, when it comes to homosexuality, O'Reilly is the equivalent of the guy in Alabama who proudly proclaims, "I don't have any problem with niggers."

Bill's progay agenda is fraught with lunacy. Let's take a look.

I TAKE YOU TO BE MY LAWFULLY WEDDED GOAT

BILL DOESN'T REALLY understand the legal system per se. Often what he considers judicial activism is simply pragmatism or an adherence to the spirit of a law. Where most people see an evolutionary change in our society, Bill sees the slipperiest of slopes. On the March 29, 2005, broadcast of *The Radio Factor*, he gave us this little gem:

> The judges in Massachusetts knew they weren't going to be impeached when they said to the state legislature, "Gay marriage is now legal in Massachusetts because we say it is. We the judges." They knew they weren't gonna be impeached. They knew the legislature didn't care. You get the government you deserve. . . . And in ten years, this is gonna be a totally different country than it is right now. Laws that you think are in stone—they're gonna evaporate, man. You'll be able to marry a goat—you mark my words!

This, of course, is the hyperest of hyperbole. After all, when the bestial unions are finally, thankfully legalized, even the most luckless carny won't have to aim much lower than spider monkey. What's with all the ungulate sex fantasies?

This is kind of like saying, "Hey, I have nothing against the concept of turning right on a red light, but if you let people do it, next thing you know they'll be driving eighty miles an hour down the sidewalk."

The truth is, it's highly unlikely that people will be marrying goats in ten years time. That would require a constitutional amendment, a sea change in cultural mores and ethics, and something along the lines of the Island of Dr. Moreau. It'll be twenty years minimum. Minimum. Liberals will most likely shoot for human-primate unions first and then work their way down the evolutionary chain. Indeed, we've been to the secret meetings and happen to know the current liberal rallying cry is, "A Goat in Every Bed Before We're Dead!"

LOSE THE MANOLO BLAHNIKS, YOU FAGGOT

BUT, AS WE noted, Bill will not abide gay-bashing, so long as gay-bashing is construed as literal bashing—as in, hey, that's a gay, don't you even think about picking up that rather large tree branch and bashing him!

> To someone gay who is the victim of discrimination or abuse, I say exchange the high heels for a sensible business suit, because that's appropriate for the playing field, and hire a lawyer who will put the screws to whatever bastards are interfering with your rights to *private sexual expression.* (*The O'Reilly Factor* book)

Yeah, he's not exactly in the vanguard of the civil rights movement with this. Seriously, what's up with the "high heels" crack? That's like saying the KKK will stop lynching black people when they put down the fried chicken and watermelon. Of course, in Bill's mind, gays are complicit in their own abuse. They bring it on themselves by—well, by being gay. Of course, when O'Reilly mentions your right to "private sexual expression," he means just that. Private. So if you're a gay couple walking down the street and happen to hold hands, then you'll get what's coming to you, homo.

IF IT LOOKS LIKE A DUCK . . . SHOOT IT

> When I'm walking down the street with a five-year-old, I don't want to have to try to explain why Jack is dressed up like Jill or Jill is wearing a buzz cut.
>
> —The O'Reilly Factor *book*

FIRST OF ALL, kudos to you, Bill, for making it through an entire authentic Southern-fried homophobic tirade without once mentioning either Adam or Steve. But, seriously, what's your point? First of all, a guy in a dress is kinda funny. It's not scary or offensive. At worst it's just silly. After all, when your kids are watching Looney Tunes, and Bugs dresses up as a girl rabbit, you don't feel the need to speculate on his sexual orientation, do you? Probably not.

And a woman with a buzz cut? Holy crap! How the hell do you explain that to a five-year-old? Seriously, if you're tucking your son into bed at night and he asks, "Daddy, you know that lady we saw today? Why was her hair so short?," do you feel compelled to say, "Well, Spencer, it's because she enjoys performing cunnilingus on other women. Good night, son"?

MARY HAS TWO MOMMIES? I WONDER HOW THEY GET IT ON

THIS IS THE essence of O'Reilly's attitude toward homosexuality: he thinks that if a child sees a same-sex couple or even hears about one, it will inevitably lead to a graphic discussion of sex acts.

Consider the O'Reilly-fueled *Postcards from Buster* controversy. In one episode of the popular PBS children's program, a little girl introduces the cartoon bunny Buster Baxter to her mommy and her mommy's female partner. Here's how Bill saw it in his February 24, 2005, column on billoreilly.com:

> In one of his adventures, Buster showed up in Vermont to check out the maple syrup industry and wound up surrounded by a bunch of lesbians and their children. The connection between the syrup business and lesbians was never really explained.

Okay, here's where Bill's substandard education really rears its head. Two lesbians is not a "bunch," it is a "gaggle." His comment about lesbians and the maple syrup industry just cinches it.

> Many Americans believe that little kids should have a childhood and not be subjected to any kind of sexuality. I don't want to be offensive here, but who in their right mind wants to explain Norma and Barbara's lifestyle to their four-year-old? Give the kids a break, okay?

Actually, Bill, any parent in his right mind would want to explain to his children that they'll encounter same-sex couples. Not

explaining it isn't giving the kids a break. What you'll want to keep
secret are the details of your trip to Thailand.

But introducing homosexuality into the little kid culture angers
many Americans who believe sex in general is an inappropriate
topic for small children, and that is a legitimate point of view
whether Barney Frank or PBS likes it or not.

Again, Bill doesn't understand the difference between discussing
sex and sexual orientation. When you tell your children, "Mommy
and Daddy love each other," let's hope they don't counter with, "Yes,
but where do you put your wee-wee? In her butt sometimes?"
Bill of course loves to fall back on the "do what you want, just
keep it away from my kids" line of argument because it makes him
seem marginally more sophisticated than the guy who tells fag jokes
at the corner bar before drunk-driving his El Camino into his
grandma's house.

MY GAY UNCLE COULD KICK YOUR GAY UNCLE'S ASS

UNFORTUNATELY, O'REILLY appears constitutionally incapable
of actually accepting homosexuals as anything other than sick
sodomites lurking in the shadows eager to recruit "normal" kids.
And while even on his best days Bill shows roughly the reasoning
capacity of your average brain stem, homos seem to really muck up
his synapses. Indeed, he rarely misses an opportunity to show both
how tolerant of and viscerally repulsed by homosexuals he can be.
For instance, in his January 30, 2003, Talking Points Memo,
O'Reilly whines that *USA Today* ran an op-ed by freelance writer
Bruce Kluger that was critical of O'Reilly without checking with him
first. (Seriously, O'Reilly complains about this, wondering, without per-
ceptible irony, "Why would *USA Today* print a hit piece like this without asking me to respond?") Then he breaks out the non sequiturs:

These drive-by attacks do little to help the cause of the left.
Kluger is a longtime liberal who has mocked President Bush on

NPR and allowed his two-year-old daughter to attend a Gay Pride parade wearing a T-shirt "I love my gay uncle."

And that's fine. Kluger is entitled to raise his child any way he wants and he's entitled to believe anything he wants. What is not fine is Kluger's agenda running in *USA Today* without challenge. That is cheap and sleazy, and the newspaper should be ashamed.

First of all, it's refreshing to know that every piece of commentary O'Reilly publishes or airs, as well as all opinions expressed by his guests, are vetted by the people or policy-makers being criticized— or else who knows how stupid his show would be every day?

Secondly, it's great to know that Kluger is raising his children to be proud of their gay relatives and that O'Reilly approves. It's odd, though, that O'Reilly would throw in something nice and support-ive about Kluger in the middle of a commentary hammering the guy. Unless O'Reilly is actually including the irrelevant factoid about Kluger's daughter's T-shirt to smear him in some way. But no, O'Reilly likes gays, doesn't he? He clearly supports homosexuals and their rights. Oh no, that's right, he's a nut.

IS THAT SANTORUM IN YOUR PANTS OR ARE YOU JUST HAPPY TO SEE ME?

OF COURSE, IF there's anyone O'Reilly supports more than homo-sexuals, it's people who say absurdly offensive things about homo-sexuals. For instance, there's this, from O'Reilly's April 23, 2003, Talking Points Memo on Senator Rick Santorum's infamous com-ments about state sodomy laws. True to form, O'Reilly disagreed with Santorum's position that the government has a right to crim-inalize certain sex acts, but he focused his criticism on those calling for Santorum's resignation:

America does not need a sex police to protect the public. It's a complete waste of time and resources, but America also does not need people who run around trying to personally destroy indi-viduals by hanging a bias label on them. That's malicious and antidemocratic. If Santorum feels homosexual activity is wrong, he's entitled to that belief without being labeled a hater.

And just for fun, here are the comments O'Reilly thought Santorum was being unfairly persecuted for. Ask yourself if this makes him a hater, a lover, or something closer to indifferent:

> If the Supreme Court says you have the right to consensual [gay] sex within your home, then you have the right to bigamy, polygamy, you have the right to incest, you have the right to adultery.

Of course, in O'Reilly's demented little world, those who called Santorum on his obvious bigotry were "witch-hunters." Coincidentally, some people have another term for, as O'Reilly says in this Talking Points Memo, "demonizing a person for holding an opinion you don't like." It's called his show. Pot meet kettle, dumbass.

WELL, I DID IT ONCE, WHEN I WAS IN THE SCOUTS

OF COURSE, THOSE who watch his show know that O'Reilly never misses a chance to stir the pot. In fact, nothing gets him going like the thought of a bunch of queers and atheists infecting institutions such as the Boy Scouts. Indeed, because this is such an emotionally charged issue, O'Reilly apparently feels the need to switch on only his limbic system before offering his opinion. While a skilled polemicist would merely cite right of free association to defend the Scouts' discriminatory policies, O'Reilly can't miss a chance to stoke this country's ever-flickering fires of antigay anxiety:

> It would be impossible for the Boy Scouts or any children's organization to admit avowed homosexuals because of the potential liability. Say the Scouts put openly gay and straight kids together and some sexual activity occurred. Well, parents could sue for millions, same way parents could sue if the Scouts put boys and girls together and underaged sex occurred. (Talking Points Memo, January 9, 2004)

Well, this is great news for parents who thought their only chance at a big payday was to get their daughters internships on *The O'Reilly Factor*. Apparently, all you have to do to sue for big bucks in this country is put your teen in a classroom and hope they screw a classmate.

Homosexuality always has and always will exist. What's changed most radically is society's attitude toward it. O'Reilly, of course, thinks he's changed with the times. Unfortunately, his public comments on homosexuality invariably make him sound about as sincere as the officiant at a Liza Minnelli wedding.

In fact, this weird bit of historical analysis, from the March 15, 2005, *Radio Factor*, about sums it up:

> You know, the Founding Fathers didn't write anything into the Constitution about gay marriage. Because back then, if you were gay, they hung you.
>
> So you couldn't get married 'cause they put you in the rack. You know, if you were running around wearing a chartreuse hat, you were in lots of trouble. So we didn't even have to worry about these people getting married, because if they come out of their closet in the log cabin, somebody'll shoot them in the head. So there really wasn't an issue back in the Founding Fathers.

Of course, the same could have been said about a black man marrying a white woman. Someone would have shot them in the head, too. So you wouldn't have had to worry about that either, huh, Bill?

6

WHO HAS DECEIV'D THEE SO OFT AS THY SELF?

Have I told any lies, sir? Why don't you come right on this program and produce some proof of that? And if you don't, you're a coward and a sleazy propagandist who deserves to be scorned.

—Bill O'Reilly, June 4, 2004

IS BILL A liar or merely insane?

As keen observers of all things O'Reilly, it's a question that has bedeviled us for some time now.

Just as quantum physicists describe both a wave nature and a particle nature of light (or, for the sake of *Factor* staff members reading this book for Bill, just as Frosted Mini-Wheats have both a sweet side *and* a wheat side), it could be there's a little lie and a little crazy in every one of his false statements. In this case, reality is truly in the eye of the beholder.

The problem with simply calling Bill a liar is that one has to be aware of one's lies for them to really be considered lies. We're not sure Bill qualifies.

Over and over again, Bill says things that aren't true. That part is easy. (And if you don't believe us, just ask the *Paris Business Review*. They've done a study.)

It's the "intent" half of the equation that complicates things. Take, for instance, what is seen by many as one of Bill's signature lies—the Peabody/Polk thing.

As Al Franken famously recounted in his book *Lies and the Lying Liars Who Tell Them*, Franken saw O'Reilly on C-SPAN one night telling an interviewer that his former show, *Inside Edition*, had won two Peabody awards. Franken checked it out, discovered it wasn't true, and then called O'Reilly.

When Franken confronted Bill with the information, Bill paused and told Franken he'd call him back. A short time later, O'Reilly returned Franken's call and told him, "It was a Polk."

Later, according to Franken's account, other media figures ran with the story, among them *Newsday* columnist Robert Reno, who wrote a column titled, "Some Factors about O'Reilly Aren't Factual."

Well, O'Reilly went ape shit, as O'Reillys are wont to do.

On the March 13, 2001, installment of The O'Reilly Factor, Bill said this:

> Guy says about me, couple weeks ago, O'Reilly said he won a Peabody Award. Never said it. You can't find a transcript where I said it. You—there is no one on earth you could bring in that would say I said it. Robert Reno in *Newsday*, a columnist, writes in his column, calls me a liar, all right? And it's totally fabricated. That's attack journalism.

Now, here's where the wave-particle duality of O'Reilly's lying comes into play. Those still operating under the Newtonian paradigm are likely to side entirely with either Franken or O'Reilly, depending on where their allegiances lie. And by sticking with just strict definitions, either could make a case.

Indeed, as far as we know, O'Reilly never actually said, "I won a Peabody Award." But in his book, Franken cited more than one instance where Bill appeared to be taking credit for those Polks/Peabodys (which the program won after O'Reilly had left), including a May 19, 2000, interview where Bill said, flatly, "We won Peabody Awards."

Now, O'Reilly's take on this is that he wasn't saying he personally won any Peabodys but was defending his old program, which interviewers had been calling a tabloid show (which it clearly is, though O'Reilly seemed reluctant to acknowledge it). Of course, if you wanted to give Bill the benefit of the doubt, you could argue that he wasn't literally saying he won a Peabody, even though he used the inclusive pronoun "we."

But most reasonable people would see it Franken's way, given the context of O'Reilly's May 19, 2000, interview with Arthel Neville, which Franken quotes in his book:

NEVILLE: You hosted *Inside Edition* . . .

O'REILLY: Correct.

NEVILLE: Which is considered a tabloid show.

O'REILLY: By whom?

NEVILLE: By many people.

O'REILLY: Does that mean . . .

NEVILLE: And even you . . .

O'REILLY: . . . we throw the Peabody Awards back? . . . We won Peabody Awards.

Now, even if Bill's sole intention was to defend the honor of his former program, this certainly makes it appear like O'Reilly is saying he won a Peabody or at the very least is implying that the show won the awards while he was host, making him a part of that success.

Imagine, for instance, we were interviewing John Tesh about his career, and the discussion moved toward his stint with *Entertainment Tonight*. And imagine if Tesh said, "we won Emmys," even though the show had actually won a Nickelodeon Kids' Choice Award a year after Tesh had left.

AMANN & BREUER: You hosted *Entertainment Tonight*...

TESH: Correct.

AMANN & BREUER: Which is considered a fluff entertainment program.

TESH: By whom?

AMANN & BREUER: By many people...

TESH: Does that mean...

AMANN & BREUER: And even you...

TESH: ... we throw the Emmys back? ... We won Emmys.

Now, aside from our kinda creepy chanting-in-unison behavior, the two things that might stand out from such an interview are: 1) Tesh is either being dishonest or is horribly deluded about the nature of the program he hosted for several years; and 2) he's either being deliberately sly about where credit lies for the awards or is making a very sloppy characterization that might understandably lead people to think that the show won awards on Tesh's watch.

Of course, Reno is not completely off the hook here either. As a journalist, he should not have made undue assumptions—the most careless being that O'Reilly is a sane man.

For instance, if Reno had read an interview transcript where OJ Simpson was defending his team, the Buffalo Bills, by saying, "does that mean we send the AFL Championship trophies back? We won two AFL Championships," he probably would have dug a little deeper (discovering that the Juice never himself won a championship), because OJ's kind of wacky.

But rather than understanding how Reno might have honestly misinterpreted O'Reilly's statement "we won Peabody Awards" as meaning that O'Reilly was saying he won Peabodys, O'Reilly flew off the handle and claimed it was a total fabrication.

No, a total fabrication is more like "Batboy has impregnated Barbara Bush" or "Jamie Farr has just inked a fifty-million-dollar, three-picture deal with Paramount." This, at worst, is sloppy reporting based on the assumption that men who host highly rated cable news shows aren't typically crazy.

Most people finding themselves in O'Reilly's position would have said something like: "Oh, I see his mistake. No, I never actually said I won a Peabody. What I meant was the *program* won the award, which I also inadvertently misidentified. It was actually a Polk. He shouldn't have written that, but, then, maybe I should have been more precise. I am a big, stupid ass."

That would have cleared up the whole thing, but O'Reilly was apparently more interested in lashing out at a perceived enemy than clearing the air.

So all this begs the question: Was O'Reilly lying? Well, not necessarily, technically, by the letter of the law, but, to paraphrase Jack Nicholson in *One Flew Over the Cuckoo's Nest*, "He, uh, he ain't honest. . . . He likes a rigged game, you know what I mean?"

But does O'Reilly *know* he was being dishonest? Well, that's one for Apollo and Zeus to puzzle over.

But here's our working theory: O'Reilly is actually more crazy than dishonest. When he's presented with a world that doesn't fit his way of seeing things, he tilts it on its axis. When he's presented with an argument with which he disagrees, he simply doesn't hear it . . . or worse, hears what he wants to hear.

We believe, then, that Bill is no more responsible for the falsehoods he peddles than John Hinckley was for shooting President Reagan. Both are too crazy to realize what they are (were) doing. What's worse, O'Reilly is his own Jodie Foster.

LIES BY REASON OF INSANITY OR MENTAL DEFECT

ON JULY 20, 2004, as the presidential race between George W. Bush and John Kerry was heating up, Bill's Impact Segment began with a very interesting teaser:

> Many Americans are worried about terrorism at the political conventions, but it is not only al-Qaeda in play here. The Ruckus

Society is a group of American anarchists who are bent on the violent overthrow of the government. And they train people to disrupt events like the conventions.

And who is funding the Ruckus Society? Well, it has received more than two hundred thousand dollars from the Tides Foundation, a far-left activist group, which in turn has been reportedly supported by the Heinz Endowment. Teresa Heinz-Kerry, of course, is part of that.

So, in a nutshell, a group of terrorists that wants to violently overthrow the U.S. government is being funded by a woman who was just a hair's breadth away from becoming First Lady. Surely you heard about this, right? No? Well, there's a reason for that. Because most of the media are not insane.

Now, Bill's contention that the Ruckus Society is "bent on the violent overthrow of the government" actually makes a lot of sense, except for the part about the violent overthrow of the government.

If you go to the group's Web site, ruckus.org, you'll see that the organization is actually explicitly involved in training people to be effective nonviolent activists. You'll see images of pro-choice rallies, Students for a Free Tibet demonstrations, and antiwar protests but, strangely, no anthrax laboratories or terrorist obstacle courses.

Granted, it's a left-wing organization that pushes the envelope at times and supports a raucous brand of civil disobedience, but it's about as close to being a violent terrorist organization as FOX News Channel is.

In fact, in its "Action Planning Manual," the Ruckus Society stresses the patriotic and distinctly American nature of its campaigns, writing, "The American experience is teeming with nonviolent direct action. One of the most famous direct actions ever, the Boston Tea Party, is patriotically taught in school."

Now, the Boston Tea Party was certainly a disruptive action that challenged the status quo. And certainly it was seen as unpatriotic by the likes of King George. Well, Bill is our modern equivalent of King George—with all the ego and just slightly more madness.

So part one of Bill's accusation is clearly built on a foundation of sand and stupidity.

But what of Bill's second point? Is Heinz-Kerry, in fact, supporting the Ruckus Society? Well, only in the vaguest, silliest, most painfully distorted sense of the word.

What Bill doesn't tell you is that the Tides Foundation, which he labels a "far-left activist group," is a large and well-respected progressive organization that has received money from some of the most reputable trusts and foundations in the country, including Pew Charitable Trusts, the Ford Foundation, the Packard Foundation, and the Charles Stewart Mott Foundation.

So does Bill think the Pew Charitable Trusts and the Ford Foundation are supporting terrorism? If so, why didn't he mention them on his show? If not, why not?

Of course, as the foundation notes on its Web site, Tides has awarded more than $300 million to hundreds of groups. So even if you were to concede that Ruckus is an unworthy recipient of grant money, you're still talking about a charity dollar's arduous trek from Heinz-Kerry's personal fortune to the Heinz Endowment to the Tides Foundation to hundreds of nonprofits, of which the Ruckus Society is merely one. We'd be surprised, then, if the amount of Heinz-Kerry money that actually went to Ruckus would be enough to pay for a 16-ounce cup of organic fair-trade coffee. We don't know that for certain, of course, but neither does Bill.

But then why should O'Reilly be the only one who gets to partake in such outlandish smear-by-association tactics? He shouldn't. So with apologies to Bill, we submit our own Talking Points Memo:

Is Bill O'Reilly Funding Pedophiles?

Many Americans are worried about men having sex with their young sons, but it's not just the neighborhood perverts in play here. The Roman Catholic Church is a group of religious leaders who have many pedophiles among their ranks. And they have hidden their exploits by moving priests between parishes and paying off victims.

And who is funding the Roman Catholic Church? Well, it has received millions of dollars from its members. Bill O'Reilly is, of course, part of that.

Heinz-Kerry may send her donation to Sweet Jesus, I Hate Bill O'Reilly Intl., c/o Nation Books.

Thank you very much.

PATTI DEUTSCH SYNDROME BY PROXY

BACK IN THE game show industry's golden age, when Patti Deutsch regularly occupied the lower-right-hand seat of the *Match Game* celebrity panel, she was renowned for giving answers that betrayed a tenuous grasp not only of the game but of English, logic, and the boundaries of space-time.

Once, host Gene Rayburn asked something like, "The White House didn't have eggs for their annual Easter egg roll so they used blank," and Deutsch confidently responded "mussels marinara."

There was no match.

Indeed, it often appeared as though Deutsch was off in some parallel universe playing some other game with entirely different questions. At times, O'Reilly appears to be afflicted with the same condition, which we have dubbed the Patti Deutsch Syndrome by Proxy.

Now, we should note that we have nothing but love and respect for Deutsch, and our appropriation of her good name to describe what ails O'Reilly should be considered an homage. Plus it sounded way better than Avery Schreiber Disease.

But while we assume Deutsch's behavior was a sort of practiced performance art, we have no clue what Bill is doing.

In fact, Bill is such a master of the non sequitur that he's made his show a nightly Zen koan for the apparent benefit of the enlightenment-poor TV-watching world.

He's either the stupidest man in broadcasting or a friggin' Buddha. Bill, if either of us achieves satori in the next decade or so while tuned in to *The Factor*, we apologize for all of this. Until then, let's take a closer look at your idiotic Jeremy Glick interview from a few years back.

Now, this interview has frequently been offered as an example of Bill's dishonesty, but we're revisiting it because we feel it demonstrates like little else the crazy nature of Bill's lying.

In February of 2003, Bill invited Glick on his show to berate him for signing an antiwar advertisement. He was particularly piqued because Glick's father had died in the 9/11 terrorist attacks, and Bill apparently thought he'd make short work of the kid.

Of course, Bill prides himself on these so-called "battles," and it soon became evident that this was going to be one of O'Reilly's trademark bully sessions. He choreographs these tête-à-têtes with the kind of excited anticipation that you'd see from Fabian Basabe lying face up in the middle of a circle jerk. For it's only a matter of time before there's an explosion.

From early on in the interview it was clear that Bill had all but made up his mind about Glick. And it soon became painfully obvious that he wasn't listening very carefully to what Glick was saying.

He's been misrepresenting Glick's position ever since. Indeed, in three years, no one has been able to get it through Bill's Igloo cooler of a skull what Glick was actually saying.

But is it insanity or true disingenuousness? Well, we'll let you make the call.

Following is a partial transcript. We pick up the interview just after the vein on Bill's left temple inflates to 55 p.s.i. and just before visible rivulets of foam begin to cascade down the sides of his mouth:

O'REILLY: You are mouthing a far-left position that is a marginal position in this society, which you're entitled to.

This is early on in the interview, and we see that Bill has already labeled Glick's position "far left" and "marginal." Clearly, the purpose of the interview is not to consider the views of a man who lost his father in the 9/11 attacks but to stress that he is wrong.

GLICK: It's marginal, right.

O'REILLY: You're entitled to it, all right, but you're—you see, even—I'm sure your beliefs are sincere, but what upsets me is I don't think your father would be approving of this.

Already Bill knows more about this kid's father than his own son does. O'Reilly has never met Glick's father. He has no idea about the man's political views. Yet he knows that the man would disapprove. You see, in O'Reilly's mind, the victims of 9/11 were not a cross section of the United States but a monolithic unit that would support the current administration in any military action against any nation, whether it was misguided or not, so long as it was swift and harsh.

GLICK: Well, actually, my father thought that Bush's presidency was illegitimate.

O'REILLY: Maybe he did, but . . .

So we see the truth. Glick's father did not support the president. In fact, he felt the election was a sham. So O'Reilly doesn't know the first thing about Glick's father. Yet he continues to speak for him:

GLICK: I also didn't think that Bush . . .

O'REILLY: I don't think he'd be equating this country as a terrorist nation as you are.

Now O'Reilly gets bolder. Rather than be content with just putting words in a dead guy's mouth, he puts words in the mouth of the guy sitting next to him. Shrewd move.

GLICK: Well, I wasn't saying that it was necessarily like that.

O'REILLY: Yes you are. You signed . . .

GLICK: What I'm saying is . . .

O'REILLY: . . . this, and that absolutely said that.

GLICK: . . . is that in—six months before the Soviet invasion in Afghanistan, starting in the Carter administration and continuing and escalating while Bush's father was head of the CIA, we recruited a hundred thousand radical mujahadeens to combat a democratic government in Afghanistan, the Turaki government.

So this is the essence of Glick's argument. He's not saying that the United States is directly responsible for 9/11. He's bringing up a valid point for discussion, which is that our foreign policy, which can be traced back through numerous administrations, may be responsible for a certain amount of blowback—that when we recruit and train killers in other countries, when we play fast and loose with other sovereign nations, occasionally it will come back to haunt us.

O'REILLY: All right. I don't want to . . .

GLICK: Maybe . . .

O'REILLY: I don't want to debate world politics with you.

GLICK: Well, why not? This is about world politics.

O'REILLY: Because, number one, I don't really care what you think.

This is a key component of O'Reilly's pathology. He brings a guest on his program but he really doesn't care to hear what he has to say.

Obviously, he brings the guy on his show not to shed light on an issue but to confront him. He can't bring himself to listen to his opinion or let him complete a thought. He has a preconceived idea of how this interview was to proceed, and nothing's going to change that. Rather than engage Glick's argument, O'Reilly hears what he wants to hear and moves on.

Sometimes you wonder why Bill doesn't just put a Rollerball court in the studio and get it over with.

GLICK: Well, okay.

O'REILLY: You're—I want to . . .

GLICK: But you do care because you . . .

O'REILLY: No, no. Look . . .

GLICK: The reason why you care is because you evoke 9/11 . . .

O'REILLY: Here's why I care.

GLICK: . . . to rationalize . . .

O'REILLY: Here's why I care . . .

GLICK: Let me finish. You evoke 9/11 to rationalize everything from domestic plunder to imperialistic aggression worldwide.

Now, this is why Glick comes on the program. Because Bill O'Reilly continually invokes the 9/11 victims. Glick is saying that his father died in that tragedy and he doesn't take kindly to people using him to forward a political agenda.

O'REILLY: Okay, that's a bunch . . .

GLICK: You evoke sympathy with the 9/11 families.

O'REILLY: That's a bunch of crap. I've done more for the 9/11 families by their own admission—I've done more for them than you will ever hope to do.

Again, O'Reilly is completely ignoring what Glick just said. It's true that O'Reilly has invoked the 9/11 tragedy over and over. Glick is correct, and O'Reilly doesn't deny it. O'Reilly answers a question Glick never asks. In O'Reilly's mind, Glick asked, "What have you done for the 9/11 families?"

GLICK: Okay.

O'REILLY: So you keep your mouth shut when you sit here exploiting these people.

Now the tables are turned. O'Reilly accuses Glick of exploiting the 9/11 families, of whom Glick is a part. What Glick had done to exploit his father and the other victims of the attack is a mystery to everyone but Bill.

GLICK: Well, you're not representing me. You're not representing me.

O'REILLY: And I'd never represent you. You know why?

GLICK: Why?

O'REILLY: Because you have a warped view of this world and a warped view of this country.

O'Reilly claims he'd never represent Glick, yet he did. He represented him when he criticized celebrities for not following the money raised for the 9/11 families. He represented him when he said war protesters were hurting the families. He represented him constantly.

GLICK: Well, explain that. Let me give you an example of a parallel . . .

O'REILLY: No, I'm not going to debate this with you, all right?

GLICK: Well, let me give you an example of a parallel experience. On September 14 . . .

O'REILLY: No, no. Here's, here's the . . .

GLICK: On September 14 . . .

O'REILLY: Here's the record.

GLICK: Okay.

O'REILLY: All right. You didn't support the action against Afghanistan to remove the Taliban. You were against it, okay.

GLICK: Why would I want to brutalize and further punish the people in Afghanistan?

O'REILLY: Who killed your father!

GLICK: The people in Afghanistan . . .

O'REILLY: Who killed your father.

GLICK: . . . didn't kill my father.

O'REILLY: Sure they did. The al-Qaeda people were trained there.

GLICK: The al-Qaeda people? What about the Afghan people?

O'REILLY: See, I'm more angry about it than you are!

There it is, folks. O'Reilly is more angry. The guy should be furious. He should be filled with blind hate and want to bomb the fuck out of everyone in the region. Glick differentiates between a terrorist group and the people of an entire nation. O'Reilly does not.

GLICK: So what about George Bush?

O'REILLY: What about George Bush? He had nothing to do with it.

GLICK: The director—senior as director of the CIA.

O'REILLY: He had nothing to do with it.

GLICK: So the people that trained a hundred thousand mujahadeen who were . . .

O'REILLY: Man, I hope your mom isn't watching this.

So Glick wants to discuss foreign policy, and O'Reilly's fixated on what Glick's mother might think. In his demented little skull, O'Reilly feels that this young man could not possibly have the support of his family. Or worse, that a 9/11 victim's family actually thinks about the big picture instead of just mouthing the administration's talking points.

GLICK: Well, I hope she is.

O'REILLY: I hope your mother is not watching this because you—that's it. I'm not going to say anymore.

GLICK: Okay.

O'REILLY: In respect for your father . . .

GLICK: On September 14, do you want to know what I'm doing?

O'REILLY: Shut up! Shut up!

GLICK: Oh, please don't tell me to shut up.

O'REILLY: As respect—as respect—in respect for your father, who was a Port Authority worker, a fine American, who got killed unnecessarily by barbarians . . .

GLICK: By radical extremists who were trained by this government . . .

O'REILLY: Out of respect for him . . .

GLICK: . . . not the people of America.

O'REILLY: . . . I'm not going to . . .

GLICK: . . . the people of a ruling class, the small minority.

O'REILLY: Cut his mic. I'm not going to dress you down anymore, out of respect for your father. We will be back in a moment with more of *The Factor.*

GLICK: That means we're done?

O'REILLY: We're done.

So there you have it. A young man whose father was killed in the 9/11 attacks comes on Bill's show. He believes our government's foreign policy decisions over the last few decades have put us at risk. He believes that the government of this country is run by a minority ruling class that's responsible for these decisions. And he doesn't want his father's death to be used to prop up an administration's case for war. That's pretty much it.

Sure, there's room for debate on these points, but O'Reilly explicitly said he didn't want to debate Glick. More important, though, is that nowhere in the interview did Glick reveal himself as a rabid conspiracy theorist who thought George W. Bush was directly involved in the al-Qaeda plot against the Pentagon and World Trade Center. He was pointing out—correctly—that the Afghan Mujahadeen, who helped spawn al-Qaeda, were financed, armed, and trained by our government during the Soviet occupation of Afghanistan.

Let's see how O'Reilly summed up the encounter more than two years later during a September 2005 interview with Phil Donahue:

> Jeremy Glick came on this program and accused the president of the United States of orchestrating 9/11. That's what he did. Right after 9/11 happened! Do you know what the pain that brought the families who lost people in 9/11?

Bill might as well have said "mussels marinara."

LYING WITH BULLSHIT STATISTICS

DURING HIS OCTOBER 5, 2005, Talking Points Memo, O'Reilly called columnists Maureen Dowd and Molly Ivins "liberal advocates who worship at the altar of *Roe v. Wade*."

We assume this means they're pro-choice, but that would be too matter-of-fact for O'Reilly. He might as well say they "suckle at the teat of *Brown v. the Board of Education*" or "dry hump the leg of *Marbury v. Madison*."

Of course, Bill's polemical hysteria is not limited to overwrought metaphors. He also loves to genuflect at the tabernacle of fake-ass statistics.

O'Reilly was taking Dowd and Ivins to task for columns they had written questioning the fitness of Bush Supreme Court nominee Harriet Miers.

In order to support his case that the country is split right down the middle on abortion, O'Reilly cited a suspiciously convenient stat:

If you belong to a conservative Christian church, these women believe you have no right to serve your country in a decision-making capacity. I mean, how crazy is that? About fifty percent of the country is pro-life. Are you telling me these people are disqualified from public service in America?

Unfortunately, the 50 percent statistic is utter crap. Now, a lapse of this sort might have been excusable had Bill been caught up in a heated debate with a pro-choice advocate, but this was part of a scripted Talking Points Memo. It wasn't just some off-the-cuff comment.

Of course, the most important consideration when citing facts as part of a written commentary is that they be true. Indeed, reporting true things instead of false things is one of the three main pillars of journalism, along with "maintain fairness at all times" and "don't scream at your guests."

But apparently, when the facts don't offer support for O'Reilly's agenda, he simply makes up new ones.

An August 28–30, 2005, CNN/USA Today/Gallup poll, the most recent available when O'Reilly cited his bogus stat, asked people point-blank where they stood on abortion: "With respect to the abortion issue, would you consider yourself to be pro-choice or pro-life?"

Only 38 percent of those questioned said they were pro-life. So, far from half the country being pro-life, the number's actually a lot closer to one third.

So where did Bill get the 50 percent stat? Probably from the same kooky library reference desk where he gets his figures on what it costs municipalities to look for runaway girls.

As we saw in Chapter 3, Bill was outraged over the "millions" Audrey Seiler cost the city of Madison, Wisconsin, when she faked her own abduction. As we showed, he was way off on the actual search-and-rescue expenses. Had Seiler disappeared in 1898 and we'd adjusted for inflation, Bill would have been pretty close, but in 2004, the incident cost the city only around fifty grand. But "millions" was more fun and proved his point.

But then, we can't figure out why he limits himself at all. Why not just say that 95 percent of Americans are pro-life and that Seiler's hoax cost the taxpayers more than the war in Iraq?

Come on, O'Reilly, that chick from Wisconsin is the real reason for the deficit, and you know it.

Sell it, man. Sell it.

LIES THAT SERVE HIS MASTER

ON JUNE 20, 2004, Thomas Kean, chairman of the independent commission that was investigating the 9/11 terrorist attacks, appeared on ABC's *This Week with George Stephanopoulos* to discuss the commission's findings:

> Our job is 9/11, and what we have concluded, there is no evidence that we can find whatsoever that Iraq or Saddam Hussein participated in any way in attacks on the United States, in other words, on 9/11.

Kean went on to say that there had been some contacts between Iraq and al-Qaeda in the past, but he was clearly stressing that no evidence existed to implicate Saddam in 9/11.

This was, of course, troubling to people such as O'Reilly, who had been hoping for a clear connection between Saddam and 9/11.

The following night, O'Reilly said this in his Talking Points Memo:

> As you may know, *The Factor* provided the link between al-Qaeda and Iraq last week. And since that time, the *Times* and other newspapers have been under heavy fire for their misleading headlines, basically saying there was no link between the two. Governor Thomas Kean says definitely there was a connection between Saddam and al-Qaeda. And he's the 9/11 investigative chief, but that's not enough for the *Times*, which continues to deny the Iraq–al-Qaeda association.

We were stunned. Is it possible that the chairman of the 9/11 commission and FOX News' most high-profile personality could have such wildly disparate takes on one of the president's chief justifications for the war? Could Bill be this far off, intent as he was on emphasizing what Kean was saying were perhaps "shadowy" contacts with al-Qaeda over the years, or was Kean deliberately downplaying the most provocative findings of his own investigation?

Luckily, O'Reilly's viewers were unlikely to notice, as they rarely watch network news programs that "spin" all the time. They just look to Bill for news analysis.

Still, we wondered how this could have happened.

A few days later, on June 24, Georgetown professor David Cole was a guest on Al Franken's radio show. Interestingly, he had been a guest on the June 21 *O'Reilly Factor* and had come away unimpressed with Bill's reporting style:

> He plays Kean's quote in which he says something like, "There is—we have found no evidence whatsoever that there is any link between Saddam Hussein and any attacks on the United States, including 9/11, however we have found some contacts between the two."
>
> And, you know, originally I think, well maybe what Al Franken said about Bill O'Reilly is false, because here he is, he's playing a balanced quote. But he immediately interrupts and says, "We can't have that quote, we've got to redo this whole thing." And two minutes later, he rerecords the whole thing, and this time, when he gets to the Kean part, he doesn't play the sound bite, and instead he says, "And Governor Kean over the weekend, head of the 9/11 commission, said there's definitely a connection between al-Qaeda and Saddam Hussein."

Later, in the middle of Bill's interview with him, Cole responded to O'Reilly's criticism of the *New York Times*, which O'Reilly was accusing of spinning its stories and misleading its readers:

So then I said, you know, why not push it a little bit further, so I said, "It seems to me, Bill, that it's the pot calling the kettle black, because I sat here not five minutes ago and heard you rerecord the introduction to this show to take out a statement from the head of the 9/11 commission saying that there is no evidence whatsoever of any link between Saddam Hussein and 9/11."

Needless to say, Bill didn't take kindly to this. Cole continued, "And [he] basically calls me an SOB repeatedly and tells me there's no way this is gonna get aired."

When Franken asked if the segment was indeed aired, Cole explained, "Yeah, and he cuts it, as he had promised. He cut it right before I accused him of basically doing exactly what he was accusing the *New York Times* of doing."

Now, in addition to promoting his program as a "no-spin zone," O'Reilly likes to point out that what you see is what you get when it comes to his show.

For instance, in July 2005, O'Reilly interviewed journalist Bernie Goldberg, author of *100 People Who Are Screwing Up America.*[1]

After commiserating with Goldberg for a while over the way Goldberg was treated on CNBC's *The Big Idea with Donny Deutsch* (a show O'Reilly felt compelled to identify as "one of the lowest-rated on cable television"), O'Reilly expressed astonishment that the program had edited Goldberg's interview:

O'REILLY: I mean, we might tell everybody on this program we don't edit it unless there's something that's libelous or obscene or something like that. Usually, in a cable news program, you do live like we're doing right now or live on tape and you don't edit.

Interesting. So to Bill's understanding, "obscene" means anything that contradicts Bill or makes him look bad. Gee, O'Reilly's sounding more and more like an Egyptian pharaoh every day.

So we ask you: How sick does Bill O'Reilly have to be to edit out key 9/11 commission findings in a report the whole world was waiting for just so he can maintain the public's illusion that Saddam and 9/11 were connected? How feeble and sad is a man who, when confronted on this, would simply edit out that portion of the segment? How ill is a guy who brags about being such a hard-boiled, fair-and-balanced reporter that he never edits his show, but then edits his show as soon as there's tape that makes him look silly?

What kind of a crazy liar is Bill, anyway?

NOTES

1. Bernard Goldberg, *100 People Who Are Screwing Up America—and Al Franken is #37* (New York: HarperCollins, 2005).

7

O'REILLY FORGETS ABOUT HIS AMNESIA

BILL HAS A little forgetfulness problem. Of course, many of us who have advanced beyond a certain age could say the same thing about ourselves. Sadly, when it comes to memory, some of us are state-of-the-art Power Macs with screaming G5 processors, and some of us are creaky old Mac Centris 610s long overdue for the recycling heap.

Bill, of course, is a circa 1973 Pong machine that's just had a 2-liter bottle of Diet Fresca spilled into it.

Whether O'Reilly has full-blown anterograde amnesia or has merely experienced a series of trauma-induced lapses is uncertain. What's clear is that when he's in the process of forgetting something, he generally has no clue he's doing it. Indeed, were he a patient in a head trauma ward, the other patients would most likely be borrowing his medications and selling them back to him later in the afternoon for lime Jell-O and hand jobs.

Sometimes Bill merely forgets what he's said; at other times he forgets his own opinions; on still other occasions he can enter a sort of mini–fugue state where he forgets the very person he was just minutes earlier.

Such episodes evoke a curious mix of frustration and amusement. It's kind of like watching a monkey trying to pull a nut from a hole that's too small for his fist to pass through. You can't help but feel a little sorry for the monkey, but, come on, it's a trapped, stubborn, exasperated monkey. That's funny stuff. So it is when Bill gets cornered with an embarrassing O'Reillyism—or when a former ally brutally betrays the O'Reilly cause.

BILL GETS A SAVAGE CASE OF FORGETFULNESS

ON HIS JUNE 18, 2004, radio program, O'Reilly rushed to the defense of right-wing talk-show host Michael Savage: "But he doesn't lie. He doesn't attack someone and just . . . and . . . and make stuff up about them. Malicious stuff. Slanderous stuff."

Okay, first of all, Michael Savage makes Ann Coulter look like Mahatma Gandhi. If he's known for anything at all, it's for saying vile and hateful things about liberals and minorities. For instance, there's this little bit of community outreach: "When you hear human rights, think gays. When you hear human rights, think only one thing: someone who wants to rape your son" (*Savage Nation*, August 3, 2004).

Now one might think the great traditionalist Bill O'Reilly would want to distance himself from such vulgar rhetoric. However, just a month after Savage's little bid for a GLAAD Media Award, O'Reilly referred to Savage as "our pal," and added, "I like Savage. I think he's very entertaining."

Yeah, okay Bill. Say, just in case your TiVo didn't catch it, here are a few other things you might find entertaining: Friday-night cockfights, lynchings, snuff films, Sally Jesse Raphael, and cosmetics testing on baby seals.

So clearly O'Reilly's a good sport when it comes to letting people run off at the mouth about whatever irks them. After all, life's too short to be so thin-skinned and politically correct. Savage is entitled to his own opinion, right? Equating gays with rapists—well, that's just good fun and well within the bounds of polite discourse. And the fact that Savage says equally provocative things about women, Asians, and peaceful Muslims is hardly worth getting upset about.

Or so it was, until Savage cruelly turned his sights on one of the few truly blessed things this nation has left to hang onto in this sad, cynical world—Bill's ratings:

> As you may know, we get hammered from extremists on both the left and the right, which tells you something. Apparently, the radio guy Michael Savage is telling his listeners that our ratings on TV and radio aren't good. This, of course, is a huge lie, as we are extremely successful in both venues, thanks to you.
>
> Now Mr. Savage is angry because no responsible media outlet will put him on the air, precisely because he doesn't tell the truth, which, of course, is ridiculous. (Most Ridiculous Item of the Day, July 13, 2005)

Now, to stress the point, Savage is the same man who complains about minorities by saying, "You can never hear about the bad things they do," and in the same broadcast says of Arabs, "I think these people need to be forcibly converted to Christianity. . . . It's the only thing that can probably turn them into human beings" (*Savage Nation*, May 12, 2005).

Yet it isn't until he says that maybe *The Factor's* ratings aren't all that great that Bill suddenly becomes a Lifetime movie heroine with a head injury.

He forgot that just a year earlier Savage was a "pal" who was "very entertaining."

He forgot that Savage doesn't attack people and just make stuff up about them.

He forgot that he himself had put Savage on the air and helped him promote his book.

All of it gone.

Perhaps it was an isolated incident.

HE'S MR. SHORT-TERM MEMORY
(HE SHOULDN'T HAVE STOOD UNDER THAT PEAR TREE)

SOMETIMES YOU'D SWEAR Bill is being fed lines through an ear-piece by a pair of drunken interns with a flair for performance art—and that they like to change shifts in the middle of each show.

On his June 17, 2004, radio program, O'Reilly was discussing the media exposure surrounding the release of Bill Clinton's new book *My Life*:[1]

O'REILLY: And [if I had interviewed Clinton] I would have been respectful to the man, by the way. I would not have been disrespectful for him. But, there would have been some real pointed discussions. And I'm interested in Clinton's philosophy of life. That's what I'm interested in. The guy doesn't seem to have any moral foundation at all.

Shortly following his far-right bomb-throwing personal smear attack on the former president, a caller challenged Bill on his characterization:

CALLER: Yeah, I just wanted to comment about Bill Clinton. He was our ex-president, and I feel like you're disrespecting him by slandering him like that.

O'REILLY: Okay, let me—all right, give me an example of how I slandered him.

CALLER: You said he has no morals.

Now, read O'Reilly's first comment again: "The guy doesn't seem to have any moral foundation at all" sounds pretty close to an attack and even closer to saying he "has no morals." If you got on the radio and said, "Gee, Bill O'Reilly doesn't seem to have any intellect at all" and then someone called you saying it was disrespectful to call such a great American stupid, you'd probably know instantly what he was referring to.

But Bill, on the other hand . . . well, let's just go to the tape, shall we?

"Did I say, Lis Wiehl, that he has no morals?" asked O'Reilly.

"I think he—Bill was asking what, I want to know this man, what are his morals?" responded O'Reilly co-host Lis Wiehl, a woman who is to obsequious banter what Señor Wences was to nationally televised hand puppetry.

Of course, to misspeak or forget something you've said—even something you've said earlier in the day—is not all that uncommon.

The difference is that most of us will take a few seconds to scan our memories and check ourselves when confronted with a statement from earlier in the afternoon. And should it be such a surprise to Bill, whose outlook on the Clintons is just a wee bit more favorable than Captain Ahab's stance toward albino sperm whales, that he might have said such a thing? But Bill doesn't think he'd ever be so disrespectful.

It's as though there's a sane little man somewhere inside Bill trying his best to do damage control, and he lets the sane little man out for a walk around the exercise yard about twenty minutes each day.

HE'LL FRUSTRATE YOU SO BUT HE'LL NEVER KNOW 'CAUSE HE'S MR. SHORT-TERM MEMORY

BILL HAD ANOTHER epic struggle with his hippocampus on the December 1, 2004, installment of *The Radio Factor*. Following an interview with Indiana University history professor Michael McGerr, O'Reilly tussled with a caller over the gist of the conversation:

CALLER: I just kind of resent . . . creating evil monsters out there, like Rush Limbaugh did. Rush went out and defined what liberals are, and said they're evil because what they really want is to . . . take from the rich and give to the poor. Let everybody stay, and that's ridiculous. I think you're doing the same thing with defining what progressives are. "What they really want is social-ism"? No . . .

O'REILLY: I didn't say that. The professor said they want economic justice. Economic justice.

Well, Bill was right about one thing. McGerr had indeed said that progressives want economic justice. Here was the full quote:

> I think, like most Americans, progressives think really only in terms of their own country, not as much being somebody else. They want what they would call economic justice, which is some-thing progressives have wanted for a century, and which they want to use the power of the state to try and create more eco-nomic equality.

But, strangely enough, Bill completely whiffed on what he him-self had said, which was: "All right, when you talk about economic justice, that means they want a socialistic system where the gov-ernment controls the money. So if you're wealthy, the government takes that from you and then gives it to other people to try to boost them up."

Stranger still, Bill didn't even try to address the substance of the caller's charge. Instead he tried to deflect the accusation by repeat-ing what the professor said.

But perhaps the oddest thing about this exchange is that O'Reilly in fact paints liberals with the socialist brush all the time. He says it like other people say "good morning." So why is he denying it in this instance, unless he's got some pathological need to greet every chal-lenge with an outright denial?

Seriously, isn't it a little freakish that Bill remembers the profes-sor's statement perfectly yet has absolutely no recollection of his own? Mind you, this all happened within the span of fifteen min-utes. The only possible conclusions are that he's lying, is so far off the grazing lands he can't come back to the herd, or has roughly the recall ability of dryer lint.

OH, HE'S CRAZY . . . CRAZY LIKE A POPE

SOMETIMES BILL'S AMNESIA mixes with a double shot of paranoia to make a fun little cocktail of crazy.

On the April 8, 2005, *Radio Factor*, O'Reilly was tending bar and serving up some frisky little concoctions:

CALLER: Thanks for taking my call, Bill. Well, I think, you know, you're doing a lot of really good work in terms of spirituality and protecting the young. But one of the things I had a question for you, is about twelve to eighteen months ago you were saying that the pope was also autocratic and senile. And you didn't like him . . .

O'REILLY: And senile? Is that what you said?

CALLER: You did say that . . .

O'REILLY: No I didn't.

CALLER: . . . on some of your radio programs if you check the archives.

O'REILLY: Well, look, you're taking the Catholic League, you're taking their pronouncement, correct? Am I correct? . . .

CALLER: Now, I don't know anything about the Catholic League pronouncement.

O'REILLY: What are you taking, then. Media Matters?

CALLER: No, I'm not taking that either.

O'REILLY: All right, well, you're taking some kind of propaganda, 'cause I never said the pope was senile. And you know, I criticized the pope when he should have been criticized, and that is for not being proactive enough in the pedophilia scandals here in the USA, and in failing to put off a cogent policy to fight terror. Now, I wrote a column, this column's posted right now. And I have said that and been very consistent. I did not change my mind. Now, you've got crazy left-wing nuts who distort what's said on this program every day. And they spit stuff out. Catholic League picked it up. Attacked me this week. You know, the usual propaganda. So, you want to buy into that . . . and live in that land, you go right ahead.

Of course, the land Bill is referring to is a little place the rest of us like to call reality. You see, back in December 2002, Bill was already questioning the sanity of John Paul II. During a segment on his television program, he had this to say to Philip Moran of the Catholic Alliance:

Well, wait a minute. Hear me out. We all know, everybody knows, even [Cardinal] Law knows. Everybody but the pope, who's too senile to know, and I say that with all due respect. I don't think the pope is lucid, I don't think he knows what's going on.

It's difficult to say which is funnier, the "with all due respect, your holiness, your brain is mush" bit or the "you're being twisted by amoral propagandists who quote me directly in context" bit.

Again, Bill is certain he never said such a thing—despite indications from concerned callers and media watchdog groups that he did—because it's simply not the sort of thing a good Catholic like Bill would say. So he has to create alternative realities where the quote simply doesn't exist.

Note that O'Reilly doesn't say, "well, that doesn't sound like me, but I'll check the transcripts and get back to you" or even "I really don't think I would have said that; I'm pretty sure you're wrong." He says, unequivocally, "no, I didn't" and writes the whole thing off as a big conspiracy against him. In his heart of hearts, he seriously thinks there are people from progressive Web sites sitting around their desks late at night wolfing down pizza crusts, guzzling warm Mountain Dew, and going, "I know, let's say O'Reilly called the pope senile!"

Of course, Bill also claims groups like Media Matters[2] "distort" what he says on his programs. What he no doubt means is that they distort what he meant to say or what he'd say now if he somehow had the opportunity to correct his idiotic blathering. And if he had fully integrated brain centers or a memory that reached back further than his last meal, he might just do that. Unfortunately, that would also require admitting he was wrong about something. And if there's anything O'Reilly forgets faster than his past, it's his fallibility.

NOTES

1. William Clinton, *My Life* (New York: Knopf, 2004).
2. On the October 4, 2005, *O'Reilly Factor,* Bill ran a segment on "political smear sites," during which he called Media Matters "vile" and said it had "no ethics or scruples." Later in the segment, his guest, author David Kline, said, "You have Web sites and political bloggers that believe that President Bush orchestrated the 9/11 attacks." Bill's response? "You mean he didn't? That's what I've been hearing from Phil Donahue and Jeremy Glick and Michael Moore, that he orchestrated it."

BILL IS MORE POPULAR
THAN YOU ARE

BART: I was wondering. How important is it to be popular?

HOMER: I'm glad you asked, son. Being popular is the most important thing in the world!

—From The Simpsons, *Episode 8, "The Telltale Head"*
Original Airdate: February 27, 1990

O**N JUNE 29, 2005,** O'Reilly read a letter from a viewer who had grown annoyed with *The Factor*'s saturation coverage of Natalee Holloway, the Alabama college student who went missing at the end of May while on vacation in Aruba: "Bill, I turned *The Factor* off for the first time in years because of the incessant Natalee Holloway coverage. Why don't you poll *Factor* viewers on this?" (Katie Barnett, Great Neck, NY.)

Now, to begin with, journalism is not supposed to be like a bad TGIF sitcom. It often is these days, but it's not supposed to be. If Urkel appears in a bit part and the ratings shoot up—allowing a banal family comedy to become marginally less banal—that's great for ABC's entertainment division. But, in theory at least, news coverage is driven by newsworthiness, so to even take seriously a letter that suggests a journalist should poll his viewers on what tomorrow's top story should be is real bush-league stuff. Ideally, journalists are driven by the relevance and importance of their work, not by how many cute, suburban missing persons they turn up.

It's a disturbing trend to be sure. Indeed, one can fairly wonder whether Richard Nixon's corrupt administration would have ever been brought down under the current infotainment regime. Had O'Reilly been the top-rated cable news personality in 1974, perhaps the only thing that could have forced Nixon out of office would have been 8 mm film of the president snorting coke off the belly of John Ehrlichman while being blown by Checkers in the Lincoln Bedroom.

But Ms. Barnett had a good point. O'Reilly had, at the time her letter appeared, dedicated twenty segments in his previous eight shows to the Holloway case—an average of 2.5 a night. Now, if he really thought giving that much coverage to an unremarkable, previously unknown young woman who climbed into a car with strangers was appropriate, he'd have likely felt no need to respond to his viewer's verbal wrist slap. Had he given similar coverage to the crisis in Sudan or the December 2004 Asian tsunami disaster, and one of his viewers wrote in to say Bill should poll his audience on whether they want to see anymore stories about gross dead foreigners, the only reasonable response would have been to delete the e-mail, because there's no way you could challenge those stories' newsworthiness without sounding stupid and crass.

So forgive us if we detected a little defensiveness on our favorite newsman's part when he responded, "Well, we do, Katie. Our ratings are huge. That's the poll."

So that's it, then. In no uncertain terms, O'Reilly was saying that the newsworthiness of a story is tied directly to the ratings it gets. The more sensational a story is, the more newsworthy it becomes.

This is the death march of journalism in the United States, and Bill is leading the way in a big, furry, drum major's hat with a baton shoved squarely up his . . . well, you get the idea.

Now, Bill is hardly alone when it comes to journalism's relentless race to the bottom these days. Laci Peterson, Jennifer Wilbanks, and Terri Schiavo all prove that. But Bill and FOX News are not only the biggest offenders, they also consistently show the least amount of shame.

A June 30, 2005, story posted on cjrdaily.org, a Web site affiliated with the Columbia Journalism Review, reported that in the preceding week "Aruba" had been uttered 685 times on FOX News. While the ideal number of mentions would be in the zero-to-ten range, CNN and MSNBC combined for a somewhat less egregious 415 citations.

It would seem, then, that there's nothing Bill likes better than a dead or missing white woman. They're like catnip to him. In fact, when Runaway Bride Jennifer Wilbanks disappeared back in April of 2005, Bill was sure there was foul play involved:

> It's got to be a crime. A woman like that with a long history of responsibility. She had a steady job. As you said, good friends who traveled to be with her on her wedding day. A fiancé who looks like, you know, he's an ordinary, regular kind of guy. She just wouldn't bolt and not tell anybody. That's cruel.[1]

Cruel indeed. The unkindest cut of all, however, may have been returning alive, which kept Bill and his fellow travelers from maintaining a solemn, highly rated vigil for a few more dozen news cycles.

O'REILLY VERSUS THE PLAYA HATAS

WHILE IT'S OBVIOUS that Bill will happily sacrifice any decent journalistic impulse he might still have to the altar of popularity, his obsession with ratings has considerable utilitarian value.

Indeed, Bill blurts out his ratings info like an octopus squirts ink. It's an automatic defense mechanism that shields him from criticism and justifies even the most blatantly sensationalistic piffle.

One of his favorite tactics is comparing his numbers to his rivals', as if enlightenment sprang lotus-like from a ratings book.

The *New York Times* thinks Bill's a know-nothing boor? Their influence with readers is waning. Al Franken slams Bill? His numbers are down in New York. Bill Press thinks O'Reilly spins everything on his show? *The Factor* is crushing *Crossfire*. MSNBC doesn't like Bill? They're a ratings disaster.

And as we discuss in chapters 7, 11, and 14, any suggestion that Bill's ratings, book sales or general marketability are not what he claims them to be is met with a response that rivals in subtlety a howler monkey marking its territory.

This pattern is so predictable that it could almost be one of Newton's laws: For every criticism of Bill's ratings, there is an unequal and opposite reaction. He's a physical oddity—the perpetual motion machine of hubris, tactlessness, and pointless bluster.

Of course, Bill has no choice but to guard jealously his reputation as a ratings bellwether because it's pretty much all he's got. Somewhere in the back of his mind he must know his program is a circus sideshow without the dog-faced boy or the dignity.

So you continually get loony analysis and non sequiturs like the following:

[Discussing Kofi Annan with former UN Ambassador Richard Holbrooke] He blows it in Bosnia. He blows it in Iraq. He blows it in the oil-for-food scandal. . . . It would be like me getting the ratings of MSNBC. Why would FOX keep me here? Okay. You have to do something and succeed to gain credibility. (*The O'Reilly Factor,* January 4, 2005)

Yesterday an analyst from MSNBC blamed part of the CBS fiasco on a FOX News executive. Now, we're used to this kind of slander, as MSNBC is a ratings catastrophe and desperate people say desperate things. (*The O'Reilly Factor,* January 12, 2005)

Now that anger extends to the media, where CNN founder . . . Ted Turner is aghast at the policies of President Bush and by the ascendance of FOX News, which is destroying CNN in the ratings. (*The O'Reilly Factor,* January 26, 2005)

Now the big picture: The editor of the *Times,* a man named Bill Keller, realizes his paper has lost power over the last few years. The rise of FOX News and other pro-America news agencies, as well as the success of radio talk-show hosts like Rush Limbaugh and Sean Hannity, have made it far more difficult for the *Times* to put out its left-wing agenda unchallenged.

So Keller has decided to help character assassins outside the paper attack those with whom it disagrees. Keller's also allowing the *Times* to promote Air America, the left-wing radio network. So far, that paper has done an astounding twenty-four stories on Air America, which loses millions of dollars, and actually has to pay some of its own stations to put it on the air.[2] (*The O'Reilly Factor*, June 15, 2005)

The Air America radio network continues to fail, with catastrophic ratings here in New York City, perhaps the most liberal market in the country. The circulations of longtime liberal newspapers like the *Boston Globe* and *Newsday* are falling. And there is not one successful stand-alone liberal commentator on cable television, not one.

Phil Donahue was fired for low ratings at MSNBC, but was actually much more successful than what they put in his place. Meantime, the FOX News Channel continues to prosper. *The Factor* has been the top-rated cable news program for 195 weeks straight.[3] (*The O'Reilly Factor*, July 26, 2005)

Now, we have to tread lightly here lest we come across as ivory-tower liberals sniffing contemptuously over our soy lattes, with *All Things Considered* humming soporifically in the background, dreadfully amused at the mere suggestion that we give a whit about mass acclaim. In our heart of hearts, we suspect everyone wants to be popular.

But seriously, come on. Bill sounds like the kind of guy who drones on about his capital gains at a cocktail party, brags about his annual sales figures at an office Christmas party, or suggests everyone line up and measure their dicks at a fraternity party.

Of course, Bill's obsession with ratings victories plays into one of this country's most hoary stereotypes about liberals: that they're so tragically sincere and naïve they can't possibly hack it in a capitalist system.

Well, it goes without saying that everyone Bill derides as a ratings leper is making a comfortable living, and many are doing so without selling out every ounce of journalistic integrity they have.

Bill is alone, however, in his constant flogging of his own ratings numbers, which begs the question: Exactly how insecure do you have to be about your own popularity to never shut up about it? Seriously, can you imagine any of the network news anchors doing this? Not any in the real world. Indeed, when it comes to cartoonishly inflated newsroom ego, Bill is about a jazz flute away from being Ron Burgundy.

Still, Bill appears to believe that ratings are the ultimate vindication—proof that he's the bestest journalist in the whole wide world and that all his critics are intellectually bankrupt because they don't get as high a Nielsen share as he does.

Of course, a quick look at late-twentieth-century pop history amply supports this:

1966: Jacqueline Susann publishes *Valley of the Dolls*, which eventually becomes the top-selling novel of all time, eclipsing such sales disasters as Fyodor Dostoyevsky's *Crime and Punishment*, John Steinbeck's *The Grapes of Wrath*, and George Orwell's *1984.*

Late seventies through the early eighties: On the strength of such quality programs as *Three's Company*, *The Six Million Dollar Man*, *Charlie's Angels*, *The Ropers*, *Mork and Mindy*, *That's Incredible*, and *The Love Boat*, ABC becomes the number one television network, destroying PBS in the ratings.

1986: *Top Gun* and *Crocodile Dundee* are the top-grossing films of the year. The pinheads at the Academy of Motion Pictures Arts and Sciences, however, award the Best Picture Oscar to the third-highest-grossing film, *Platoon*, while nominating such box-office also-rans as *Children of a Lesser God, Hannah and Her Sisters, A Room With a View* and *The Mission*.

1998: *The Jerry Springer Show's* ratings surge ahead more than 100 percent in one year. The previous ratings winner, *The Oprah Winfrey Show*, founders behind the newly crowned daytime talk-show king.

2004: *People* magazine is listed by the Magazine Publishers of America as the twelfth-highest-circulation periodical in the country, crushing *Newsweek, U.S. News and World Report,* and *The New Yorker.*

August 2005: McDonald's announces an increase in comparable sales of nearly 5 percent over the previous year. The french-fry cooks and bun toasters there continue to outsell the loser chefs at Spago by a huge margin, which makes one wonder why the restaurant keeps them around, since you have to do something and succeed to gain credibility.

Bill, you are the McDonald's and *People* magazine of broadcast news. Congratulations on your huge success. Really. Bravo.

NOTES

1. Incidentally, on June 9, 2005, Bill said, just three days after saying Natalee Holloway was probably dead, "As you may know, we do not speculate here on *The Factor.* We have no idea what happened to Natalee or why she left the bar with some Aruban men. I've heard some irresponsible media speculate about that, and it makes me angry."
2. As we discuss further in Chapter 14, when O'Reilly launched *The Radio Factor,* conservative Web journalist Matt Drudge reported that radio stations were paid as much as $300,000 to carry the show.
3. When MSNBC canceled Donahue's program in February of 2003 during the run-up to the Iraq war because of low ratings, it was the network's top-rated show.

9

BILL JUST DON'T UNDERSTAND . . .

WE ALL HAVE our blind spots. It comes with being human. But listening to Bill O'Reilly proffer his homespun wisdom can be a little like watching Mr. Magoo talking to a fire hydrant. It's embarrassing for everyone involved, but it's unlikely anyone will really get hurt.

Indeed, O'Reilly is so often clueless on topics related to government, religion, ethics, and general knowledge that you begin to wonder if stupid pills are an actual product currently being tested by the Food and Drug Administration.

Bill suffers from two handicaps when it comes to forming cogent arguments. One, he doesn't know much, and two, he thinks with his sense of outrage rather than his brain.

BILL JUST DON'T UNDERSTAND . . . THE CONSTITUTION

IN A FEBRUARY 2002 newspaper column, Bill basically argued that the New York state and city governments are violating the Constitution because he gets stuck in traffic a lot:

The founding fathers were very wary of the power of the State to punish individual Americans and said flat-out in the preamble to the Constitution that the government was formed to "establish justice, insure domestic tranquility, provide for the common defense and promote the general welfare."

It is the "general welfare" clause that concerns me the most.

Right now, many big cities in America have tremendous traffic problems. Boston, Los Angeles, San Francisco and New York City—just to name a few—are choked with vehicles for most of the day. Instead of coming up with innovative solutions to alleviate the traffic mess—which by the way wastes tons of fuel and heavily pollutes the atmosphere—our leaders have decided to punish those of us who drive cars.

Now, strict constructionists are often highly critical of the rights some judges find inherent in the Constitution, arguing that those rights that are not explicitly prescribed in the document cannot be assumed to exist. It's a classic dispute between those constitutional scholars who advocate a more literal interpretation of the Constitution and those who see it as a living, breathing document. But only O'Reilly could argue that James Madison intended that Bill not be late for the season finale of *Desperate Housewives*.

There can be little question that O'Reilly wrote this because he was fuming in gridlock traffic one day and he suddenly remembered he had a deadline the next morning. But instead of simply writing a column bemoaning the poor condition of local roads, he treats us to a classic O'Reilly overreach.

That Bill failed to find an implicit message to the pinheads at the New York Department of Transportation in the Sermon on the Mount or the Bhagavad Gita is just a little surprising. Seriously, he might as well argue that the Wal-Mart he goes to is violating the Constitution because they ran out of Count Chocula.

Of course, O'Reilly loves to rip into "activist" judges every chance he gets when he doesn't like their decisions. Indeed, he frequently talks about judges' arrogant flouting of majority opinion, which shows he also doesn't understand the whole three branches of government, separation of powers thing the founding pinheads gave us.

But while Bill can't seem to fathom how a strict wall between the public and religious spheres might be implicit in the First Amendment's establishment clause, he can't get past the first paragraph of the Constitution without thinking it means big, loud Irishmen with cable TV shows should be protected from taking the subway.

Boy, is he ever looking out for you.

BILL JUST DON'T UNDERSTAND . . . TREASON

IN JANUARY AND February of 2005, University of Colorado professor Ward Churchill became a cause célèbre of the right for a time after it came to their attention that he'd written a column saying the United States brought the 9/11 attacks upon itself because of its own foreign-policy decisions. In the column, he famously referred to certain of the World Trade Center victims as "little Eichmanns."

So when O'Reilly found out that Churchill was giving a speech at Hamilton College, a tiny liberal arts school in New York State, and that Churchill looked like one of those sixties throwback academic types with lots of brains and no common sense, he pounced.

Now, MIT professor Noam Chomsky has built a reputation as one of the world's most dogged critics of U.S. foreign policy and is considered by many a champion of left-wing anti-imperialist thought. He's a relatively high-profile (though fringe) character who at least seems lucid on the few occasions he's been invited to appear on network television. In other words, while Chomsky is a much more appropriate standard-bearer for the brand of left-wing rhetoric the little-known Churchill aspires to, O'Reilly would probably have had to read a book first if he'd taken on Chomsky.

No, Churchill was the perfect foil. If he wasn't literally made of straw, he looked as if he might be. His feral, gray locks and brusque, arrogant demeanor snugly fit O'Reilly's idea of what an aging hippie left-wing college professor should be. Indeed, Bill couldn't have found a better opponent if he'd commissioned Hanna-Barbera himself.

So, fine. O'Reilly found an angry idiot hardly anybody knew about, turned him into an unlikely celebrity, and used the opportunity he'd created to wax indignant for a while. It's a little sleazy, but, well, the guy needs to keep his ratings up. Maybe we could cut him a little slack, huh?

Oh, but ya know there's gotta be more to this story, right? Here we go: On the February 9 *Factor*, O'Reilly suggested that Churchill was so egregious and so distressing to the American public that he was literally guilty of treason. When his guest, an expert in international law, disagreed, O'Reilly quipped, "certainly he's demoralizing particularly Americans who lost people on 9/11, and giving aid and comfort to al-Qaeda."

Now, we've argued throughout this book that it's actually O'Reilly's stupidity and insanity rather than any core dishonesty that fuel his most outlandish assertions. But, come on, he's got to know he's full of shit on this one, right?

First of all, the right to unpopular speech is at least as important to the functioning of a healthy democracy as the right to clog the highways and pollute the air with your car. While Churchill wasn't making many friends with his comments, they are clearly protected by the First Amendment. That's pretty much indisputable.

Secondly, Churchill's "demoralizing" remarks, which would have ordinarily fallen on the ears of a few dozen potheads at the University of Colorado and Hamilton College, were instead broadcast to millions on O'Reilly's show—including, presumably, the families of 9/11 victims, U.S. military personnel, and maybe even a few of the less intelligent members of al-Qaeda. It's like hearing someone give away the ending to *Fight Club* while you're standing in line to see it and then going on the air and letting all your viewers know that some asshole told you Ed Norton's character and Brad Pitt's character were the same guy. Well, actually, it's nothing like that. It's more like giving aid and comfort to al-Qaeda, which is clearly an act of treason punishable by either life in prison or execution.

Anyway, we can all consider ourselves fortunate that *The O'Reilly Factor* wasn't on the air during the Julius and Ethel Rosenberg espionage trial, or the U.S. government would currently be struggling to sustain a credible nuclear deterrent against your drunk cousin Larry.

BILL JUST DON'T UNDERSTAND . . . PRESIDENTIAL AUTHORITY

WHEN AUTHOR AND George W. Bush confidante Doug Wead released his book *The Raising of a President*[1] in January of 2005, it was widely publicized that he had secretly recorded phone conversations with Bush before Bush was elected president.

The tapes, while revealing, were not particularly damning. Still, O'Reilly was incensed and thought Bush should come at Wead with both guns blazing.

Here's Bill's trenchant analysis from the February 21 O'Reilly Factor: "I hope Bush gets him. I hope Bush audits him. I hope Bush has guys follow him around and gets him. That's what I would do."

Now, missing from most of the public tittering over Bill's October 2004 I'm-too-sexy-for-my-wife-and-family scandal was this rather spooky excerpt from FOX producer Andrea Mackris's affidavit:

> **O'REILLY:** If you cross FOX News Channel, it's not just me, it's [FOX President] Roger Ailes who will go after you. I'm the street guy out front making loud noises about the issues, but Ailes operates behind the scenes, strategizes and makes things happen so that one day BAM! The person gets what's coming to them but never sees it coming. Look at Al Franken, one day he's going to get a knock on his door and life as he's known it will change forever. That day will happen, trust me.

If genuine, the excerpt dovetails nicely with O'Reilly's public comments on Wead to create a lovely, Hieronymus Bosch–like portrait of a truly sick mind. Why do we get the feeling that hidden somewhere in a folder deep within Bill's secret porn stash on his PC is a Nixonian enemies list with the names of Mackris, Franken, Bill Moyers, Michael Kinsley, Hillary Clinton, and now Doug Wead?

Why do we also get the feeling that, were Bill ever actually to become president, Personal Vendettas would soon become a Cabinet-level department?

That Bill "hopes" Bush "gets," audits, and has guys follow an

author around is a large living-room picture window into his
demented psyche.

BILL JUST DON'T UNDERSTAND . . . HIS OWN RELIGION

BILL IS A Catholic. According to Catholicism, Jesus Christ, a poor,
humble carpenter from Galilee, died on the cross to take away the
sins of the world and save the souls of all mankind. Well, you could
have fooled Bill.

On page 104 of O'Reilly's book *The No Spin Zone*,[2] Bill, who
opposes the death penalty, argues that Jesus would have likely been
against it too because He considered all life sacred (probably true)
and that "since [Jesus] was a victim of it, he may have a rooting
interest in seeing it abolished."

Unfortunately, had some smart Roman lawyer convinced Pilate
to commute Jesus's sentence to life in prison, as O'Reilly's "Jesus
as victim" comment seems to imply would have been a more favorable outcome, Catholics wouldn't have had an ancient, mysterious,
soul-saving faith so much as a nice Sunday morning wine and
book club. The death and resurrection of Christ is the linchpin of
the whole deal. Without it, no salvation. Jesus couldn't consider
himself a victim of crucifixion any more than God the Father
could consider himself a victim of creation. It's the whole reason
He was here.

But Bill does understand some tenets of his faith. For instance,
he appears to know that one of the earmarks of Christianity, as well
as its antecedent, Judaism, is that the monotheistic Christian god is
a personal god. Unfortunately, Bill takes this to mean that Jesus
watches *The O'Reilly Factor*.

> The FOX News Channel and its commentators stand in the
> way of the secular agenda. Demonizing us sends a message to
> others who may challenge the secular cabal. Do it and we slime
> you badly. So what's going on? Another vicious battle in the
> American culture war. Somewhere Jesus is weeping. (*The O'Reilly
> Factor*, December 20, 2004)

Yeah, well let's hope that's not why that tsunami hit Asia six days later, because Christ was too busy crying over Hannity's ass.

But as if eager to prove crazy is a forty-hour-a-week job, the very next day O'Reilly topped himself:

> The truth is that the federal holiday of Christmas should be respected in public. Its images are a threat to no one. If you are offended by a snowman or the image of a baby, you need therapy, with all due respect. (Talking Points Memo, December 21, 2004)

And if you think that the ACLU is filing suit against public Christmas displays because they have some sort of shifty-eyed animus against Frosty the Snowman and nondescript, secular infants, you need a frontal lobotomy followed by a Xanax and Percodan smoothie.

Unless we missed something and last year's *Michael Newdow v. Rankin-Bass* decision has become a watershed in the secular movement to destroy winter fun and frolic, we're pretty sure it's O'Reilly who needs the therapy.

Seriously, if you equate symbols like a light-up plastic Blitzen to God's gift to the world of His only begotten son, you just need to stop talking. Particularly if you're under the delusion that you're some sort of Christian.

BILL JUST DON'T UNDERSTAND . . . POLITICAL DISSENT

IN AUGUST 2004, Bill interviewed Democratic Congressman Anthony Weiner of New York. The subject was protests surrounding the Republican National Convention.

After saying, "But I think they help President Bush, when mainstream America sees these people get naked and saying these crazy things," Bill claimed, "These are true radicals. These are people who want a socialist government, who don't think America is a good country."

Weiner, of course, disagreed with Bill's interpretation:

WEINER: There is nothing more patriotic than what those two hundred thousand-some-odd people did. Just as there is nothing as patriotic as what's going on here. This is what democracy is all about.

O'REILLY: No, but there's a difference. . . . Isn't there a difference, though? If you wanna tear the country down, I don't think that's patriotic.

WEINER: I don't think someone goes out and protests because their agenda is to tear the country down.

O'REILLY: Well, what about the anarchists and things?

WEINER: They're exercising perhaps the most important right that you and I are exercising today. Isn't that what this country is all about?

Do we even have to respond to this one? Seriously, after a while you start to feel a little ashamed, like you're kickboxing toddlers.

First of all—anarchists and things? Dude! You sound like an eight-year-old boy giving an oral book report on George Orwell's *Animal Farm* after forgetting to read it.

Finally, Weiner was right. There's nothing more patriotic than political protest, even if they were socialists (which the majority certainly were not), anarchists (ditto), or naked (again, no, but please don't use the word "naked" on a night Ohio governor Bob Taft is giving a speech ever again).

BILL JUST DON'T UNDERSTAND . . . POLL QUESTIONS

ONE OF O'REILLY'S most curious regular features is his poll question. Polls are usually meant to gauge public opinion on a specific issue, but Bill's are usually just a regurgitation of his own views. He uses them to pump up his own ego by showing how his opinions are firmly in line with those of his viewers. Each is a self-fulfilling prophecy.

For example, Bill might do a story on how, if gays are allowed to marry, there will be nothing preventing people from marrying triplets or dogs. The Factor poll will then ask whether gays should be allowed to marry. Gee, what will the results be? Will they herald a grassroots movement in favor of bestiality and polygamy? Only his viewers can say for certain.

On July 21, 2004, it could have been different. There were a lot of things happening in the world at that time . . . important things. Bill's poll question could have dealt with the 9/11 Commission report due out the following day. He could have asked a question about waning support for the Iraqi War. Or how about a question on the grand jury inquiry into alleged Halliburton ties to Iran? Indeed, any conscientious, marginally intelligent journalist would have had no problem coming up with a worthy, thought-provoking question.

For the record, here's what Bill came up with: "Who is worse? Michael Moore or Al Franken."

Now to be perfectly fair, Bill is not the first person to do a poll like this. A very similar poll was started by Terrance Yakes some years ago in the classroom of this book's coauthor, Joseph Amann. Joseph was in seventh grade, and the poll was passed to him in history class. The choices then were Amy Hawkins and Christy Cornue, but otherwise it was basically the same poll. So if Bill were thirteen, this would be a perfectly acceptable question. Since Bill is not thirteen, this makes him a moron.

You see, Bill wants to be a news source. He really does. He thinks CNN and MSNBC are a joke. He finds the network news programs tedious and fatally infected with liberal bias. He constantly talks about FOX News and the fantastic ratings they have. He brags about how influential he's become in the news game. Then he pulls shit like this. If these questions were any more masturbatory, he'd have to end each program with a money shot.

Incidentally, in honor of Bill, we ran a little poll of our own the following night on sweetjesusihatebilloreilly.com. Here were the results.

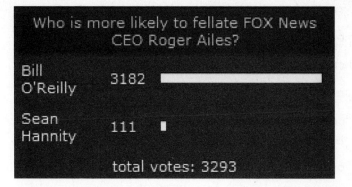

BILL JUST DON'T UNDERSTAND . . . THIRD-GRADE MATH

ON SEPTEMBER 13, 2005, Bill started off his program with a Talking Points Memo titled "America and the Poor." He took time out of his busy schedule to confront critics who felt the poor were losing ground under the Bush administration: "Halfway through President Clinton's tenure in office in 1996, the poverty rate was 13.7 percent. Halfway through President Bush's tenure, the rate is 12.7 percent. A full point lower."

Of course, we had no idea Bush had reduced the number of people living in poverty in the United States. Well, that could be because he hadn't.

In 1993, Clinton's first year as president, the poverty rate was 15.1 percent (up from 12.8 percent in 1989, when George H. W. Bush's term began).

By 1996, Clinton had lowered it to 13.7 percent, and in 2000, Clinton's last full year in office, the poverty rate was 11.3 percent.

Enter George W. Bush. People living under the poverty line rose to 12.1 percent in 2002, to 12.5 percent in 2003, and to 12.7 percent in 2004.

So, clearly, the poverty rate had escalated every year under Bush while consistently falling under Clinton. And, just as clearly, O'Reilly looked like an idiot.

But the next day on his radio program, Bill was still defending his fuzzy math:

110 JOSEPH MINTON AMANN & TOM BREUER

CALLER: Let's see, poverty is up since George Bush took office.

O'REILLY: That's not true.

CALLER: It is true.

O'REILLY: I have the stats right here, Larry.

CALLER: I just looked at the figures. Gun crime is up since George Bush took office.

O'REILLY: All right, Larry, hold it, hold it, hold it. Let's deal with one at a time. The only fair comparison is halfway through Clinton's term, halfway through Bush's term, okay? That's the only fair comparison. You gotta go real time.

CALLER: Bill, I . . .

O'REILLY: Poverty is down, Larry, one full percent in real time from 1996, halfway through Clinton, 2004, halfway through Bush. That is the truth, Larry, and if you're not willing to acknowledge that's the truth, this conversation is over.

Why "real time" has to be considered halfway through a president's term is a mystery, but Bill was sticking to his own no-spin interpretation.

Of course, by his standard, one could argue that George W. Bush is a better slave emancipator than Abraham Lincoln. Halfway through Lincoln's presidency, very few slaves had been emancipated. Halfway through Bush's tenure, all of them had been freed. So why isn't George W. Bush's face on the $5 bill?

Now, it could be that O'Reilly simply needs a remedial math course. For his benefit, then, we submit the following third-grade story problem:

Billy and Sean both take trips to Thailand. Sean shows up in January at a time when 15.1 percent of the prostitutes in Bangkok have chlamydia. When he leaves at the beginning of March, only 11.3 percent of the prostitutes have chlamydia. Billy arrives in

March at the same time Sean is leaving. Just halfway through Billy's trip at the beginning of April, 12.7 percent of the prostitutes have chlamydia. Halfway through Sean's trip, 13.7 percent of the prostitutes had chlamydia.

Assuming Billy stays one more month, whose picture will Bangkok brothels most likely post at their front desks with a note attached saying, "Don't Have Sex with This Man"?

Answer: Billy's. But you knew that already.

BILL JUST DON'T UNDERSTAND . . . RIGHT-TO-DIE BATTLES

IT WAS MARCH 23, 2005. Bill declared that he had a solution to the ongoing Terri Schiavo case. We were anxious to see what lotus flowers of wisdom would blossom from our little no-spin Buddha. We weren't disappointed:

> But this whole ordeal can end right now if Michael Schiavo simply stops the litigation. He should stand up and say that he tried to implement his wife's wishes, but the greater good is now served by allowing her family to care for her as they want to do.

Now, we realize you're all thinking, "How is this a solution? It's just giving up." But that's the genius of O'Reilly. You can just imagine him in protracted divorce negotiations with his wife as he suddenly exclaims, "Hey, I've got it! How about you just walk away now and let me keep everything!"

Brilliant.

But he wasn't finished: "Michael Schiavo keeps his thesis that Terri did not want extraordinary care, but shows compassion. And Terri's family gets to keep her alive. Again, where's the downside?"

His thesis? Michael Schiavo was trying to let his wife die with dignity, and O'Reilly talks about it like he's writing a term paper. Keeping her alive, trapped in a lifeless brain . . . that was the downside. Moron.

And now for the clincher: "So do that, Michael Schiavo. Rise above the bickering. Your wife can't feel anything. A miracle could happen."

Bill is possibly the dumbest man in broadcasting. He makes Ryan Seacrest sound like Confucius. If God were to intercede on Terri Schiavo's behalf, couldn't he just as easily do it after she died? Hell, it would even be more dramatic that way. Did God just need more time? Was He still hemming and hawing about what to do on this one?

Of course, the best thing about the Schiavo case is that it allows us to keep our thesis:

Bill O'Reilly is really quite dumb.

NOTES

1. Doug Wead, *The Raising of a President: The Mothers and Fathers of Our Nation's Leaders* (New York: Atria Books, 2005).
2. Bill O'Reilly, *The No Spin Zone: Confrontations with the Powerful and Famous in America* (New York: Broadway Books, 2001).

10

MEA CULPA SORTA: O'REILLY AND THE ART OF THE HALF-ASSED APOLOGY

BILL O'REILLY IS not a humble guy. He admits as much. Indeed, on page 170 of his book *The No Spin Zone*, he writes, "I have to admit that I am not a humble guy." Of course, true to form, in the very next sentence he manages to pin his lack of humility on someone else: "But that's not my fault, as all of my ancestors were conceited louts."

O'Reilly appears to be joking here,[1] but his disavowal is really quite telling. Indeed, while in a rare moment of clarity it's obvious even to Bill that he's a loud, arrogant, confrontational boob, he remains self-aware enough to know that nothing is ever really his fault.

There are many examples of this. We've collected just a few.

NOT FONDA 'POLOGIES

ON MAY 17, 2005, O'Reilly had the following exchange with Nick Gillespie, editor-in-chief of the libertarian *Reason* magazine. O'Reilly claimed that during Jane Fonda's visit to Hanoi, she had passed to the North Vietnamese notes American POWs had given her.

GILLESPIE: But, but here is, and certainly, one of the things that's fascinating about [Fonda's autobiography, *My Life So Far*[2]] is when she talks about visiting Hanoi in 1972, which is the reason why we still talk about her and why she's such a large . . .

O'REILLY: Yes, but Mr. Gillespie, you're giving her too much credit. Hold on just for a second. You're giving her too much credit. She didn't talk about the big thing that she did wrong, and that's the messages that were slipped to her by the POWs . . .

GILLESPIE: Yes, but that story's not true.

O'REILLY: Well, it is true according to the POWs. See? They believe . . .

GILLESPIE: That story has been debunked.

O'REILLY: By whom?

GILLESPIE: By, if you go to Snopes.com. The urban . . .

O'REILLY: Who?

GILLESPIE: Snopes.com.

O'REILLY: Snope? See, look, I'm believing, I'm believing the guys who were there. I'm not going to believe Snope.com.

GILLESPIE: Okay, well, Bill, if you don't, if you read any, any history of the Vietnamese war that talks about that, it is absolutely not true. And you know, I'm not, I don't have any stock in Jane Fonda.

O'REILLY: Just to clear the air here . . .

GILLESPIE: Bill . . .

O'REILLY: The POWs themselves stand by the story and say that their interrogators told them what happened.

So what do we know so far? A damaging story has been circulating about Jane Fonda that sounds a little too good to be true and a lot like an urban legend.[3]

Now, a good journalist would know that at this point anything relating to the Hanoi Jane legend should be checked out, as so many bogus stories have attached to that period in Fonda's life.

An average but conscientious journalist would take pains to confirm this particular story because it sounds kind of hyperbolic and urban-legend-y, and extraordinary claims require extraordinary proof.

A really shitty first-year journalism student, on the other hand, would make an inflammatory accusation based on a false story that had been debunked almost six years earlier, when his guest tries to set the record straight, interrupt by simply repeating the bogus claim, and the next day, upon discovering the accusation has been thoroughly discredited, imply that it's still kinda sorta an open question though probably wrong, because it's been proven beyond a shadow of a doubt to be dead wrong.

Here's Bill:

> Time now for the Most Ridiculous Item of the Day: setting the record straight on Jane Fonda. Now, last night I told Nick Gillespie of *Reason* magazine that I was not willing to give Ms. Fonda a pass on the accusation she turned over notes from American POWs to the North Vietnamese during her trip to Hanoi. A Web site called Snopes.com has investigated and debunked that accusation. They say it's not true.
>
> Well, we decided to research it. We spent the day doing it. And the indication is that Snopes is correct. The story is bogus. So at this point, lacking any definable evidence to the contrary, Jane Fonda did not turn over any POW notes to the Vietnamese.
>
> We're happy to clarify the record. It would be ridiculous not to do so. All right. Way to go, Snopes.com.

Now, if you were in a bar and you started shooting your mouth off about one of your neighbors, saying "I heard he once stole a

Hanson cassingle from Big Lots" or "I heard he collaborated with the Vietcong during the Vietnam War," and then later you found out it was nothing but a vicious rumor circulated by people who hated your neighbor, you'd probably feel pretty bad and more than a little embarrassed.

You'd want to set the record straight in the most abject possible manner and you'd be fiercely apologetic if you ran into your neighbor and discovered he'd heard about the smear. What you most likely wouldn't do is say, "the indication is that you're not a traitor to our country" or "lacking any definable evidence to the contrary, you did not shoplift 'Mmm Bop.'"

In fact, such a response would be especially bad form if you had made no effort to check the story out beforehand, particularly if doing so would have taken about three mouse clicks and twenty keystrokes on any standard search engine.

Clearly, what this situation required was an apology and a retraction, not a half-clarification. Of course, not only did O'Reilly not apologize, he left open the possibility that the accusation might be true. It's kind of like saying, "Well, the indication is that Bill O'Reilly is not in fact a pedophile, so at this point, lacking any definable evidence to the contrary, he has not molested any eight-year-olds. That we know of. Good night, everybody!"

PISSED AT THE POST

WHEN BILL DOES on the rare occasion manage to eke out an apology, he reminds one of the little boy who's forced to tell his sister he's sorry for hitting her, then, under his breath, utters a scarcely audible "poopyhead."

On the January 19, 2005, *Radio Factor*, O'Reilly called California senator Barbara Boxer "a nut." What followed was pure O'Reilly.

On the January 25 *Factor* TV show, *St. Louis Post-Dispatch* columnist Sylvester Brown, Jr., cited O'Reilly's reference to Boxer as an example of how Bill's bare-knuckles style is similar to Jerry Springer's influence over television:

BROWN: Well, let me, let me explain the Springer comparison. You can talk about Brokaw, you can talk about Russert, you can talk about Cronkite, everybody else who works for the liberal media, but you don't see these guys calling people idiots on the air. You don't see them calling them nuts on the air. You don't see them calling names on the air. You don't see them . . .

O'REILLY: And the last time I called somebody an idiot was?

BROWN: But you did it, Bill . . .

O'REILLY: When?

BROWN: . . . and you know you did it.

O'REILLY: When?

BROWN: You did it last week. You did it last week on—with Barbara Boxer. You called her a nut. You called the voters who voted for her loony. Is that not true?

O'REILLY: That's not true. I mean, what I do is I say, there are loony left-wing people or "this is nuts," but I never say "she's a nut" or "this person is a loon."

BROWN: Bill, I suggest you . . .

O'REILLY: Come on.

BROWN: I suggest you play your tape. You did call Barbara Boxer a nut last week.

O'REILLY: I—her position is nutty on certain issues. I do not call her a nut. And, you know, we'll pull it [the clip], and we'll show that you're wrong. But here's the deal. You write for a liberal newspaper . . .

BROWN: It's your radio program.

Of course, as the far-left bomb-thrower Web site mediamatters.org has pointed out, O'Reilly frequently calls people loons. In fact, Media Matters documented nine cases where he did just that from June 2004 through January 2005. Among the honored were Sharon Stone, Howard Dean, the folks at moveon.org, and half of all people who call themselves liberals.

And how might one refer to someone who vehemently claims he's never said something that he has in fact said numerous times? That's right—meshugah.

Well, needless to say, when O'Reilly did pull the tape, he realized his error. So a humble apology to Brown was clearly in order. Even though the two disagreed politically, fair was fair, right? Well, sort of:

> Last night on *The Factor*, a left-wing columnist for the *St. Louis Post-Dispatch*, Sylvester Brown, demonstrated his anti–FOX News bias to the nation right here.
>
> While Mr. Brown is generally misguided, in my opinion, he did challenge me at one point, saying that I had called Senator Barbara Boxer a nut. Now, I denied doing that, and I didn't on television. But on the radio, uh oh, I forgot that I indeed did apply that word to Senator Boxer while analyzing her strategy, or lack thereof, to fight terrorism.
>
> So Brown was right and I was wrong, which makes me the Most Ridiculous Item of the Day. I hate that.

Okay, so O'Reilly set the record straight, even if he was kind of an ass about it. Surely, though, he would be more conciliatory on his radio program, where he first slammed Boxer. Or maybe not:

> If you saw *The Factor* last night, that was a wild program on television. Had a guy named Sylvester Brown on, who's a left-wing columnist for the *St. Louis Post-Dispatch*. And Brown is like [Ted] Turner and like many in the liberal press in that they hate the success of the FOX News Channel and *The Radio Factor*. I mean, they just despise it. And the reason is because they disagree a lot of times with our political point of view.
>
> So instead of debating the issues and trying to figure out why we're so successful and the other enterprises are failing, including

the *St. Louis Post-Dispatch*—it's losing circulation and, I think, losing money—they attack us in all kinds of varying ways.

Anyway, one of the attacks that Brown leveled against me on television last night was that I called Barbara Boxer a nut. And on television, I did not do that. But on radio I unfortunately did. And I shouldn't have. But I didn't remember.

Now, to extend the little-boy analogy with which we started this section (which, to be honest, at this point seems a bit unfair to little boys who say "poopyhead"), this is kind of like saying, "Yes, I hit my sister, but it's not really my fault because she disagrees with me on a lot of things, reminded me that I did something I don't remember doing, and, frankly, is not as popular as I am. Look at her lemonade sales. Horrible."

Of course, any fair observer would concede that Brown is owed a sincere apology, and one day he may actually get it. Just not from Bill.

HOW DARE YOU WRITE THAT EDITORIAL YOU DIDN'T WRITE!

ALMOST ALL REPORTERS will tell you that one of their biggest fears is getting a story wrong. It's embarrassing and reflects poorly on them as journalists. Unfortunately, all journalists err from time to time, and when it happens, they're forced to eat crow.

Of course, Bill likes to send the crow back with a few harsh words for the chef.

On May 10, 2005, O'Reilly took aim at a *Houston Chronicle* editorial that criticized Florida's new Jessica's Law, which, among other provisions, required convicted sex offenders to wear tracking devices when released from prison.

Judging from his comments, it was immediately obvious that Bill either didn't read the editorial thoroughly enough or didn't understand it.

The same day the *Houston Chronicle* piece ran, O'Reilly took after it, claiming the editorial had said the law was too harsh and implying that the *Chronicle* had called for counseling sexual predators in lieu of imprisoning them.

On May 12, the *Chronicle* attempted to set the record straight:

> The editorial, citing extensive research on this subject, said hooking GPS monitors to sexual predators released from prison might prove less effective than closer supervision by parole officers and other low-tech strategies. The *Chronicle* did not call for lighter punishment; it called for the adoption of the most effective measures to protect our children.

Oh, so case closed, right? The misunderstanding was cleared up. It was evident that Bill had missed the basic gist of the editorial and would surely, at the first opportunity, set the record straight. No biggie. It happens to everyone, particularly in demanding, high-pressure jobs like his.

Oh, but you know our Bill. The guy makes Narcissus look like Droopy Dog.

Indeed, on the May 12 *O'Reilly Factor*, Bill did his best to clear the air by taking another swing at the *Chronicle*:

> You know, one of the interesting things that they attacked me on today was that they didn't say the Florida law, twenty-five to life, first offender, molesting a kid under the age of twelve, was too harsh. And they didn't. They didn't actually say that.
>
> But from everything that I extrapolated from the editorial, why would they bother to write the editorial if they didn't think it was too tough?

Indeed, that will go down as a mystery for the ages, right up there with the ineffable nature of God and the elusive unified field theory. Why did the *Houston Chronicle* write an editorial about the most effective way to monitor released sex offenders instead of the editorial O'Reilly originally thought they had written about the law being too harsh or the editorial Bill later extrapolated in his head?

The world may never know.

NOTES

1. One can never be quite sure when O'Reilly is joking, as he's really quite horrible at it. See *The O'Reilly Factor, The Radio Factor, The O'Reilly Factor*—the book, *The No Spin Zone, Who's Looking Out for You?, The O'Reilly Factor for Kids, Those Who Trespass,* Bill's newspaper column, and the Andrea Mackris sexual harassment affidavit, featuring the comedy stylings of Bill O'Reilly.
2. Jane Fonda, *My Life So Far* (New York: Random House, 2005).
3. Fonda did visit Vietnam in 1972 and cozy up with the North Vietnamese, but that doesn't make every subsequent rumor circulated about her worth repeating.

LIBERALS, SECULARISTS, ATHEISTS, AND MOORE

▼

11

O'REILLY VERSUS HILLARY: THE FAKE RACE THAT NEVER WAS (AND HE STILL LOST)

ON **SEPTEMBER 23, 2003,** Bill O'Reilly's most recent literary masterpiece, *Who's Looking Out for You?*, hit bookshelves across the United States. O'Reilly was in all his pompous glory as he declared he would debut at the top of the *New York Times* bestseller list. He tirelessly pitched his book day after day on his television program, ensuring a lengthy stay.

There was a problem, though. Books by liberals Al Franken and Michael Moore would soon knock him from the perch his ego fondly calls home.

This was problematic for Bill and his fragile psyche. So how could he pump up book sales? Well, he could peddle it every single day on his highly rated cable "news" program. Consider it done. Still, there must be a way to sell more. But how?

LET THE FAKE RACE BEGIN

ALTHOUGH HIS ARCHRIVAL Al Franken's satirical book *Lies and the Lying Liars Who Tell Them* would seem a likely object of his ire, Bill seemed more preoccupied with Hillary Clinton's *Living History*.[1] Suddenly, he announced there was a race between sales of his book and Clinton's.

It was a curious race to be sure. Why was there a race? Why would the race be with Hillary and not Al Franken, who put a rather nasty photo of Bill on the cover? In fact, Franken had dedicated an entire section of his book to O'Reilly's lies. Hadn't Franken already established himself as the Moriarty to O'Reilly's dashing Holmes?

But would a race with Al Franken spur his book sales? Probably not. Who would Bill be able to position his book against? Enter Hillary, the long-established bête noire of the lunatic right. It was clear the race was going to be a heated one, except for the inconvenient fact that Ms. Clinton apparently had no idea she was in it. Still, it was up to "the folks" to show her. Bill had found a whole new way to tap into the common man's latent love of literature: spite.

THE EVIDENCE STARTS TO POUR IN

JUST OUT OF the starting gates, however, ol' Bill was already looking like a long shot. Hillary had quite a head start. Her initial printing was 1 million copies, followed quickly by another printing of 300,000. Bill's initial printing was 750,000, with an 82,000-copy second run. Advantage Hillary. Oh, it was gonna be a helluva fake race. So how could Bill gain the edge?

It looked bleak, but then some stunning surprise evidence surfaced.

In the December 15 installment of *The O'Reilly Factor*'s homage to Voltaire, The Most Ridiculous Item of the Day, glad tidings came from the heartland's humblest of outposts: Costco.

> While I was signing [the book], a Costco manager handed me a sheet of paper with sales figures. As you know, we are in a fight with Hillary Clinton for best-selling nonfiction book of the year. Since September, in Costco stores across the country, *Who's Looking Out for You?* has sold 96,000. Hillary's book has sold less

than 9,000 copies. Ninety-six thousand. Nine thousand. We've got a real shot at overtaking Mrs. Clinton. We have two weeks to do it. Ridiculous? Only if you're rooting for her.

Okay, there are like ninety things wrong with this statement. Here are three:

1. "As you know, we're in a fight"? Who started the fight? Does Hillary know this thing has escalated from a fake race to a fake fight? It was becoming abundantly clear that Bill needed to up his meds.
2. Are the sales at Costco a representative sampling of total book sales across the United States? No. No, they're not.
3. "Only if you're rooting for her"? People are rooting? Rooting for what?

This is where you start to realize how skewed Bill's reality actually is. Obviously he was making a joke, but when you make a joke over and over, night after night, somewhere in your head it ain't no joke. By keeping his viewers updated on the fake race and by creating a sense of urgency, he had convinced himself that people were, in fact, rooting.

ENTERING THE HOMESTRETCH:
CLINTON 1,084,520, O'REILLY 430,407 (FRANKEN 674,024)

WITH TWO WEEKS left in the year, conservative Web journalist Matt Drudge got hold of the sales figures and reported that O'Reilly wasn't even close to hitting Clinton's number. In fact, he was also getting slaughtered by Franken.

This report would infuriate O'Reilly to no end. He stopped at nothing to spin this one, but Drudge's story, which simply reported the Nielsen numbers, was all but spin-proof. The only figures O'Reilly had seen fit to report up to this point had been meticulously gleaned from a Long Island Costco manager.

SHE'S CHEATING! SHE'S CHEATING!
SHE'S CHEATING IN THE FAKE RACE!

ON DECEMBER 18, the fake race was once again the subject of The Most Ridiculous Item of the Day . . . ironic, we know.

> As for the race between Hillary's book and *Who's Looking Out?*, we are closing in. Broadway Books has gone back for a sixth printing since September, bringing the total of *Who's* in print to close to a million. The senator has sold around a million, but a good amount of those were purchased by the Democratic National Committee. That doesn't count, Senator.

Okay, we hate to use online chat jargon, but ROTFLMAO. "That doesn't count, Senator" is truly a classic line. Is he serious? Is he sending her a personal message? Is he accusing her of cheating in the race? THE FAKE RACE?!?

I'M TOO BUSY FOR YOUR STUPID RACE THAT I STARTED

In the same Most Ridiculous Item of the Day when O'Reilly claimed Hillary and the Democrats were conspiring to rig the game, he also whined that he was unfairly handicapped:

> *The Palm Beach Post* is reporting that Senator Hillary Clinton signed books for hundreds of people down in Florida—but the average time they got with her? Each person? [Just] eight seconds. Eight! Whoa. Mrs. Clinton has had time to do scores of signings around the country, but I've only had time to do four because I have to work. I'd love to be down there in South Florida signing copies of *Who's Looking Out for You?* Believe me, you'd get more than eight seconds with me, although some folks think that's too much time.

Classic O'Reilly. First he says Hillary isn't spending enough time with each person at her book signings and then in the next sentence he says Hillary is spending all her time gallivanting around the country doing signings while he has to "work"—implying she doesn't or, at the very least, is shirking her duties. So she's spending *only* eight seconds with each person, but she shouldn't be spending *any* time with them at all. So what is his point?

And then the best part: Even though he won't do additional book signings, if he were to do more he'd spend a lot more time with you than Hillary does. But he can't. So he won't.

What?

Oh, but if O'Reilly proves anything, it's that nothing's so crazy that it's not worth saying over and over again. On January 1, he let his viewers know why he was losing the fake race. Apparently he was too busy looking out for the folks:

> I've received a ton of letters asking why I don't travel around the country doing signings for *Who's Looking Out for You?* Hillary Clinton has dozens of events for her book, and the smear people are all over the place. But I have to work doing both radio and TV daily, and air travel throughout the USA is brutal.

Poor, poor Bill. He has to work up to five days a week. Can you imagine? Oh, and first-class air travel is such a bitch.

FINISH LINE FOR THE FAKE RACE ARRIVES

SO THE RACE is over. Wow, it must have been a close one. Bill tried so hard to win. Maybe he did. Maybe it was close. And even if Hillary did edge Bill out, it was because she cheated. Would Bill be just ahead of Hillary? Would he win in spite of his fake nemesis's lies and cheating? Would he be just a shade behind Hillary? Yeah, but then he could still claim moral victory because of all the DNC copies.

Well, it takes a couple months to calculate book sales after the year's end, but Bill knew he'd lost the race.

But still he fought his delusions (January 7, 2004): "[Drudge] has repeatedly misled his readers about book sales. He quotes the Nielsen Group and says Hillary's book is this and that, the smear books are this and that, and O'Reilly's book doesn't measure up, na da da da da. Nonsense. And Drudge knows it."

Okay, so Drudge quoted a report from Nielsen. He didn't make up anything. Unlike O'Reilly, he didn't make it personal at all. He quoted facts.

And where did he say O'Reilly's book didn't "measure up"? Again O'Reilly shows how his delusional paranoia, wild conspiracy theories, and painfully low self-esteem cloud nearly every bit of his reality. Even though O'Reilly's the one who started the fake race, the moment someone shows actual evidence regarding said race, it becomes a personal attack on Bill.

Then Bill once again showed his love of irrelevant evidence that doesn't support his claim but sounds like it might. "This coming Sunday will mark the fifth week *Who's Looking Out for You?* is No. 1 on the *New York Times* best-seller list."

That's great for O'Reilly, but it really doesn't change the fact that he got his Irish arse kicked by a fiery lass from County Pulaski.

Of course, it doesn't even matter who sold more books at this point. Bill's all alone in the race. He's just a pathetic ranting lunatic. He even dragged his poor publisher into his silly battle.

"My publisher actually sent Drudge a letter saying that the Nielsen Company does not count book sales from many major department stores and other places. *Who's Looking Out for You?* does great business in these venues."

Now if you think for one second that a book publisher was sitting around reading the Drudge Report, saw the Nielsen info, and subsequently fired off a letter, well, then you're as loopy as O'Reilly.

"For example, at Costco, we've outsold Hillary since September nine to one."

Jesus Christ, the imbecile just brought up Costco again.

A PHOTO FINISH?
IF YOU USE A REALLY, REALLY WIDE-ANGLE LENS

THE FINAL 2003 book sales were printed in the March 22, 2004, issue of *Publishers Weekly*:

Hillary Clinton: 1,546,000
Bill O'Reilly: 932,750

You see, Bill was down by more than 600,000 copies, just as Drudge had originally reported before Bill basically called him a liar. So who's the real liar? Who's the delusional king-sized nut bar? Who's chock-full o' fibs? O'Reilly? Naw, can't be.

NOTES

1. Hillary Clinton, *Living History* (New York: Simon & Schuster, 2003).

12

MILLION-DOLLAR CRYBABY: O'REILLY VERSUS HOLLYWOOD

They wanted to tell everybody how bad Bush is and how their rights in Bel Air are being infringed upon. I can't get my Jaguar out of the driveway anymore, there's so much pollution. Come on.

—*Bill O'Reilly on* The O'Reilly Factor, *April 2, 2004*

AS **ANY COMIC** book fan knows, a staple of every comic book world is the supervillain.

Superman has his Lex Luthor, Batman his Joker, Spider-Man his Green Goblin, Professor Charles Xavier his Magneto, Electra Woman and Dyna Girl their Empress of Evil.

It's a complex relationship wherein the hero, who is on the side of truth and justice, is evenly matched for a time by the villain, whose only real advantages are guile and treachery. Through his machinations, the villain will often temporarily get the upper hand before truth, good, and justice ultimately prevail.

O'Reilly, of course, thinks he's Superman, fighting the evil elites on behalf of "the folks." Unfortunately, he doesn't fit the profile. Spotty fifty-six-year-old men who threaten to tear the children of 9/11 victims to pieces are rarely considered for the role. Would Superman lose his cool and storm out of an NPR interview because he thought the host was being mean to him? Could you see Superman wheedling his bosses into suing an author who put an unflattering picture of him on a book, claiming the letter "S" is a registered trademark of the Justice League? Not likely.

This isn't to say O'Reilly doesn't have a place in the comic book world. He does. Indeed, he's the classic supervillain. And when it comes to O'Reilly, his arch-nemesis and the voice for truth, justice, and the America way is the dashing George Clooney.

Consider: the supervillain usually despises the superhero because he represents everything good and just in the world. The supervillain has only hate and falsehoods on his side.

The superhero has a cleft chin, chiseled body, and rugged, all-American good looks. The supervillain usually has some sort of deformity, such as an embarrassing skin condition.

The superhero is adored by millions, whereas O'Reilly—sorry, the "supervillain"—commands only his toadying minions.

The superhero has women throwing themselves at him. The supervillain is forced to thrust himself awkwardly on unsuspecting associate producers.

And most important, the supervillain's wife spends her nights dreaming of the superhero flying through the window and standing at the foot of her bed, rather than being forced to endure the shriveled old body that climbs on top of her twice a week.

This is why Bill O'Reilly hates George Clooney.

But O'Reilly doesn't reserve his rage just for Clooney. He hates all "Hollywood celebrities." They are indeed the Justice League to his Legion of Doom. Those flashy, successful do-gooders are adored by the masses. Nothing wounds his ego more. He has to stop them. It's the only way.

THEY MAY USE PRICEWATERHOUSECOOPERS, BUT THEY'RE ACCOUNTABLE ONLY TO O'REILLY

ABOUT A MONTH and a half after 9/11, Bill O'Reilly criticized several Hollywood celebrities for not appearing on *The Factor* to address accusations that the money they had raised for the September 11 Fund wasn't getting to the victims' families.

Clooney responded with a sharply worded letter:

On the evening of October 31st you ran a story that has no basis in truth. What is not important is your attack of the performers who gave their time to raise money during the telethon for the September 11th fund. What is important is your accusation that the fund is being mishandled and misused. That sir, as you know, is nothing short of a lie.

The fund is intact and has already handed out some 36 million dollars to victims' families (fifteen thousand checks), with over $230 million more to be allocated as The United Way sorts through the complicated process of who is in the most need. To have given out all of the money only six weeks after it was raised, would truly be irresponsible. If you were a journalist you would have known that.

Sadly, O'Reilly is not a journalist. He's a guy on TV who wanted Ed McMahon to show up at grieving families' doors with giant photocopies of checks.

But the most interesting thing about this whole scrap as it pertains to O'Reilly wasn't whether or not the United Way had fumbled the operation but how Bill reacted to it. A better journalist—say Jim Lehrer, Mike Wallace, Bill Moyers, or MTV's Martha Quinn—would have focused more on the charity itself, not on the stars who donated a small fraction of their time to it. After all, if you think something's fishy with the Muscular Dystrophy Association Telethon money, you don't harangue Shecky Greene for two weeks. You go to the top.

But like the true supervillain, who both seethes with anger over and secretly admires his foils, Bill just had to get these stars to acknowledge him.

Indeed, on March 26, 2002, O'Reilly still hadn't let up on the notion that Hollywood do-gooders were accountable to him personally:

"Talking Points" hopes the [Rosie] O'Donnell interview will send a message to the powerful people in America. You can't hide behind your handlers anymore. If you want respect, you

have to step up and answer the questions. . . . We encourage people like John Ashcroft, Charles Schumer, and George Clooney
to do the same thing. We have questions for you guys, and you'll
be treated fairly.

Hmmm, let's see . . . the attorney general of the United States,
a New York senator who coauthored the federal assault weapons
ban, and the guy from *ER*. He might as well say "Henry Kissinger,
Kofi Annan, and Jaleel White, TV's Urkel."

Again, O'Reilly calling out George Clooney five months after his
original dustup with the Hollywood heartthrob is rather revealing.
The superhero/supervillain homoerotic subtext, while disturbing,
is self-evident.

Of course, O'Reilly's little schoolboy crush was far from over. In
January 2005, in the wake of the tsunami disaster in Asia, Bill
again banged his demented little drum:

If George Clooney and other stars go on TV and ask you to
give, then they had better be involved all the way down the line.
Now I don't expect the celebrities to audit the books, but if problems are brought to their attention, they must help solve those
problems. Sending billions of dollars into chaotic areas is fraught
with danger, even if it is the right thing to do. Americans must
demand reasonable accountability.

First of all, Americans demand very little other than an ever-
expanding selection of cable channels and new variations on
microwaveable pocket-type products. What O'Reilly demands is
that anyone he challenges on anything is from that point forward
personally accountable to him.

He's like a twelve-year-old boy who throws himself a birthday
party and then has a tantrum when the popular kids don't show up.
Make no mistake about it, O'Reilly's rage at Clooney is displaced
anger over some long-buried junior high school incident, possibly
involving a summer pool party, a pair of ill-fitting swim trunks, a girl
he liked, the girl's strapping beau, and a freakishly small Irish penis.

WE'RE SELLING TONS OF LEX LUTHOR GEAR, AND WONDER WOMAN IS NOT HAPPY ABOUT IT

O'REILLY KNOWS HIS audience well. Like all evil people, they hate Hollywood. And when it comes to Hollywood celebrities—particularly liberal celebrities—O'Reilly is like a deranged sea captain chumming the waters for sharks. Sometimes he offers up a morsel, sometimes a meal.

Indeed, there are at least four distinct techniques he uses during the course of his broadcasts to get his viewers churning the seas for another feckless anti-Hollywood feeding frenzy:

The Out-of-Left-Field Streisand Reference

Both *The Factor,* which we'll give you the address in a moment, and billoreilly.com offer a wide variety of gifts to please everyone except Barbra Streisand. There just is no pleasing that woman. (*The O'Reilly Factor*, December 16, 2003)

That's an example of a morsel—just a taste to get his viewers' attention. It can be used to entice, as in "Barbra Streisand doesn't want you to know this, but . . . " or it can be invoked as a call to action, as in "Barbra Streisand is at it again, and we'll let you what you can do about it."

Or it can be used as a cheap ploy to get people to buy his crap.

The "They're Democrats . . .
Not That There's Anything Wrong with That" Reference

As part of our election coverage, we are going to tell you which powerful and famous people are rooting for which candidate. John Kerry collected some big money last night in Hollywood, more than three million bucks from people like James Taylor, Larry David, Leonardo DiCaprio, Jennifer Aniston, Kevin Costner, Meg Ryan, and, of course, the omnipresent Barbra Streisand. Nothing wrong with supporting your guy. It's not ridiculous at all, and we can't wait to tell you about the big Hollywood-for-Bush fund-raiser. But we may have to wait a loooong time for that. (*The O'Reilly Factor*, March 31, 2004)

Yeah, Bill has the bad guys on the ropes now. He's bustin' this story wide open, and those Beverly Hills types can't hide from the exposure. The truth is out; some Hollywood stars are Democrats! In your face, Costner! In your face!

Thank God a crusading journalist is finally telling us which famous people are supporting which candidates. Can you imagine how invaluable it would have been to have O'Reilly toiling away for the fourth estate back in the seventies? Just think how much better off the world would be now if the American public had known Lindsay Wagner was voting for Carter or that Vic Tayback was squarely in Ford's camp.

Knowledge is power, and you couldn't find more knowledge than this unless you tuned in to E! or *Entertainment Tonight*.

The Muddled and Confused Reference

You can also expect to see left-wing actors Sean Penn, Tim Robbins, and Alec Baldwin all be nominated for Academy Awards next March, and these guys deserve the nominations. They're great actors. But, again, the entertainment industry is going to unite to put forth a powerful anti-Bush message in all of these awards programs. (*The O'Reilly Factor*, December 5, 2003)

O'Reilly loves a mixed message. Mind you, we have no idea what point he's trying to make here, other than perhaps a primitive Solomon Grundyesque "Hollywood BAAAAD!"

The "They Better Watch Out" Reference

The final results of our billoreilly.com poll, which asked the question, "Are your movie choices affected by the politics of the actors appearing in them?" Ninety percent of you said yes. Just

10 percent said no. About twenty-five thousand people voted on billoreilly.com. (*The O'Reilly Factor*, October 27, 2003)

O'Reilly's online poll questions are, of course, the funniest displays of vox idiotus populi in the Western world. He just *loves* leading questions.

But seriously, who's taking a pass on *Shrek 2* because Cameron Diaz is an outspoken liberal? Well, 90 percent of O'Reilly's viewers, that's who.

But when push comes to shove, most people probably base their moviegoing decisions on things like previews, newspaper reviews, raw star power, and word of mouth. Judging by their many box-office triumphs, it's unlikely that most liberals, who probably see a lot more movies than conservatives, are boycotting films headlined by Hollywood conservatives such as Arnold Schwarzenegger, Bruce Willis, and Mel Gibson. Even Gibson's own directorial efforts are rarely blackballed by the majority of liberals. Now, if Mel's father, Hutton Gibson, starts making movies, the reaction from the left-wing pinheads might be different.

But that would likely have less to do with anticonservative bias than the fact that nobody wants to see a film about a brave Holocaust denier who falls in love with a woman who thinks Vatican II was a Masonic plot backed by Jews to undermine the Catholic Church and install a series of illegitimate antipopes. Unless he could get Tom Hanks and Meg Ryan to star. They're just so cute together.

HISTORY 101 WITH PROFESSOR O'REILLY

IN A MARCH 2003 newspaper column, O'Reilly wrote the following:

I would like to give Susan Sarandon, Julianne Moore, Martin Sheen, and the other anti-war stars a history quiz. I want to ask them what they know about the Treaty of Versailles, the appeasement conference at Munich and the structure of the German police state as it compares to Saddam Hussein's tyrannical rule of Iraq. Also, I want to discuss Saddam's human rights record with Richard Gere, who for years has been chanting with the Dalai Lama about freeing Tibet.

First of all, O'Reilly attempting to speak from authority on history is about as funny as it gets. This is the same guy who apparently believes the phrase "all men are created equal" is in the Constitution (Talking Points Memo, December 2, 2002),[1] thinks Louis XVI would have loved secular America (*Who's Looking Out for You?*, p. 119), and claims Hitler, Stalin, and Mao would have been card-carrying members of the ACLU (*The Radio Factor*, January 19, 2005).

Of course, that O'Reilly received a degree in history from Marist College does more to trash that poor school's reputation than it does to establish O'Reilly's bona fides. As long as we're throwing around exaggerated Nazi comparisons, you could say that being the college that gave O'Reilly a bachelor's in history is kind of like having to admit that Josef Mengele graduated from your med school. It might be true, but it's not exactly a point of pride.

If the Hollywood crowd could pass my quiz and answer my rather boorish questions, I'd apologize and listen intently as they told me that chief UN weapons inspector Hans Blix should have had more time to find anthrax in an uncooperative country the size of California. I would sit enraptured as Sean Penn explained the benefits of living under Saddam, Uday and Qusay Hussein. I would pin the dove on Meryl Streep's gown as she regaled me with her vision of peace and understanding in the age of Al Qaeda.

You mean the same Hans Blix who found no WMD months before the United States concluded there weren't any? The same al-Qaeda that the 9/11 commission stated had no collaborative relationship with Saddam Hussein? That Hans Blix and al-Qaeda?

But what exactly is Bill saying here? These celebrities only get to sit in on Bill's show—the same show where O'Reilly pitches highly spun questions and gets final edit—after they pass a quiz? That's the reward for knowing more about history than O'Reilly?

Of course, the supervillain will always try to lure the superhero to his lair, but few are stupid enough to fall for it.

"But most anti-war stars are not big on complicated history questions. It is easier to flash peace signs to like-minded compatriots at award programs, then retire to eat lavish dinners paid for by fawning sycophants."

Hey Bill, here's a complicated history question for you. The phrase "all men are created equal" is in the Constitution. True/False?

But you know what's even easier than flashing peace signs to like-minded compatriots? Taking potshots at highly paid celebrities when you yourself are one and accusing them of being misinformed and flighty just because they don't agree with you and then driving home to a wife who you publicly embarrassed her because you couldn't control your sexual fetishes and then tucking in your children who will almost certainly grow up to hate you. That would be even easier. Oh, just teasin' ya, Bill.

YOU'RE EVEN PRETTIER WHEN YOU SHUT YOUR PIEHOLE

O'REILLY'S ATTACK on the bubbleheaded celebs continued:

> In the midst of the verbal insanity streaming out of Hollywood came one very cogent comment that passed virtually unnoticed. Renée Zellweger, an excellent actress, admitted that the war unsettled her but told one reporter that she wasn't going to speak out because she didn't know enough about the big picture. Renee, thank you. You are exempt from the quiz, and I will tutor you free of charge.

First and foremost, keep your wrinkled, flaccid penis in your pants, Bill. Zellweger ain't buying what you're selling. But O'Reilly's comments here are actually very telling. After all, there's nothing he likes more than a cute blonde who keeps her opinions to herself and doesn't worry her pretty little head over politics.

Of course, as a journalist, O'Reilly should know that the main reason things go virtually unnoticed by news outlets is that they're not news. An actress saying she has no opinion on something isn't even remotely newsworthy unless you're Joan or Melissa Rivers. You're not, Bill. You are so not.

But what, exactly, would Bill prefer to a press indifferent to a cute actress's ignorance of world affairs? A phalanx of reporters and paparazzi chasing her at high speeds into a tunnel to get more details until she finally dies?

Maybe Bill needs to do some entertainment reporting of his own on his show to fill this yawning void. We can just imagine it:

> Coming up next on *Bill O'Reilly's Hollywood Minute*: Tiffani-Amber Thiessen tells us she has no opinion on the Nunn-Lugar Cooperative Threat Reduction Program. And we'll have the inside scoop on Drew Barrymore's total lack of input on the genocide in Sudan's Darfur region. And what does Denise Richards think about the Abu Ghraib scandal? Nothing. The former Bond girl and ex–Mrs. Charlie Sheen says she has no idea what we're saying. But it *was* torture on the set of her latest movie. We'll have a report.

But all this begs the question: Why is O'Reilly's opinion so well informed compared to any other intelligent American's? Why is his take on the war valid while anyone else in the entertainment industry who disagrees is merely spouting "verbal insanity"—or in the case of Shields and Yarnell,[2] nonverbal insanity.

But come to think of it, maybe nonverbal is the way to go. You know, something subtle, like a simple, dignified symbol of peace:

> Hey, Adrien Brody, glad you won the Best Actor statuette, but do you really understand the true nature of evil, the force that enveloped your character in *The Pianist*? If you do, I'm glad. If you don't, you might want to rethink that dove on your lapel.

Jesus H. Christ. The man can't even wear a dove pin without taking flak from O'Reilly. A Hollywood celebrity is wearing a universal symbol of peace and understanding. You'd think O'Reilly would let that one slide. Crazy knows no limits.

DON'T WORRY, NELL, I'LL SAVE YOU . . . RIGHT AFTER I PROMOTE THIS BOOK

OBVIOUSLY, O'REILLY THINKS Hollywood is populated chiefly by money-hungry, self-aggrandizing types who care more about themselves than the charities they claim to support. That's why O'Reilly went on *The Today Show* in November of 2001 to selflessly raise awareness about the plight of the 9/11 families.

Oh, it went a little something like this:

(TODAY HOST) MATT LAUER: Is it not a little disingenuous, though—when we booked you for this show, you know what your publicist—we won't call that person a pinhead publicist. Do you know what the publicist told our producer?

O'REILLY: Mention the book.

LAUER: Yeah, "Bill will not appear on the show unless you show the book."

O'REILLY: Well, that's what publicists do. They say—they said, "Mention the book." And you know why they said that?

LAUER: But are you promoting a book, or are you talking about the families?

O'REILLY: Do you know why they said that?

LAUER: Why?

O'REILLY: Because you guys wouldn't book me on this program for two and a half years. That's why. So they didn't—they didn't know what your intentions were.

LAUER: If you're accusing the celebrities of doing something for publicity as opposed to the good of the people—isn't it a little case of the pot calling the kettle black?

O'REILLY: I'm not calling anybody anything. I got up at five in the morning to come in here to tell you what the truth is about these charities. Now if you think I'm a self-promoter, then you go right ahead and think that. My publicist has a duty to try to get all the projects that we're working on in the public eye. I'm interested in helping these families.

Oh, Bill. Not even Lex Luthor would sink that low.

NOTES

1. "In 1870, President Grant made Christmas a public secular holiday, and the federal government gave workers the day off. The reason was a holiday . . . to honor a man, Jesus, whose philosophy that all men are created equal and that one should love your neighbor helped the Founding Fathers of the United States craft the Constitution."
     Dumbass.
2. The authors wish to officially announce their campaign for the National Book Awards' Best Seventies TV Mime reference.

THE ACLU RAT PACK:
HITLER, STALIN,
AND THE CHAIRMAN, MAO

IN 1965, BERNARD Fein and Albert S. Ruddy launched their seminal portrait of life in a Nazi prisoner-of-war camp. The program broke new ground in the understanding of the German zeitgeist in World War II Europe through its depiction of a cruel commandant and his oafish harlequin of a sidekick.

It was a watershed in mankind's decades-long struggle to make sense of the Nazis' heartless rule and their brutal implementation of a eugenics program that would ultimately destroy millions of innocent lives across the continent.

That show, of course, was *Hogan's Heroes*.

We mention this extraordinary artistic achievement only because it's been almost three decades since anyone's captured the reality of life under the iron boot of Nazism as well as the immortal Werner Klemperer, Bob Crane, and Richard Dawson. But at last, we have Bill O'Reilly to shine the eternal light of compassion and reason on these monsters' terrible crimes and make us whisper solemnly to ourselves, "never again, never again."

On the January 19, 2005, *Radio Factor*, Bill was in a mild-to-severe froth over the ACLU's opposition to the Dover, Pennsylvania, School District's decision to teach the controversial intelligent design theory as a complement to evolution.[1]

> [The Dover School District] won't even tell you in the state-ment what intelligent design entails. They won't mention a cre-ator, a deity, a God. You know why? Because the ACLU then can haul them into court and cost them a hundred thousand dollars to defend themselves. Fascism, fascism, fascism. Okay? Ah, drive me nuts! Hitler would be a card-carrying ACLU member.

Drive him nuts? Bill arrived safely at nuts about a half-decade ago.

Of course, while the claim that the foremost civil liberties organ-ization in the country promotes fascism is a seductive argument, the notion that Adolf Hitler would have been a member is particularly tantalizing. Bill sure is an astute observer of history.

Take, for instance, the following excerpt from the World Book Encyclopedia[2] on Hitler's Germany:

> By mid-July 1933, the government had outlawed freedom of the press, all labor unions, and all political parties except the Nazis. The Gestapo (secret state police) hunted down the enemies and opponents of the government. People were jailed or shot on suspicion alone.

Yes, the similarities to the ACLU are eerie. As everyone knows, if the ACLU stands for anything, it's outlawing the freedom of the press, labor unions, political pluralism, and representative government—and agitating for extralegal detention and execu-tions. They're downright Nazi-riffic. And you should see them on casual SS Fridays.

Okay, so fine. Pointing out that the ACLU is in fact diametrically opposed to the values and goals of Nazism is fish-in-a-barrel stuff. Maybe it's not fair to take O'Reilly to task for his off-the-cuff comments here. So he had a brain lapse. It happens to everyone. And after all, Bill was talking specifically about the ACLU's stance on intelligent design. Surely Hitler would have supported the ACLU's efforts to keep religious instruction out of public schools. Right?

Here's Adolf:

> Secular schools can never be tolerated because such schools have no religious instruction, and a general moral instruction without a religious foundation is built on air; consequently, all character training and religion must be derived from faith . . . we need believing people. (April 26, 1933, from a speech made during negotiations leading to the Nazi-Vatican Concordant of 1933)

Now, while comparisons of contemporary figures to Hitler and Nazism are generally overwrought, overused, and uncalled-for, it's hard not to notice that the above Hitler quote sounds a lot more like one of Bill's arguments than anything the ACLU would say. Indeed, throw in a comparison between Nazis and twenty-first-century liberals, a couple of Natalee Holloway references, and a gratuitous "pinhead" or two, and it could easily be a Talking Points Memo.

So at the very moment in history that Hitler was greasing the skids for fascism, dictatorship, suppression of political and journalistic freedom, and the brutal repression of minorities, he was also speaking out against secular instruction—much like O'Reilly himself.

Hmmm, sounds a little like a case of the swastika calling the jackboot black.

ACLU—THE "C" STANDS FOR COMMIE

OF COURSE, O'REILLY wasn't done. The first rule of moronic, inflammatory arguments with no basis in truth, logic, or common sense is that they work best with numerous examples.

After saying Hitler would have gleefully joined the one organization most likely to oppose his rule, O'Reilly added, "So would Stalin. Castro probably is. And so would Mao Tse-tung."

Bill O'Reilly was once a high school history teacher. We mention this partly to provide context and partly because it's the easiest laugh anyone is likely to get in any published work this year.

With apologies to C students everywhere, let's take a closer look at these claims.

"So Would Stalin"

In reference to Stalin's many well-known atrocities, the online encyclopedia Wikipedia writes:

> It is generally agreed by historians that if famines, prison and labor camp mortality, and state terrorism (deportations and political purges) are taken into account, Stalin and his colleagues were directly or indirectly responsible for the deaths of millions. *How many* millions died under Stalin is greatly disputed. Although no official figures have been released by the Soviet or Russian governments, most estimates put the figure between 10 and 50 million.

Needless to say, the ACLU generally frowns on such roughhousing.

"Castro Probably Is"

Other than a rumored gay affair with Hollywood Squares center square Paul Lynde, Castro has shown few signs that he might want to join such an organization. Oddly enough, Lynde was reportedly the pitcher. Yeah, we don't get it either.

Of course, Castro is a mixed bag when it comes to upholding the civil liberties the ACLU consistently advocates for. On the one hand he outlaws all political opposition. On the other hand he jails prisoners of conscience without fair trials.

"And so would Mao Tse-tung"

Someone remind us how this guy got on television.

HOW DARE THE ACLU FIGHT FOR CIVIL LIBERTIES!

OF COURSE, AS any thinking person knows, Nazism, Stalinism, Maoism, and whatever you call what Castro does would be impossible in an open, transparent democracy that upholds the American values of free speech, free assembly, freedom of the press, free religious worship, and the accused's rights to counsel and a fair, speedy trial.

Every American should feel grateful that we live under such a system, but the ACLU refuses to take it for granted. The organization knows that unless there's an effective firewall between citizens' rights and the worst instincts of government, the Constitution could very well become a toothless document.

But Bill sees it differently. He thinks the ACLU actually hates America. Here's how he put it on the February 18, 2005, broadcast of *The O'Reilly Factor*: "As you know, I believe the ACLU has become a partisan progressive organization no longer interested in expression of liberties. Rather, it wants to advance a political agenda."

As the ACLU itself points out, our government is founded on the counterbalancing principles of majority rule and individual rights, which limit the power of the majority. It's this second part Bill seems unable to grasp.

Indeed, the Bill of Rights was designed to protect citizens' freedoms and prevent government abuse of power, and the ACLU works tirelessly to uphold these freedoms. As Bill sees it, to fight for such founding principles is to "advance a political agenda."

Now the ACLU has filed a number of information requests, designed to spotlight atrocities by the U.S. military in Iraq and Afghanistan. What this has to do with civil liberties, I don't know, but I do believe the military should be held accountable for what it does, so I have no problem with the request.

Hmmm, Bill says he has no problem with the request, but guess what he's about to compare the ACLU's actions to?

1. The Founding Fathers' struggles to establish and maintain an open democracy with checks and balances and limits on executive power.
2. The passage of various twentieth-century sunshine laws designed to make government more transparent.
3. Witch-hunts.

Ding ding ding ding ding.

But, again, Bill shows his ignorance with regard to the founding principles of our country.

The ACLU wants to know exactly what government officials knew about prison abuse in Iraq. It believes, as should every real American, that the government must remain open and accountable to the American public.

A radical move toward government secrecy is a dangerous precedent that makes actual fascism a much more realistic possibility.

So what does this have to do with civil liberties? Everything!

The latest expositions released today from the ACLU involve pictures some American soldiers took, pointing weapons at detainees and the beating of an Iraqi accused of rape. Those are the highlights of a thousand-page report. The ACLU has been after military scandals since October of 2003, about the time the Abu Ghraib situation hit. Once again, accountability is necessary but witch-hunts are not.

And where does accountability end and witch-hunts begin? Bill doesn't say. But the accusation allows him to imply that the ACLU is fundamentally unpatriotic. It's kind of like saying, "Dissenters are necessary, but pansy liberal faggots are not."[3]

"Talking Points" firmly believes the ACLU wants to undermine the military effort in the war on terror. The ACLU opposes the Patriot Act, Guantanamo detentions without lawyers, military tribunals, coercive interrogation, the war in Iraq, and pretty much all aggressive action against terror.

So the American Civil Liberties Union opposes government actions that blatantly run afoul of civil liberties? What a bunch of pricks! You know what we really hate about MADD? Their constant whining about vehicular homicide. Other than that, they're pretty cool.

> Now I'd really like to know exactly how the ACLU would wage war against terrorists, or if it even would. Unfortunately, the ACLU does not answer those kinds of questions, being too busy criticizing any and all action taken [in the] terror war.

Now, asking the ACLU how we should wage war against terrorists would be an odd question, given that they're the American *Civil Liberties* Union and not, say, the Pentagon.

If the kids over at the ACLU are sitting around giant chalkboards devising attack strategies for Fallujah, they should probably change their mission statement . . . because it's not what they're supposed to be doing.

Of course, by O'Reilly's logic, there's no reason to support Easter Seals either. They haven't done jack-shit to stop terrorism.

AL-QAEDA AND THE ACLU—TWO GREAT TASTES THAT GO GREAT TOGETHER

ON HIS JUNE 2, 2004, radio program, O'Reilly threw the gauntlet down once again:

> Finally, the ACLU—we talked about this yesterday and I—and, you know, I have to pick on the ACLU because they're the most dangerous organization in the United States of America right now. There's by far. There's nobody even close to that. They're like, second next to al-Qaeda.

And, of course, rounding out the top five are the Peace Corps, Doctors Without Borders, and the Aryan Nation.

Of course, most commentators would have heard those words come out of their mouths and immediately looked into joining a twelve-step program for crazy, but on the March 1, 2005, broadcast of *The Radio Factor*, Bill was in full lather again:

> This ACLU has no strategy to fight the war on terror at all. Everything the United States government does—everything—they oppose. Everything! Nothing they like in defending ourselves against terrorists—nothing.

This argument is really starting to make sense. Seriously. If Easter Seals doesn't come up with a plan to stop the insurgency in Iraq right quick, they're dead to us. It's like they hate America or something.

> No-fly list, remember that? National Transportation Safety Administration put a no-fly list of travelers who they considered a threat. ACLU sued, challenged it. Can't have a no-fly list. Okay? That's number one.

What Bill doesn't tell you is that the ACLU's challenge to the no-fly list was filed because too many ordinary citizens were being caught up in the government's security dragnet. Furthermore, these people couldn't get information as to why they were on the list in the first place and they couldn't clear their names.

According to an August 2004 *Washington Post* story, Sen. Teddy Kennedy was stopped at East Coast airports repeatedly in March of 2004 because his name was on the list. According to the *Post*:

> Federal air security officials said the initial error that led to scrutiny of the Massachusetts Democrat should not have happened even though they recognize that the no-fly list is imperfect. But privately they acknowledged being embarrassed that it took the senator and his staff more than three weeks to get his name removed.

The fact that a U.S. senator was on the no-fly list doesn't seem to bother O'Reilly. Would he be so accommodating if it had been him? If he'd had to spend weeks or months trying to get it removed? Well, you can be sure it would have been the topic of each and every Talking Points Memo until his flying privileges were restored.

Patriot Act? Uh uh. No Patriot Act. Can't be listening on floating wiretaps like you do on drug dealers, uh uh. Can't try to catch terrorists like that. Can't be looking at people checking out weird things in the library. Uh uh. Okay? Nope, sued.

Again, the ACLU is looking out for the folks by making sure the government, in its zeal to protect the American people, doesn't overstep its bounds and take away the very freedoms it's trying to defend. It's not all that complicated, yet Bill seems unable to grasp it.

Immigration, all right? ACLU sued, filed a federal lawsuit challenging an initiative by Ashcroft to enlist state and local police in the routine enforcement of federal immigration laws. No, no, can't do that. Can't have the local police or the state police help the feds enforce immigration laws—no way! Can't do it!

Of course, the ACLU was hardly alone in its objection here. In fact, Ashcroft's initiative ran afoul of long-established federal policy. In a June 2002 letter to Ashcroft, the ACLU outlined its objections:

According to a 1996 Office of Legal Counsel (OLC) memorandum, while state and local police may lawfully assist the Immigration and Naturalization Service (INS) in certain respects, "(s)tate and local police lack recognized legal authority to stop and detain an alien solely on suspicion of civil deportability, as opposed to a criminal violation of the immigration laws or other laws." We believe this analysis is sound, and that any change would be vulnerable to legal challenge.

More important, the ACLU pointed out that there's a logical reason for this:

Involving state and local law enforcement in immigration status issues will have a severe impact on the civil rights and civil liberties of immigrant communities. Such a policy will increase racial profiling and other unjustified stops, not only of undocumented workers, but also of legal residents and United States citizens who "look foreign." As you are aware, many of these problems have plagued earlier efforts of state and local law enforcement officers to become involved in civil immigration enforcement.

We realize that O'Reilly and his followers would rather not trouble themselves with such ambiguities. But it's not that Bill doesn't want to understand. He simply can't understand. He's not very smart.

Guantanamo Bay—all of 'em have to have civilian lawyers. No enemy combatants—no way, uh uh. Come on. Come on. Every single thing the United States government tries to do to protect us against terrorism, these people oppose and they'll sue—just like Christmas. Same thing. Same thing. We'll sue you—put the crèche in the main part of town, sing a Christmas carol—we'll sue you. Sue, sue, sue, sue, sue.

The Guantanamo Bay/Christmas connection is a powerful one to be sure. The idea that the ACLU loves al-Qaeda with all its heart while reserving all its hatred for the baby Jesus is only logical.

So look, I'm declaring war on the ACLU. I think they're a terrorist group. They're terrorizing me and my family. They're terrorizing me. I think they're terrorists. Can I get some lawyers to help me out here? Can we sue 'em? They're putting us all in danger.

In all seriousness, O'Reilly's assertion that those organizations fighting hardest against the erosion of civil liberties in this country are not only unpatriotic but in fact terrorists is vile.

Would O'Reilly rather have Americans give up their privacy rights? Does he want us to live in fear and surrender what generations before us have fought so hard to defend? Isn't that the most unpatriotic thing of all? Wouldn't the terrorists' best-case scenario be instilling a crippling fear and stealing our freedom?

In light of that, isn't O'Reilly actually aiding the terrorists? You bet your sweet ass he is.

THE NEW POPE HATES US BECAUSE OF THE ACLU

"Talking Points" expects the American media to go after the new pope because he is conservative. And that will confirm his opinion that we're all a bunch of godless secularists over here. Remember, it is the American Civil Liberties Union which is now behind all abortion on demand, euthanasia, and, coming soon perhaps, infanticide for impaired babies.

—Bill O'Reilly on The O'Reilly Factor, April 19, 2005

FIRST OF ALL, Bill is simply confused. "Infanticide for Impaired Babies" is actually the new slogan for the Democratic National Committee.

Secondly, Bill's stock accusation that the ACLU suppresses religious freedom and expression and is hell-bent on creating a secular America that's hostile to Christianity is at best ignorant and at worst outright deceitful.

It may be hard for Bill to understand, but religious freedom means being allowed to worship freely and being free from religious coercion. This means keeping the public and religious spheres separate—that is, keeping religion out of government and keeping government out of religion. The ACLU does both. Indeed, listed below are just some of the battles the ACLU has fought on behalf of expressly religious folks, taken directly from the organization's Web site. (Journalists can find a more complete list by going to aclu.com, clicking on "Religious Liberty" and then clicking on "ACLU's Defense of Religious Liberty." Bill, on the other hand, can just continue to make shit up.)

December 22, 2004: ACLU of New Jersey successfully defends right of religious expression by jurors.

November 20, 2004: ACLU of Nevada supports free speech rights of evangelists to preach on the sidewalks of the strip in Las Vegas.

November 9, 2004: ACLU of Nevada defends a Mormon student who was suspended after wearing a T-shirt with a religious message to school.

August 11, 2004: ACLU of Nebraska defends church facing eviction by the city of Lincoln.

July 10, 2004: Indiana Civil Liberties Union defends the rights of a Baptist minister to preach his message on public streets.

June 9, 2004: ACLU of Nebraska files a lawsuit on behalf of a Muslim woman barred from a public pool because she refused to wear a swimsuit.

June 3, 2004: Under pressure from the ACLU of Virginia, officials agree not to prohibit baptisms on public property in Falmouth Waterside Park in Stafford County.

May 11, 2004: After ACLU of Michigan intervened on behalf of a Christian valedictorian, a public high school agrees to stop censoring religious yearbook entries.

March 25, 2004: ACLU of Washington defends an Evangelical minister's right to preach on sidewalks.

February 21, 2003: ACLU of Massachusetts defends students punished for distributing candy canes with religious messages.

We'd go on but, frankly, it's a bit exhausting.

Of course, to most fair-minded Americans, obstructing appropriate private expressions of religion is just as objectionable as forcing religion down others' throats through official government sanction. The ACLU understands this. Unfortunately, Bill is about two scoops of gray matter removed from really understanding the ACLU.

NOTES

1. The ACLU of Pennsylvania argued in a press release that, "Intelligent design is a Trojan Horse for bringing religious creationism back into public school science classes."

   This is pretty obvious when you think about it. The idea that the universe was created by a supreme intelligence is a legitimate belief held by billions of intelligent people but it has nothing to do with science if for no other reason than it's not falsifiable. As any scientist could tell you, this alone makes it *not science*. Hence including it in a science curriculum is bogus and irresponsible. It could very well be true but, by definition, it can simply never be considered science.

   Of course, teaching kids how to be unscientific during science class defeats the purpose of school. It would be like teaching beach volleyball during organic chemistry or teaching kids how to cook meth in home ec.

2. *World Book Multimedia Encyclopedia,* Version 9.0.2.1 Chicago: World Book.

3. A tip of the pen to blogger Henry Quinn, from whom this quote was shamelessly lifted.

14

MOORE AND AIR AMERICA AND SOROS, OH MY!

HEARING O'REILLY deny his conservative bias is like listening to your closeted gay friend in high school talk about his girlfriend in Chicago. You know he's lying, but confronting him only makes things more awkward.

Well, O'Reilly's girlfriend is named Independent and he ain't never met her. Whether he's giving Roger Ailes a deep-tissue massage or wanking off to WorldNetDaily, O'Reilly is a closet conservative and an embarrassingly obvious one at that. It would be easier to buy into the nuptials of Bruce Vilanch and Anna Nicole Smith than to accept O'Reilly's political self-assessment.

Indeed, you can tell a man by his enemies. And there's no question O'Reilly reserves his most potent venom for liberals.[1]

MICHAEL MOORE (HATES AMERICA)

BILL REALLY GOT on the anti–Michael Moore bandwagon after seeing the filmmaker's controversial polemic *Fahrenheit 9/11*.

Moore's documentaries have always been a little on the sly side, and critics certainly had room for challenging the tone and context of some of *Fahrenheit 9/11*, if not the relevant facts. But there were broader themes presented in the movie that are harder to discount, such as how and why we enter wars, how we recruit youth to fight in them, and how and why the current administration makes its decisions.

Love it or hate it, it's hard to deny that the sort of robust challenge Moore leveled against our country's power elite is not only a valued American tradition but, indeed, the very thing our nation was founded on. Republicans did it for eight years while Bill Clinton was in office and questioned him vigorously during the Kosovo campaign.

But O'Reilly was having none of it. It wasn't enough for him to disagree with the gist of the film, he had to sling accusations of disloyalty.

"Far Left Spin?" was the title of the Impact Segment on June 28, 2004. Bill brought on Cass Sunstein, a professor from the University of Chicago, and posed the question in the most fair and balanced way possible.

Okay, Bill. Jingo all the way:

Here's my problem, Professor. You know, I've said many times, if you wanna go see this Moore movie, go knock yourself out, but when it's shown overseas it's going to incite anti-American violence, I believe. It's going to even make things worse for America, and in a war on terror, I dunno, that crosses the line from dissent into something else, does it not?

When the professor refused to buy into his take, Bill added: "What if the dissent is simply not true?"

Mind you, this is smack-dab in the middle of the No Spin Zone. Go see the Michael Moore movie if you want, but it will hurt our nation and bring violence to our countrymen. Other than that, giddy up.

Now one obvious question is: Among whom exactly was this film supposed to incite violence? al-Qaeda and fundamentalist Islamo-fascists? They hate us already. Iraqis? They already know what's going on in their country, and anyway, the lights are never on long enough over there to get them through a *Spider-Man* trailer. Europeans? They loved the movie and, unlike O'Reilly, are smart enough to draw a fair distinction between what a government does and what its citizens do. Besides, if any film is going to incite anti-American violence in Paris, it'll be *Baby Geniuses 2*.

Also, why is it so difficult to understand that people who criticize their government's most crucial decisions might be doing so out of love for their country rather than hatred for it?

Unfortunately, of the millions of colors in the visible spectrum, O'Reilly sees only two, and white shows up only when he squints.

We don't take loyalty oaths to our presidents, and the divine right of kings was out of fashion even before all that "consent of the governed" jibber-jabber Jefferson stuck in the Declaration of Independence. In a healthy democracy, dissent doesn't undermine government, it fixes it—or at the very least keeps it on its toes.

Besides, disagreeing with someone or something doesn't mean you love him, her, or it less. If you're a die-hard Yankees fan enjoying a friendly conversation with another Yankees fan and he criticizes George Steinbrenner, you don't scream at him and accuse him of really being a Red Sox fan. Grousing about the government is a hallowed American tradition and vital to keeping our democracy strong. In this sense, *Fahrenheit 9/11* was an act of true patriotism.

Of course, in O'Reilly's mind it was just the opposite. It "crosses the line from dissent into something else"—that "something else" being left to the vivid imaginations of his viewers. Clearly, Bill doesn't think Moore set out to challenge the Bush administration; he thinks he set out to hurt and betray the United States and its citizens:

> Increasingly, the bully America is being portrayed as the devil. And the far left in this country is gleefully piling on. Guys like Michael Moore running around the world telling everybody what a bad place America is. Moore and his enablers should be very proud of themselves. (Talking Points Memo, July 8, 2004)

He is a subversive in the sense that he doesn't like the capitalistic system. He doesn't like any of our politicians. He's a socialist. (*The O'Reilly Factor,* July 14, 2004)

So that's it, then. If you criticize the Bush administration, you think America is a "bad place," and if you criticize any corporation, you're a socialist. This is the brilliant, nuanced reasoning of the most powerful man in cable news.

AIR AMERICA (NO, NOT THE SUCKY MEL GIBSON FILM)

ON SEPTEMBER 14, 2004, Bill had a very promising teaser at the top of his show: "Is right-wing talk radio out of control? Caution, you're about to enter a no-spin zone. *The Factor* begins right now."

Bravo, Bill. Bravo.

Yes, it looked like O'Reilly was finally going to toss his more left-leaning dogs a bone. Indeed, when the Factor Follow-up Segment logo popped up on the screen, O'Reilly's liberal viewers, Chet and Heather, no doubt waited with a sense of keen anticipation. Who might Bill bring on the program to discuss the vile hatred and lies being spread by right-wing radio? Though he plied his trade on Rupert Murdoch's media Death Star, this would surely be Bill's way of finally bringing balance to the Force. He would prove his independence once and for all.

Wait for it.

Ahem . . .

When the segment began, Bill introduced his guests, conservative radio hosts Curtis Sliwa and Steve Malzberg. It seemed a curious choice, bringing on two conservative radio hosts and no liberals for a segment that promised to hold conservative radio's feet to the fire. Still, his teaser left nothing to chance. He was gonna pummel these guys. Maybe he would even "dress them down." Happy day.

However, soon after the segment started, rather than discussing the state of far-right talk radio, as promised, O'Reilly and his guests started talking about the situation over at CBS. After a little jovial conversation (i.e., no "dressing down") they concluded that Dan

Rather had unwittingly accepted fake documents because he so desperately wanted to find dirt on President Bush.

Um, at the risk of appearing indelicate, what the fuck does that have to do with right-wing radio being out of control? Nothing! It actually supports right-wing radio!

Shakes fist in air

You got us again, O'Reilly! You got us again!

But this wasn't enough. Bill wanted to kick his left-leaning dogs square in the jewels. After commiserating with Sliwa and Malzberg about the Rather scandal, he proceeded to advise them on their shows' direction:

> Look, you don't wanna be Air America. You don't. . . . You don't
> want to be those people. . . . They are the leper colony of the media.
> They have twenty affiliates. Let 'em go. You don't wanna be that.
> And I think that some right-wing talk-show hosts are gettin' close.

So basically, far-right talk radio is out of control . . . so out of control that it's coming dangerously close to the lowest depths of journalism . . . currently occupied by far-left radio? That's the story? Seriously? He can't . . . is he really? . . . come on . . . *for the love of God!*

Of course, what O'Reilly's swipe at Air America really proves is that he's still smarting from his infamous BookTV dustup with Al Franken. Make no mistake about it, O'Reilly's attack on the liberal radio network is really an attack on Franken. What O'Reilly won't tell you is that to compare an individual syndicated radio show to a start-up radio network is not so much apples and oranges as apples and orange groves.

O'Reilly's *Radio Factor*, for instance, is syndicated by Westwood One. In radio, it's relatively easy for syndicates to place programs and for stations to buy individual programs. On the other hand, finding affiliates for a full slate of network programming is a much more daunting task. It's like the difference between selling a sofa and a duplex.

So even though it should have been effortless for O'Reilly, an established media figure, to launch a radio version of his popular cable show, it evidently was not.

On May 7, 2002, Web journalist Matt Drudge reported on pay-offs that were being made to stations as an inducement to pick up O'Reilly's new radio show:

> In a dramatic reversal from normal radio practice, stations are being paid big bucks to carry Bill O'Reilly's new nationally syndicated talk show, the Drudge Report can now disclose. O'Reilly's radio flagship in New York City, WOR-AM, alone is being paid $300,000, according to sources, just to carry the cable star's radio program, which launches on Wednesday.
>
> Difficulty clearing O'Reilly in the Washington, D.C., market raised the payout price to $200,000, according to insiders—a payout that was rejected by all major stations in the region! . . . Incentives to carry O'Reilly came after WESTWOODONEIN-FINITYVIACOM had trouble placing the controversial TV host and best-selling author.

And in case any of you were wondering if this had ever happened before in radio, the report went on to say:

> Unlike his targeted radio competitor Rush Limbaugh, who has never paid stations to carry his broadcast, O'Reilly launches this week under a cloud of controversy. "This is without precedent in the spoken word format of commercial radio," noted a broadcast executive who personally rejected an O'Reilly offer.

So if, as O'Reilly claims, Air America's radio hosts are nothing but untouchable lepers, then O'Reilly is a leper you wouldn't cross the street to piss on—even if you were paid $200,000 to do so.

Here's how our levelheaded correspondent responded to Drudge's report, on *Imus in the Morning:* "I just want to tell everybody that Matt Drudge is smoking crack, right now, in South Miami Beach on Washington Avenue. . . . And the authorities should know it."

Of course, Bill's limp jibes notwithstanding, Air America is, as we noted, a comprehensive network that carries a full day's worth of programming and should thus be much more difficult to launch than a single show.

That said, despite its leper status, as of this writing Air America is heard on more than sixty stations throughout the country and is carried on XM Satellite Radio.

GEORGE SOROS (IS HE CRAZY BECAUSE HE'S LIBERAL OR LIBERAL BECAUSE HE'S CRAZY?)

ON HIS JUNE 1, 2004, radio program, O'Reilly was in full smear mode over billionaire financier George Soros. The far-left bomb-thrower Web site mediamatters.org reported that O'Reilly described Soros as an individual who is "as far left as you can get without moving to Havana" and "a total radical on all the issues that Americans care about."

O'Reilly also said Soros "wants abortion even out of the womb—out of the womb!" and said Soros wanted to "turn this country completely upside down."

And despite Bill's well-documented distaste for personal attacks and smears, he had previously called Soros "a real sleazoid" on his May 18 radio show.

Of course, George Soros is one of the great philanthropists of our age, having given away billions of dollars of his personal fortune. O'Reilly's beef is that he chooses to give to liberal causes. Information on his Open Society Institute and Soros Foundations Network can be found at www.soros.org.

But all you really have to do to understand O'Reilly's hatred of Soros is to read Soros' own words:

> The supremacist ideology of the Bush administration stands in opposition to the principles of an open society, which recognize that people have different views and that nobody is in possession of the ultimate truth. The supremacist ideology postulates that just because we are stronger than others, we know better and have right on our side.

Of course, this is contemptible to O'Reilly, who sees himself as the idealized American—a man of wealth, power, and influence, and a man whose views are not just well informed but absolutely and undeniably correct in every way.

Even the barest whiff of cultural relativism is anathema to Bill. To his mind, all roads lead to Levittown, the cultural and philosophical epicenter of the world.

O'Reilly has nothing to learn from someone with a different worldview, much less a lib foreigner like Soros. That a great many Americans share Soros's views is irrelevant. Those people are simply out of touch with real Americans—meaning those Americans who agree with O'Reilly.

Then, on July 21, 2004, in an *O'Reilly Factor* interview with Newt Gingrich, Bill said this after calling the *New York Times* a brochure for the far-left progressive movement: "But see, there are powerful forces at work here. George Soros money has created a lot of smear Web sites on the left and we're in a cultural civil war . . . "

Yeah, we're in a cultural civil war all right, and O'Reilly is Cooter the one-legged supply clerk. Unfortunately, he does nothing to foster understanding between the two sides. Instead he labels every unapologetic liberal Web site a "smear site" and many left-of-center views attacks against America.

That big money has lined up behind liberals for once instead of churning out a few more influential right-wing think tanks or underwriting a thinly veiled conservative cable network is to Bill a seditious act.

To O'Reilly's thinking, liberals are hippies with nose rings who bathe once every six weeks and use the profits from the pot they grow in their parents' basements to maintain their meager stocks of bean curd and Che Guevara T-shirts. They're not supposed to make hit movies, launch national radio networks, or finance influential foundations and Web sites that challenge a Republican president's decision to go to war, even if that decision was based on a tissue of falsehoods.

But they do, and some dare call it treason.

NOTES

1. Another O'Reilly tactic is to set the locus of fringe right-wing orthodoxy so far out into space, while casting comparatively moderate left-wing thinkers as equally unhinged, that the "centrist" position ends up being what most observers would consider right-wing.

   For instance, in his book *The O'Reilly Factor*, Bill cites Rev. Al Sharpton as a prime example of a racial demagogue. Now, Sharpton *is* fairly far out in the wobbly orbit of left-wing thought, which may be part of the reason Democratic voters overwhelmingly rejected his bid for the 2004 presidential nomination. But while he's a bit of a showman and can be a shameless opportunist, Sharpton's clearly not a rabid black supremacist. So who does O'Reilly proffer as the other pea in the reverend's pod? David Duke.

   Bill might as well have paired up Tom Daschle and Generalissimo Francisco Franco. Asshole.

15

SECULARISTS AT THE GATE

That's why nobody sticks up for Christmas except me. Did Peter Jennings stick up for Christmas last night? I don't believe he did. How about Brian Williams, did he? Did Rather stick up for Christmas? How about Jim Lehrer—did he? Did Larry King [say] "Hello, I love Christmas"—did he? No.

(Bill O'Reilly on The Radio Factor, *December 9, 2004)*

IN A DECEMBER 2004 Talking Points Memo, O'Reilly proved once again that, when it comes to cogent political analysis, he's a greasy ponytail short of being Steven Seagal.

"Christmas under siege" was the very FOX-like teaser at the top of the segment, and then Bill took the off-ramp to Loopyland for a happy skip down Candy Cane Lane:

All over the country, Christmas is taking flak. In Denver this past weekend, no religious floats were permitted in the holiday parade there. In New York City, Mayor Bloomberg unveiled the "holiday tree," and no Christian Christmas symbols are allowed in the public schools. Federated Department Stores, [that's] Macy's, have done away with the Christmas greeting, "Merry Christmas."

Yes. It's so bad, in fact, that Santa thinks the children of the world no longer care about Christmas, so he's decided not to come this year.

There's just no more Christmas spirit, is there? It could be the year without a Santa Claus. Can Bill save Christmas in time? Stay tuned.

Of course, O'Reilly isn't content simply to say the true meaning of Christmas is waning in importance and maybe that's kind of sad. No, that would be the pussy NPR take. To Bill's mind, secular holiday greetings do nothing less than empower al-Qaeda and herald the collapse of Western civilization.

Indeed, O'Reilly goes from Macy's employees saying "Seasons Greetings" to the war on terror in fewer moves than Kevin Bacon to Dame Judi Dench.

But first there's a little detour to the Island of Misfit Gays:

> Secular progressives realize that America as it is now will never approve of gay marriage, partial birth abortion, euthanasia, legalized drugs, income redistribution through taxation, and many other progressive visions because of religious opposition.

Damn, Bill figured out the master plan. A few more Christmas parades sans nativity and we'd have had our stockings stuffed with lesbians who get late-term abortions, euthanize any parent with a head cold, and shoot smack into the webbing of their adopted kids' toes while waiting for their check from Uncle Sam.

But it's not just the prospect of a future dystopian holiday with faggy pudding, partial-virgin-birth abortions, and Colombian gold, frankincense, and myrrh that's got Bill up in arms. Denver's holiday parade is threatening not just Christmas but our very welfare and safety:

> Americans will lose their country if they don't begin to take action. Any assault on Judeo-Christian philosophy should be fought. . . .
>
> "Talking Points" is convinced that the USA cannot defeat terrorism and any other evil without a strong, traditional foundation that clearly defines right from wrong. The struggle today is not about Christmas but about the spirit of our country.

Yes, if history shows us anything, it's that Christian nations locked in epic struggles with Muslim lands should surrender decision-making to their clerics. That's a time-honored formula for peace and prosperity.

Of course, people have been saying for at least fifty years that the true spirit of Christmas is in decline. And second-rate pundits looking to score cheap applause have been pointing this out for at least forty-nine. O'Reilly is just another in a long line of doomsayers. In fact, no one's gone this far out on a limb since the last time a DJ played "My Heart Will Go On" at a Green Bay wedding reception. Yet Bill appears to believe he's stumbled on a new wrinkle.

When the first towheaded little scamp saw to it that his new Stretch Armstrong would be found in flagrante delicto with his sister's new Dressy Bessy when she toddled down the stairs on the way to the family hearth roundabout 1976 or so—that's when Christmas went off the rails. Atheists, Jews, and Muslims are the lamest of scapegoats.

Of course, there's no shortage of bona fide Christmas celebrations, greetings, worship services, TV shows, and news stories every year to remind people that there's a religious holiday going on.

That might have something to do with the 84 percent[1] of Americans who identify themselves as Christian.

Somehow, we think a two-thousand-year-old holiday that's celebrated the world over should be able to withstand the many depredations of Macy's pockmarked teenage sweater-folders.

GET RICH AND SAFE NOW—ASK ME HOW

O'REILLY IS AT his best when he's at his most desperate. As he continues to fight his battle against the evils of secularism, he begins what could only be described as a marketing campaign for Christianity:

> About four million people came to Rome to honor the life of John
> Paul II, and his funeral this morning was an amazing spectacle. The
> ancient rites of the Roman Catholic Church were on full display to

a world that is largely retreating from spiritualism, especially in the industrialized countries. (Talking Points Memo, April 8, 2005)

Actually, religion and the ancient rites of the Catholic Church have been declining in importance since at least the eighteenth century, when Europe kicked off the Enlightenment. Once again Bill is right on top of the story:

> Now, many young people were enthralled by the demonstration because in many parts of the world, including the USA, public spectacles like this are rare. Secular forces have succeeded in blunting public displays of faith. So the exposition in Rome was new to many people.

Sure, the death of the pope was a sad event for many people, but we doubt it garnered even a tenth of the coveted tween market that, say, the DVD release of *New York Minute* or reruns of *The OC* did.

We can promise you, no kid took a break from playing Grand Theft Auto to call his boys with, "Yo, pick up, dawg! JP2 just totally kicked it."

Indeed, the April 2005 *Tiger Beat* with Aaron Carter, Orlando Bloom, and Joseph Ratzinger on the cover was one of the worst-selling in the magazine's history.

And, again, public spectacles like the exposition in Rome have been in decline since the Protestant Reformation, which had pretty much nothing to do with secularists. Sure, Bill's only five hundred years late on this story, but it can hardly be good for your reputation as a journalist to get scooped by Johannes Gutenberg.[2]

O'Reilly is complaining about the inexorable fade of a phenomenon that's barely existed for decades. Indeed, outside of St. Peter's Square, where exactly does he think these grand, baroque displays of religious devotion have taken place? This sort of thing was new to young people because the last pope hung on like Jason, not because the world doesn't care about God. It had exactly nothing to do with the sinister influence of the secular world.

If secularists really were able to shut down public displays of faith, you wouldn't have Billy Graham filling up football stadiums and Christian rock fests wouldn't continually draw thousands of enthusiastic fans. Public Christian displays are pretty much everywhere you look; they're simply no longer gilded with ancient pomp and tradition and no longer sanctioned by governments. You'll forgive Michael W. Smith if he doesn't walk around the Illinois State Fairgrounds with a censer and a miter chanting invocations in Latin.

> Here in America, the pope coverage is a big plus for those of us who believe that spiritualism rather than secularism should be the dominant philosophy. Baby boomers like myself are really the last generation to be raised in the Judeo-Christian tradition that was fostered by the Founding Fathers. . . .
>
> The founders didn't want any one religion given preference by the new government, but they did want people to behave; because the new federal government was so weak, the founders understood that religious convictions could restrain bad behavior. And the more spiritual people were, the more law-abiding they would be.

So Bill is basically saying that because of secularism, people born during the baby boom—which, according to the online encyclopedia Wikipedia, started in 1946 and ended in 1964—must in some real sense be superior people, having experienced a greater spiritual grounding than subsequent generations.

Bill snugly fits within this cohort, having been born in 1949. And it's not too much of a stretch to say that this makes Bill, by his own reckoning, a better, more spiritual person than most of those born later, who, according to Bill, are less likely to be law-abiding because of the baleful influence of secularists.

Well, on certain measures—such as the number of college girls mysteriously disappearing while on vacation in Aruba, the frequency of women fleeing to New Mexico to avoid looming nuptials, and the number of people with video cameras who get attacked by wild animals—the country may indeed be sliding off a cliff. But according to Department of Justice statistics, it's not.

To quote from a September 2004 Associated Press story:

> The nation's crime rate last year held steady at the lowest levels since the government began surveying crime victims in 1973, the Justice Department reported yesterday.
>
> The study was the latest contribution to a decade-long trend in which violent crime as measured by victim surveys has fallen by 55 percent and property crime by 49 percent. That has included a 14 percent drop in violent crime from 2000–2001 to 2002–2003.

Hop on over to the Bureau of Justice Crime and Victims Statistics Web page at www.ojp.usdoj.gov/bjs/cvict.htm, and you'll see just how far crime has fallen since 1973, when the survey was first conducted. Both the violent victimization and property crime victimization trends show a pretty steady decline. In fact, if you squint, the charts depicting this look uncannily like O'Reilly's ratings numbers over the last three years.

In 1973, Bill was a young man just starting to feel his oats, as were many others of his generation—"the last generation to be raised in the Judeo-Christian tradition." But it was a generation that also did a lot of messed-up shit. Then, apparently, the secularists came along to save the day. We've had low crime rates ever since. Indeed, based on casual observation, it would seem crime is in fact inversely related to the number of "Season's Greetings" uttered at Macy's and positively correlated with the spike in papal coronations in the late seventies. Thanks, secular America!

"Talking Points hopes that all Americans will begin thinking about the traditional versus the secular in America. Which philosophy is best for all of us? Which one will keep us safe and prosperous?"

Yes, Pope Falsius Dichotomus XIV strikes again. On one hand you have the philosophy of accepting Jesus Christ as your personal savior. On the other hand you have the philosophy of painful death and economic ruin. Gee, they both just look so good.

Of course, it's typical of O'Reilly to use the pope's death to push his agenda. Sadly, for a great number of Americans, it was just another news cycle sandwiched neatly between Terri Schiavo and the Runaway Bride. In fact, of the three, the pope received the least amount of coverage . . . by far. O'Reilly was, of course, one of the worst offenders.

Still, it's up to you to decide. Just remember, a secular America is an unsafe and economically precarious America. Thanks, Bill.

HEY DUDE, IT WOULD BE TOTALLY COOL OF YOU NOT TO BLOW UP OUR BUILDINGS

I believe organized religion can be a champion of human rights and provide resistance to secular societies which, if they progress much further, will never be able to defeat the fanatical Islamic fundamentalists. The more permissive the Western world becomes, the more it rejects discipline and avoids confronting evil, the greater the danger to freedom will be.

—*Billoreilly.com, April 21, 2005*

IT'S A BIT of a mystery why Bill seems to think a secular society can defend neither human rights nor itself. Bill's use of "permissive" is curious as well.

It seems that the only thing a secular society permits more than does a Christian society is personal freedom. Does Bill really believe gay marriage will make us more susceptible to an al-Qaeda attack? Would an onslaught of Adam-and-Steve nuptials force the country into a lethargic stupor of post-gay-sex euphoria?

This is the world O'Reilly fears, where church and state are truly kept separate: no placement of the Ten Commandments in public buildings, no "under God" in the Pledge, no nativities on public grounds.

Picture legalized marijuana, regulated like alcohol. Can you imagine how often we'd be attacked by terrorists? Why daily, of course. Why? Because God would certainly turn his back on us.

Yes, even if we still prayed daily and sought to live principled, fair, and charitable lives, it would never be enough. Everyone knows that prayers don't count if they're not said in government buildings and that even the most Christ-like individuals will die in fiery collisions if they dare say "Happy Holidays." And if you have the temerity to sign a card "Merry Xmas" you might as well shoot yourself in the head, 'cause you're looking at a slow and painful death.

JESUS LIKES 'EM REPRESSED, RICH, AND READY TO BOMB

As the Blues Brothers once remarked, "We're on a mission from God." The *Times*, of course, would remove God from that quotation. The paper is definitely on a mission, and the gloves are off. Arthur Sulzberger and his tribe want a secular nation with few judgments on personal behavior, income redistribution through taxation of the affluent, and a foreign policy that seeks consensus at almost all costs.

—Billoreilly.com, June 17, 2004

WHETHER SECULARISTS REALLY want few judgments on personal behavior is arguable. It could be that secularists want to create a moral framework based on what's best for everyone rather than what's considered moral by any particular sectarian worldview. You might say they want a society where everyone can practice their faith freely or not practice at all, according to their own consciences—and where people treat each other with kindness and respect regardless of their religious beliefs. That's probably what secularists would say.

As for Christ's well-known opposition to the progressive income tax, we can only quote Scripture:

And it came to pass that an order was sent from Herod decreeing that those with vineyards and oxen producing talents far beyond their worldly needs should cede a part equaling one score and nineteen from every hundred talents earned by their yields. The wicked Herod allowed that these talents should be apportioned to the sick and lame who toiled in their masters' fields, and to the soldiers who defended their cattle and fine stocks, and for the repair of the roads that had borne their stores of wheat these many years. And Jesus wept.

The truth is, of course, that Bill's peculiar brand of Christianity relates about as much to Scripture as Tibetan Buddhism to the works of Jacqueline Susann.

On the other hand, there are probably dozens of passages in the Bible praising those who seek nonviolent solutions to conflicts and admonishing us to look after the poor. And Jesus himself said worship should remain as private as possible (Matthew 6:5–6) and that religion just might function best without government entanglement (Matthew 22:21—"render unto Caesar what is Caesar's").

That these passages happen to jibe with the very secularism O'Reilly claims will be our downfall may just be a coincidence. Or it could just be that the very same people O'Reilly claims are godless heathens bent on the destruction of our nation know a bit more about Christianity than Bill does.

NOTES

1. According to a 2004 end-of-year Gallup summary.
2. For the record, Gutenberg died circa 1468 and Martin Luther didn't nail his protest theses to the church door until 1517, so we're fudging this a little bit. There. We just proved we know more about history than Bill.

16

THE ELITE MEDIA:
THEY THINK THEY'RE SO DAMN ELITE

They'll never get it until they grab Michael Kinsley out of his little house
and they cut his head off. And maybe when the blade sinks in, he'll go,
"Perhaps O'Reilly was right."

—Bill O'Reilly on The Radio Factor, May 17, 2005

O'REILLY HAS ALWAYS seen his show as an alternative to—
and indeed a remedy for—the mainstream media's supposedly liberal slant.

To him, the *New York Times*, CBS, CNN, and most metropolitan
dailies are everything he and the Boys of Levittown have always
stood against—supercilious, effete, contemptuous of the masses,
and out of touch with the real world.

It's perhaps revealing that O'Reilly was once part of the so-called
elite media himself, as a correspondent for CBS and ABC.[1] But he
was not long for the rarefied atmosphere from which ivory-tower
intellectuals like Barbara Walters have long drawn breath. After
leaving network news, he went on to host the syndicated tabloid
show *Inside Edition* and then finally *The O'Reilly Factor*. In the world
of journalism, that's a little like being a waiter who couldn't crack
the glass ceiling at Denny's and so decided to open up a Burger Chef
just down the street.

Of course, even the most intractable loon will eventually be asked to explain what the hell he's talking about, and this was certainly true of O'Reilly and his favorite bugaboo.[2]

On March 8, 2004, O'Reilly sat behind his desk at FOX and proudly stated, "Some viewers have asked me to explicitly define the fabled elite media, and so I will try with some illustrations and examples."

This should be good.

THE PASSION OF THE O'REILLY

THAT NIGHT, BILL offered all the fair and balanced analysis he could muster:

> *New York Times* writer Frank Rich continued his savage attacks on *The Passion of the Christ* movie yesterday.
>
> Even though most who have seen the film—including the head of the Jewish Anti-Defamation League[3]—believe it is not hateful towards Jews, Rich is smarter than all of us. If you see merit in this movie, you are either a moron, a sadist, and/or an anti-Semite, according to Mr. Rich.
>
> And that is the foundation of the elite media: It knows—you don't. Their slogan might be, "We report. You're a dope."
>
> Frank Rich's rantings have now become embarrassing both to him and to the *Times*. I mean, disagreement about an issue is one thing. Trying to destroy someone like Mel Gibson is quite something else.

Yeah, no kidding. How can you justify saying stuff like, "I want to kill him. I want his intestines on a stick. . . . I want to kill his dog." That's just sick.

Oh wait. That's what Gibson said about Rich. Here's what Rich wrote about Gibson in the March 7, 2004, *New York Times*, in a wry nod to Gibson's *Braveheart*-like invective: "*The Passion* is far more in love with putting Jesus' intestines on a stick than with dramatizing his godly teachings, which are relegated to a few brief, cryptic flash-backs."

This is, of course, a statement not of opinion but of fact. The fact of the matter is that the film spent much more time showing the gore of crucifixion than the more important teachings of Christ. Regard-less of how O'Reilly wants to spin that, it's fact.

"There is no question that it rewrites history by making Caiaphas and the other high priests the prime instigators of Jesus' death while softening Pontius Pilate, an infamous Roman thug, into a reluctant and somewhat conscience-stricken executioner."

Again, this is a valid point. Why would O'Reilly be so infuriated about a man questioning the very important characterizations of key figures in the story?

As for O'Reilly's contention that Rich sees all the fans of this film as morons, sadists, or anti-Semites, that's flatly contradicted by Rich's own words. Here's what Rich actually had to say about the movie's fans:

> My quarrel is not with most of the millions of Christian believers who are moved to tears by *The Passion*. They bring their own deep feelings to the theater with them, and when Mr. Gibson pushes their buttons, however crudely, they generously do his work for him, supplying from their hearts the authentic spirituality that is missing in his jamboree of bloody beefcake.

You see, O'Reilly reads "authentic spirituality" and sees "morons." It's an easy mistake to make . . . if you're a lunatic.

THE ELITE MEDIA THINK TACOS ARE BETTER THAN JESUS

O'REILLY'S DEFINITION OF "elite" continued:

> The *New York Times* is ground zero for the elite media, and you would think executives at that paper would understand how detached from American reality it has become. But they don't. In

fact, one day before Rich's column, a *Times* music critic gave thug rapper Ludacris a positive review. That's right: In the world of the *New York Times*, Ludacris is good; *The Passion of the Christ* is bad.

Now, think about this for a second. Really think about it. A newspaper on one day gave a rapper's album a good review. The next day the same paper gave a critical review to a film about Jesus Christ.

Do you think—or do you think maybe hardly anyone in the world besides O'Reilly thinks—that the subject matter of a piece of art in and of itself determines its value or quality? Might some people—many of them sincere, devout Christians—believe that films about Jesus Christ should be held to a higher standard than songs about bitchas, hos, and bling-bling?

Is it fair to the thoughtful, independent-minded Christian that Mel Gibson's film should stand as some kind of litmus test for the depth of one's faith or that one's emotional response to the gruesome *Passion* should be a test of one's patriotism? What if Gibson had made a film about Jesus in which Pontius Pilate was played by Wilford Brimley in a pair of denim overalls and Caiaphas sported horns and cloven hooves and devoured babies? And what if, despite all that, it was a box-office success? Would it then be un-American to challenge its tastefulness or historical accuracy?

Willie Aames of *Eight Is Enough* fame sells episodes of a show called *Bibleman* in which he runs around in a cape and fights bad guys with names like The Fibbler and Dr. Fear. Are we all obliged to show that program deep and abiding respect because it's about God? It's Tommy Bradford in a purple foam superhero outfit. We have a constitutional right—some would say a patriotic duty—to make fun of it. In fact, you could say that if you don't make fun of it, you're detached from not just American reality but pretty much reality in general.

Or imagine if Frank Rich had written something positive about a new Mexican restaurant. Would O'Reilly then argue that Rich thinks tacos are better than Jesus? That's right, people. In the world of the *New York Times*, meat-filled tortillas are better than our Lord and Savior.

And what of the rest of the elite media? Do they agree that we should worship south-of-the-border cuisine? Do they tout the power of prayer to the great and powerful enchiladas in the sky?

Of course, Bill's nonsensical attack on Rich's *Passion* review is just the fulcrum that hoists his greater grievance—that the elite media is a propaganda arm in the battle to oppress white, wealthy Christians:

> The pendulum has swung. It is the majority that is now under siege in this country. Today the special interests are often the ones doing the oppressing.
>
> It goes without saying that the elite media will almost always favor political candidates that espouse high taxes for the evil rich; higher spending on the poor—even if the programs are wasteful and ineffective—and more restrictions on corporations, which the elites believe are oppressors as well.

It's hard to know which part of this argument to dissect first—the "crazy" part or the "not true" part. Well, let's kick the crutch out from under his premise first.

While it's become an article of faith among conservatives in this country that the mainstream media are predominantly liberal, there's plenty of evidence that they're not. Eric Alterman's book *What Liberal Media?*[4] is one notable attempt at refuting this idea.

By way of example, one can look at the official positions of the nation's newspapers to prove that they certainly do not "almost always favor political candidates that espouse high taxes for the evil rich."

For instance, while *Editor and Publisher's* Web site reported that John Kerry received more newspaper endorsements than George W. Bush in 2004—213 to 205, representing 20,882,889 and 15,743,799 readers respectively—*E&P* also noted that this is an unusual occurrence: "We can see this was a rare occasion when the Democratic candidate for president [got] more editorial nods than the Republican."

In 2000, major newspapers endorsed George W. Bush over Al Gore by a wide margin. While it's true the *New York Times* endorsed Gore (which is probably a faithful reflection of that newspaper's own readership), not all big-city papers did. O'Reilly can gerrymander his elite-media definition to include only Gore endorsers if he likes, but that would mean excluding prominent urban papers such as the *Chicago Tribune*, the *Chicago Sun-Times*, the *Cincinnati Enquirer*, the *New Orleans Times-Picayune*, the *Indianapolis Star*, and the *Houston Chronicle*, with which O'Reilly has publicly feuded (see Chapter 10) and which he refers to as a "mainly progressive paper."

Secondly, you can say a lot of things about white, wealthy, Christian CEOs of major corporations, but "oppressed" is generally not one of them. Bill is dangerously close to completely falling off the beam on this one. Indeed, we are anxiously awaiting the "Are There No Prisons? Are There No Workhouses?" Talking Points Memo, which seems as inevitable as Bill's next producer-related impropriety.

Of course, in O'Reilly's world, whenever anyone even discusses higher taxes on upper-income earners, these earners are being treated as the "evil rich." Perhaps the elite media actually see them as the "fortunate few," but O'Reilly could never admit as much. If you discuss social programs, they are invariably "wasteful and ineffective." Any restrictions on corporations to limit pollution, empower workers, or protect consumers are an attack on capitalism itself.

These are clearly not the arguments of an independent or even a conservative. This is the sort of thing you'd expect to hear from a Gilded Age robber baron being faced with the institution of income and property taxes. That O'Reilly blames the "elite media" for turning common folk against regressive tax structures, the elimination of social programs, and corporate deregulation is not just sad, it's a little sick.

CRAZY LIKE A FOX ANCHOR

Bill's attack on and marginalization of the elite media continued:

> Now if you go up against the elite media, it's not going to be pretty. You will be branded a bigot, racist, anti-Semite, homophobe. You will be called a fundamentalist, or an ultra-conservative. Elites don't debate. They attack and marginalize.

See also: irony.

"Think back eight years ago when FOX News Channel did not exist."

Seriously, do that now. Close your eyes and lie back. Do you hear the babbling brook? The refreshing forest breeze? Oh, off to the left now . . . a little doe gently nibbling the brown pointed bud of a sugar maple.

> Outside of the *Wall Street Journal*, which puts forth a conservative philosophy, the elites had the national information flow pretty much to themselves; no one could stand up to them.
>
> Now the landscape has changed. And while our competitors at NBC and CNN still can't figure out how FOX News has become so powerful, it's simple: We are not the elite media. For example, we don't feel the 66 percent of Americans who oppose gay marriage are fools and bigots. And we don't think that our opinion has more validity than your opinion, no matter what it is—we give voice to all points of view, including the elite one.

That's an interesting take, and we have no doubt O'Reilly believes it. And technically he's right that FOX airs diverse viewpoints. But, unfortunately, FOX is conservative in much the same way Ivory Soap is 99 44/100 percent pure. It's obvious which part is soap, but you're not quite sure what the other 56/100 percent is. It may be liberal, it may be centrist, but you can be damn sure the manufacturers consider it an adulterant.

In 2001, the media watchdog group Fairness and Accuracy in Reporting (FAIR) tested FOX's "fair and balanced" mantra by monitoring nineteen weeks of *Special Report with Brit Hume*, which FOX called its signature political news show. (It's true that FAIR is a *liberal* watchdog group, but that doesn't mean its staff can't count.)

Among FAIR's conclusions:

The numbers show an overwhelming slant on FOX towards both Republicans and conservatives. Of the 56 partisan guests on *Special Report* between January and May, 50 were Republicans and six were Democrats—a greater than 8 to 1 imbalance. In other words, 89 percent of guests with a party affiliation were Republicans.

FAIR also monitored CNN's *Wolf Blitzer Reports* over the same period and found an oddly different pattern: "Of Blitzer's 67 partisan guests, 38 were Republicans and 29 were Democrats—a 57 percent to 43 percent split in favor of Republicans."

Now, if FOX is so careless about the party affiliation of guests on its shows that one of the gems in its crown can be allowed to present a greater than 8-to-1 ratio of Republicans to Democrats, it doesn't seem that far a leap to suggest that its commentators also skew to the right when they offer their own opinions.

And while most of the broadcast media are reluctant to offer their own opinions, FOX is only too happy to fill in that yawning opinion-free gap.

While we can state with a fair degree of certainty that the *CBS Evening News* has never reported that Americans who are opposed to gay marriage are fools and bigots, what you find at FOX News these days are lots of commentators who are more than willing to offer their opinion on a story.

As we saw in Chapter 1, the Project for Excellence in Journalism at Columbia University studied the cable news outlets' reporting of the Iraq War and the 2004 presidential election, concluding that FOX was far more opinionated in its coverage than were its competitors:

FOX journalists were even more prone to offer their own opinions in the channel's coverage of the war in Iraq. There 73 percent of the stories included such personal judgments. On CNN the figure was 2 percent, and on MSNBC, 29 percent.

The same was true in coverage of the presidential election, where 82 percent of FOX stories included journalistic opinions, compared to 7 percent on CNN and 27 percent on MSNBC.

Those findings seem to challenge FOX's promotional marketing, particularly its slogan, "We Report, You Decide."

That damn, nonbiased, no-opinion-givin' elite media. O'Reilly will get you yet!

YOU SAY POTATO, I SAY FLAMING QUEER

IF THERE'S ANYTHING Bill hates more than illegal immigrants and gays, it's positive stories about illegal immigrants and gays. On June 21, 2005, he let them both have it:

> Impact Segment tonight. As you know, Governor Schwarzenegger was viciously attacked after he called for the Mexican border to be secured, and in the *Miami Herald* some pinhead called CNN's Lou Dobbs and me, your humble correspondent, anti-Hispanic for wanting the border secure as well. That's one tactic being used to keep the borders open, but there's another, more subtle one in play as well.
>
> In the past few months, at least twelve articles have appeared about students in this country illegally who have done very well academically. The articles appeared in the *New York Times, Boston Globe, Houston Chronicle,* and other mainly progressive papers. In addition, the *New York Times* has run more than a hundred gay-related stories in the past six months—a hundred!—the majority very positive.

Damn that elite media and their feel-good stories about nonwhite, nonheterosexual people!

Of course, Bill has an interesting take on "fair and balanced." In his mind, if you run twelve stories about illegal immigrants who are doing well academically, you're obliged to also do twelve stories on illegal immigrants who smoke in the boys' bathroom and are hot for teacher.

And if you do a hundred gay-related stories, fifty can be positive, but fifty should be about how sick and wrong homosexuality is. It's like saying if you have a hundred stories about white, heterosexual women who run small businesses, fifty of those stories need to be about how they'd be better off staying at home making babies.

While Bill (who, incidentally, claims at least in some small way to support gay rights—see Chapter 5) may not recognize gays and lesbians as worthy of respectful treatment, a lot of people do. But Bill's bigotry toward gays is glaringly obvious.

Imagine, for instance, he'd said this: "In addition, the *New York Times* has run more than a hundred Jewish-related stories in the past six months—a hundred!—the majority of them very positive." Indeed, substitute any ethnicity, profession, or other group for "gay-related" and see how it sounds. "The *New York Times* has run more than a hundred Catholic-related stories in the past six months—a hundred!—the majority of them very positive."

It's a fun little game, isn't it?

Of course, O'Reilly appears to forget that the *New York Times* is the *New York Times*. That means it's in New York, where gays roam the prairies and people for the most part think being gay is just fine. One hundred stories in six months averages out to about four a week. That's not really all that many considering how thick that paper is and how many gays read it.

It's like saying the *Atlanta Journal-Constitution* should limit the number of stories it runs on NASCAR and make certain at least half of those stories are negative. Or that Bill should run a bunch of stories on how ignorant FOX News viewers are instead of gradually turning his show into *Missing White Woman Weekly*.

NOTES

1. Note that in the Talking Points Memo referenced in this chapter, O'Reilly does not explicitly include the TV networks in his definition of the elite media, which he says consists mainly of the *New York Times*, a large number of urban newspapers, National Public Radio, and PBS: "Many think TV network operations and Hollywood executives are part of that club, but there is a subtle difference: Entertainment and TV news operations need you, the folks, to survive. Thus, while they are mostly sympathetic to the elites and generally follow their lead, they have to be careful."

    So while they mostly trumpet elite causes, according to Bill they are not elite because they need an audience, whereas newspapers apparently survive mainly on wishes and fairy dust.

    Later, of course, he appears to contradict at least the spirit of his earlier comments, saying, "And while our competitors at NBC and CNN still can't figure out how FOX News has become so powerful, it's simple: We are not the elite media."

2. Note that this should not be confused with O'Reilly's favorite Bugaloo, Joy, as portrayed by Caroline Ellis on the eponymous Sid and Marty Krofft production from the early seventies.

3. Later that year, in his December 9 radio program, O'Reilly would call the Anti-Defamation League, "an extremist group that finds offense in pretty much everything. Abraham Foxman is the national director. These are the people who accused anybody of liking *The Passion of the Christ* as being anti-Semitic."

    In O'Reilly's defense, the ADL was at the time accusing Bill of being insensitive for telling a Jewish caller he should go to Israel if he was offended by the idea of Christmas carols or gift exchanges in schools.

4. Eric Alterman, *What Liberal Media? The Truth about Bias and the News* (New York: Basic Books, 2003).

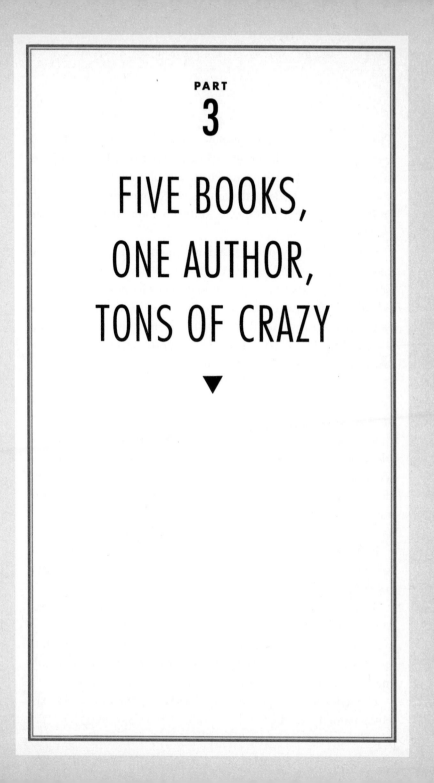

PART

3

FIVE BOOKS, ONE AUTHOR, TONS OF CRAZY

▼

THERE'S A SMALL but burgeoning cottage industry of anti-O'Reillyism taking hold in this country. In addition to our humble efforts, mediamatters.org does an excellent job of monitoring O'Reilly from the broadcast side, and many mainstream medianauts have alit on Planet O'Reilly when they've suddenly found themselves a target of Bill's ire.

But few O'Reilly detractors have stepped into the steaming, muddy jungles of Bill's prose. And fewer still have emerged without feeling they'd rather have caught malaria or typhus.

Unfortunately, when it comes to the world of literature, the best thing you can say about Bill is that he's written five times as many books as Paris Hilton's dog. Even more unfortunately, we had to read them—all of them: *The O'Reilly Factor*, *Escape from the O'Reilly Factor*, *Beneath the O'Reilly Factor*, *The O'Reilly Factor Goes to Monte Carlo*, and *Those Who Trespass: This Is So Fucking Horrible It Almost Makes Me Miss the O'Reilly Factor*.

Actually, the truth is, only one of us read these. That's the disadvantage of sucking hind teat in the coauthorship of a book. You get the shit jobs. While Amann blithely skipped about these volumes gleaning useful material, I was deep within the mines slowly contracting black lung: "If you please, gov'ner, Mr. O'Reilly wrote a nasty bit 'bout 'illery 'ere. Is it useful to ye?"

Rest assured, when this project lets up I will definitely look into Amann's rather odd and, I suspect, wholly apocryphal claim that Friedrich Engels used to scrub Marx's linens.

But such is the life of a writer. It's far less glamorous than it looks. And, I grant you, it doesn't look all that glamorous.

Anyway, knuckles bloodied and my pickax and dignity worn to the nub, I eventually emerged from my research assignment a little angry and ready to come out swinging.

The following first-person book reviews are the result. My existential pain, my credit.

—*Tom Breuer*, writer, reader, laundry boy

17

THE O'REILLY FACTOR
FOR KIDS

THE FIRST LINE in the foreword to Bill O'Reilly's latest opus starts out "I wish I'd had this book when I was a teenager."

Really Bill? You wish you'd had a book written by you as a fifty-five-year-old man? You know, I also wish that as a teenager I'd had a book written by a future me. The first line of my book would have been, "In about twenty years, a spectacularly obtuse TV personality named Bill O'Reilly will write a piece of dreck called *The O'Reilly Factor for Kids*.[1] Whatever you do, for the love of Jehovah, DON'T READ IT."

While Bill's ridiculously inflated ego is more than evident in the first line of this piffling waste of pulp, one would have thought it impossible even for someone as delusional and self-important as O'Reilly to think he could actually pull this off.

Indeed, it may not be all that much of a stretch to say that Bill O'Reilly, in the Year of our Lord 2004, has written the worst book in the history of publishing.

This is an impossibly stupid effort. Seriously, I'm waiting for

God to come jumping out of a closet any second to tell me my entire life has been one long, embarrassing practical joke and this is the punch line.

Honestly, if you were a publisher casting about for someone to write a book that speaks to teens frankly and in their own language about the pitfalls of growing up, it's hard to imagine a worse choice than FOX News's loudest, dumbest, and most meretricious newsman.

I myself have spent a good part of the morning trying to imagine a worse choice and all I've been able to come up with so far are Rip Taylor, Pope Benedict XVI, John Holmes, and Fred "Rerun" Berry.

Unfortunately, Taylor had prior commitments, Holmes and Berry are dead, and Benny is probably too busy, so O'Reilly, working for the Bizarro wing of HarperCollins, apparently got the gig by default.

The O'Reilly Factor For Kids's putative purpose is to give teens some honest, straightforward advice from a guy who's been there and who, as a father himself, knows how to rap with the kids. Instead, it's a deeply confused tract on everything from sharing, to reasoning with bullies, to proper skin care (we'll get to this one later). At times, Bill sounds like he's talking to five-year-olds ("You have to learn—and believe me, I know how awful these words can be when you want something—to share"); sometimes he appears to be counseling the elderly ("But excessive sun exposure, according to the U.S. Office of the Surgeon General, can lead to skin cancer and other skin growths, cataracts, premature aging of the skin, and several other types of health problems"); but most of the time he sounds like a deranged Carmelite nun trying to relate to teenagers on their own level ("The adult doesn't have to be in the room snappin' to OutKast, but one of these specimens must be somewhere on the premises").

Is this a joke? Wait, perhaps I haven't explored that possibility thoroughly enough. Bill, seriously, is this a joke?

Well, it must be a joke, because there's a belly laugh on every page. Don't believe me?

Page 3 (following the above-mentioned, stunningly idiotic

foreword): "Almost everybody watched the TV show *Friends* on NBC. Unfortunately, some kids think that's what real friends are like. . . . In real life, true friends stand by you when things get rough."

(Yes. Now let's go visit Mr. Green Jeans and see what he thinks.)

Page 4: "Okay, you know I've made money. It was a long time coming, so I don't usually spend much of it and I certainly don't show it off."

(Okay, Bill, obviously you do show it off. You're now averaging one reference to your huge salary every two pages. [Page 1: "I have a career that's lots of fun and makes me a lot of money."] For God's sake, Bill, these are *kids*! Can you possibly be this insecure? Do you flash a fat roll of Benjamins in front of the dog every morning, cooing, "Who's your daddy?")

Page 5: "Now, I don't want you to think that I sat around when I was your age and carefully chose my companions because of their virtues."

(*Carefully chose my companions because of their virtues?* Are you kidding with this? Who are you talking to? 'Cause I guarantee you, all the kids have left. You sound like Truman Capote, for God's sake. Can you possibly be this tone deaf? You might as well quote Ralph Waldo Emerson while you're at it.)

Page 7: "'Keep your friendships in repair,' warned Ralph Waldo Emerson."

Page 6: "If a kid lies to his parents, he or she will lie to you."

(Okay, Bill? I haven't used the word gaywad in probably twenty-five years. Please don't force my hand.)

Page 8: "Growing up on Long Island just a few miles outside New York City, I had tons of friends in the neighborhood. They were all guys, because at that time women's lib had not kicked in and the girls played differently than we did."

(Think. Who is your audience? The last time anyone said "women's lib" these kids' *parents'* were zygotes. Just stop talking. You are beyond embarrassing. I guarantee your kids are plotting your death right now.)

It's actually quite stunning that this book ever saw print. It's certainly not intended for kids—not any on this planet anyway. In fact, there's no question that either this has to be a cynical ploy to sell books to those O'Reilly fans who are still teed off about NBC's decision to cancel *Bonanza*, or O'Reilly is irretrievably insane and is sincerely hoping to reach today's teenagers with lines like, "If you knew that a few minutes spent with an older person could ease his loneliness, why would you ever choose to spend those minutes alone with your Game Boy instead?"

I can say with confidence there is not one teenager in the nation who will read past page 3 of this book and want to continue . . . or at least there are very few. And when I say very few I'm talking roughly the same number of death row inmates who subscribe to *Redbook*.

Indeed, if I were a PR flack and had my choice between taking a job with Union Carbide's Bhopal office circa 1984 or being responsible for promoting this crap, I think I'd take the Union Carbide gig.

While he claims to believe he's helping kids out, what O'Reilly has actually done is consigned hundreds of innocent children of *Factor* viewers to the worst Christmas break they've ever had.

There's absolutely nothing interesting, fresh, or insightful here. The book is little more than an assortment of dull anecdotes from O'Reilly's childhood alongside regurgitated bromides from elementary school health classes and old fifties hygiene films. The thing makes *Reefer Madness* look cool.

Throughout the book, for example, there are "instant messages" from O'Reilly where he delineates the difference between "pinheads" and "smart operators."

According to O'Reilly, "a pinhead is a kid who brags about how much money she has or how much money she's spent on something." (No argument there.)

"A smart operator is a kid who gets a decent night's sleep so that everyone else doesn't have to suffer with him the next day."

He's got four whole chapters full of this crap. It looks like he lifted stuff straight out of a 1946 copy of *Boy's Life* and then removed all the edginess.

In Pinheads and Smart Operators: Instant Message Number 3, Bill writes:

IMNSHO [which O'Reilly and all teens apparently know means 'In my not-so-humble opinion'], a pinhead gets sunburned. Okay, a nice even tan can make you look healthy and sexy. Or it can advertise to your friends that you've had a great winter vacation at the beach. But excessive sun exposure, according to the U.S. Office of the Surgeon General. . . .

—and then on he goes about those legendary teen bugaboos, cataracts, as well as studies from Boston University and the Centers for Disease Control. (Or the BU to the CDC, as O'Reilly might put it.)

First of all, Bill, I hate to be crass, but have you seen your skin? You look like something Ed Gein made after he was finished upholstering the settee. Do you think you're really going to reel kids in with your thoughts on proper skin care? If they didn't bail out after your take on gangsta rap (page 85, I'm not even kidding), you've definitely lost them now.

Secondly, these kids are teenagers. Honestly, what do you think you're accomplishing? Why not just write, "A pinhead finds blood in his stool and ignores it. A smart operator gets regular colorectal screenings and eats a diet rich in fiber"?

Unfortunately, this book will impress no one—not the teens whom it's supposedly written for nor the grandparents whom O'Reilly was probably actually hoping to fleece. It's just plain too stupid.

I'm forty now, and I know it's sometimes tough to remember what it was like to be a kid, and trying to make heads or tails out of teens' culture, attitudes, and beliefs years removed from your own painful adolescence can be a Sisyphean task, to be sure.

But that's hardly the point. I remember fondly my grandmother on my mother's side. She and I hardly had anything to talk about other than the typical grandma/grandson stuff. As O'Reilly himself might say, she was "squaresville." For instance, she had a picture of Pope Paul VI on her wall—ten years after he was dead. When I was a teen I used to mow her lawn; she'd give me $5 and some cookies when I was finished. I'm fairly certain that when I was twenty-three, she still thought I was in the Scouts.

I wish she were alive, principally because she was my grandma and I loved her dearly, but close behind that reason would be the opportunity to show her this book. I'm almost certain that by page 2 she would have started rolling her eyes and done one of those forced-vomit pantomimes.

I have to admit now, in the interest of fairness, that I didn't read all of *The O'Reilly Factor for Kids*. I took a cue from O'Reilly himself, who walked out of the middle of *Fahrenheit 9/11*, and ditched before I was done with it.

Yeah, I can almost hear O'Reilly now—"a pinhead reviews a book he hasn't read in its entirety while a smart operator gives it an honest shake." But c'mon, Bill. It's not that difficult to extrapolate from beginning to end. If I didn't get your wisdom on searching for changes in moles and freckles, you'll just have to forgive me. But the truth is, there's nothing here even remotely worthwhile. If your book had been a TV show, it would have been canceled at the first commercial.

You had to know that. Or is it possible you're really just this dense?

NOTES

1. Bill O'Reilly, *The O'Reilly Factor for Kids: A Survival Guide for America's Families* (New York: HarperEntertainment, 2004).

18

WHO'S LOOKING OUT FOR YOU?

WHEN IT CAME time for me to review *Who's Looking Out for You?*,[1] the penultimate work in the O'Reilly oeuvre, I was a bit reluctant.

My earlier review of O'Reilly's recent children's book, *The O'Reilly Factor for Kids*, was aided mightily by the fact that O'Reilly is simply nuts—nuts enough to think he could engage today's teenagers with his thoughts on gangsta rap and *Friends* while relying on a writing style that evokes an eight-year-old Nepalese transfer student channeling Mr. Green Jeans.

That book was not just bad, it was so off-the-beam bad that I was convinced that level of craziness simply could not be duplicated. In short, I was skeptical that lightning of this sort could ever strike twice.

Well, dear reader, lightning *can* strike twice, and, once again, here are my testicles to serve as grounding wires.

While there's off-the-charts, brimming-drool-cup lunacy on nearly every page of *Who's Looking Out for You?*, it's perhaps most remarkable for its flat-out terrible writing.

Indeed, you know you're in trouble when the most inspired prose in your book is an excerpted Enrique Iglesias quote from *Parade* magazine. Believe me, "It's not a normal relationship. After I sold millions of records he [Julio] would say 'but you'll never win a Grammy,'" was like a cool breeze in the desert after six days lodged in a camel's uterus. Thank you, Enrique Iglesias. Thank you, thank you, thank you.

Reading *The O'Reilly Factor for Kids*, one got the impression that O'Reilly was dumbing down his writing to appeal to youngsters. One is stunned to discover after just a few pages of *Who's* that that's just the way he writes. Indeed, this, his "adult" book, is basically the same as the children's drivel, only with more politics, more on Clinton's blow job, and, bizarrely enough, less advice on how to avoid cataracts.

After *Who's Looking Out for You?* had spent twenty-three weeks on the *New York Times* best-seller list, O'Reilly made much of the *Times*'s lack of interest in reviewing it. No doubt O'Reilly imagines that the Old Gray Lady ignored his magnum opus because of some institutional left-wing bias. Please. Three pages into *Who's*, you'll realize that the *Times* chose not to review it for the same reason they don't send a food critic to Chili's or an art critic to check out a potato chip that looks like Dale Earnhardt.

Of course, the *Times has* published reviews of books by William J. Bennett, Dinesh D'Souza, William F. Buckley, Jr., and even Dan Quayle, all darlings of the right.

Bill, try to get this. The *New York Times* is not on a malicious crusade against you; they're on a malicious crusade against wooden prose and underpants-shitting insanity. The *Times* ignored your book because it sucks ass. It's really that simple.

O'Reilly reveals once again in *Who's Looking Out for You?* that he is a howlingly funny mix of cognitive dissonance, narcissism, projection, and garden-variety madness.

Indeed, one of the funniest things about O'Reilly is his ability to hold two competing thoughts in his head simultaneously. For instance, he continually presents his childhood as some kind of Dickensian nightmare and once said, "You don't come from any lower than I came from on an economic scale." Yet after he made his millions, his mother continued to live in his childhood home. See? Nuts.

Of course, *Who's Looking Out for You?* is full of these kinds of contradictions, so much so that you begin to seriously question the man's grip on reality.

For instance, what could possibly be going through his head when he writes, "Which media operations are looking out for you, the regular American who wants a good life for your family? Which editorialists are fighting for your children to experience a childhood free from degradation? Unfortunately, there are very few press potentates who give a fig about you or your kids," and then in the *very next paragraph* says, "I'll talk about some specific press people in a moment, but first let me quote from an article I wrote for the January 2003 edition of *Playboy* magazine."?

(Who knows, but my guess is something like, "I'm so glad I received the moral grounding provided by a traditional Roman Catholic upbringing. . . . Wow, get a load of the rack on that Lindsay Lohan. Oh, to be fifty-two again.")

Later, he calls out Bill Moyers for claiming not to be left-wing (in reality, Moyers simply denied being an ideologue). Of course, considering the content of his former PBS show, *NOW*, and the fact that he served on LBJ's administration, it would be quite remarkable if Moyers actually did claim to be a political centrist. But if he does, it only proves that he's as crazy as O'Reilly, who goes nuts whenever anyone suggests he or FOX News are conservative when it's painfully obvious both are.

O'Reilly also telegraphs his ongoing obsession with the Clintons. While the conservative press in general walked around for about a month after Clinton left office like the Borg after their queen was killed, O'Reilly *still* can't let go. After telling the story about the fourteen-year-old girl who was caught giving fellatio to a sixteen-year-old boy on a school bus, he snidely implies that this might have been President Clinton's influence. (Actually, if you want to get technical, at least 99 percent of the blame goes to Ken Starr.)

He does have a point, however. Public figures are very influential. So if a high school girl gives a guy a hummer on a bus, that may

or may not be Clinton. On the other hand, if he rubs Middle Eastern food on her vagina while threatening to inject wine into her arm,
you can be lead-pipe certain that's some O'Reilly mojo workin'.

Toward the end of his section on Clinton, O'Reilly claims he was
told by a guy "in a position to know" that O'Reilly was mentioned
by CBS brass as a potential debating partner for Bill Clinton when
Clinton signed up with *60 Minutes* as a commentator. "Apparently the
former president found that prospect, well, let's say, unappealing,"
writes O'Reilly. "I'll leave it to you to speculate about the reason."

Okay, Bill. I'll speculate. Now, I know you think Clinton turned
down the offer because he was afraid you were too much of a no-
nonsense, plain-talking, jus'-folks kinda guy and would make short
work of him and his phony veneer. But I can just about guarantee
you that if this story is in fact true, the president heard "Bill
O'Reilly," and it was like hearing "Tootie from *Facts of Life*" or
"Coreys Haim and Feldman." He's not afraid of you; he simply
doesn't want to share the stage with someone who has all the journalistic integrity of Ron Popeil.[2]

O'Reilly really flips out when he starts talking about Hillary's
book, however. He's had it in for Hillary ever since he challenged
her to a contest over book sales that she didn't know about and then
lost. (Well, to be fair, that was actually a contest over *Who's Looking
Out for You?*, but the whole thing's just too rich not to rate a mention.)
Referring to the $8 million book advance Hillary received for her
memoirs, O'Reilly writes, "Mrs. Clinton herself likes the concept of
personal money a lot." (Awkward phraseology aside, this is hilarious coming from O'Reilly, who has done for financial modesty
what Jeffrey Dahmer did for Ambrosia Chocolates.)

About her book, O'Reilly notes that Hillary's publisher "stuffed
her pocketbook with cash for a book she didn't even write."

Okay, Bill? You're not in the second grade, and Hillary didn't just
beat you in the science fair. Whether Hillary got her dad to write the
book for her or she used ghostwriters, there's a lesson in here for you.
Namely, some celebrities are smart enough to use ghostwriters.
Next time around you may want to look into it. I'll put your agent
in touch with Enrique Iglesias.

Unlike *The O'Reilly Factor for Kids*, which was a laugh riot from the beginning to about page 30, where I stopped reading it,[3] the only truly entertaining bits in *Who's Looking Out for You?* are where O'Reilly relates experiences from his own life. Since the whole point of this book is to help the reader decide who is looking out for them (this gets really annoying, by the way, as he constantly asks "was so-and-so looking out for his countrymen/viewers/children, etc.?"), he tries to impart the wisdom of a fifty-some-year-old man who has lived long and learned by doing it. Unfortunately, most of these stories reveal deep-seated character flaws instead.

For instance, in his chapter on religion, O'Reilly writes about intimidating funeral mourners to increase his altar-boy tips, presenting the whole thing as boys-will-be-boys high jinks:

> Many times [the funeral directors] would "forget" to provide the saintly altar boys with the expected gratuity for performing the funeral ceremony with dignity and compassion. On occasions like these I, having control of the incense pot, might become just a tad bit exuberant with it, causing large clouds of smoke to form over the grieving congregation. Of course, the priest would shoot me a dirty look, but the message was sent: The living must be taken care of.

Bill, a little advice: There are some childhood reminiscences you'll want to keep under your hat. As youthful indiscretions go, this isn't exactly the same as fondling your cousin in your neighbors' tree house, but it's close. Think about it. You were baiting the bereaved for cash. Whether you're eleven years old or fifty, it's just bad taste.

His most delightful story, however, is about the time he went to a big event hosted by a wealthy philanthropist in Aspen, Colorado. O'Reilly writes that he doesn't usually go to such events because he's (I'm not kidding) not "comfortable among the swells." He says the crowd was (still not kidding) "big-name city." The guest list included Rudy Giuliani, Martha Stewart, Tom Brokaw, Diane Sawyer, Roger Staubach (you mean, of the Kennebunkport Staubachs?), Prince Andrew, Lance Armstrong, John Glenn, Queen Noor, Alan

Greenspan, Karl Rove, and Charlie Rose. Then he calls the thing (I shit you not) a "giant flea market of power" (ghostwriter, Bill!) and relates how he pissed off Queen Noor of Jordan by saying Arabs won't give the United States a break because we support Israel and many Arabs hate the Jews.

He might as well have pinched her bum and called her "toots," but he presented the encounter as though he were a regular guy striking a blow for Joe Sixpack.

Seriously, you couldn't make stuff like this up if you were pushing peyote buttons directly into the folds of your brain. Again, we all have embarrassing stories from our pasts. But most of us don't put them in a book and then beg people every fifteen seconds to buy it.

There's far more insanity to be had in *Who's Looking Out for You?* For instance, O'Reilly somehow comes to the conclusion that Louis XVI would have loved secular America.

But this isn't about O'Reilly's tenuous grasp of history. It's much deeper than that. The man needs help, as do I. These headaches won't go away. Tomorrow, I'll settle in with a fresh *New York Times*. Thankfully, that's still an O'Reilly-free zone.

NOTES

1. Bill O'Reilly, *Who's Looking Out for You?* (New York: Broadway Books, 2003).
2. Check out Factor Gear online at www.billoreilly.com or just wait about two minutes, and he'll provide ordering information on his show.
3. Okay, to tell the truth, I skimmed the rest of it to strike a reasonable balance between thoroughness and my mental well-being.

THE O'REILLY FACTOR: THE GOOD, THE BAD AND THE COMPLETELY RIDICULOUS IN AMERICAN LIFE

I SIT HERE like a house cat that's just been dunked in a thick stew of stinging nettles, hydrochloric acid, and Elmer's glue, unsure of whether to meticulously cleanse my body of the latest O'Reilly extract at great pain to myself or simply jump in a river and drown.

My task this time was to review Bill's *The O'Reilly Factor: The Good, the Bad and the Completely Ridiculous in American Life*,[1] and, needless to say, my patience is wearing thin.

Now, here's the part I don't get. They didn't make a sequel to *Showgirls*, Germany didn't decide to give Nazism another try, the *Hindenburg II* is not shuttling small children around America's theme parks, and yet O'Reilly has written five books. And I've read three of them. So who's dumber, O'Reilly or me?

Well, my excuse is that I'm reading these eminently unreadable volumes for the purpose of savaging them in print. But I have to say that I've more than once been panicked during the course of this project about the possibility that a longtime friend or, worse yet, a dating prospect might send me one of those e-mail surveys that includes a question about the last book I read. It makes me want to go out and quickly grab a copy of *Valley of the Dolls* or *The Turner Diaries* so I'll have a better answer.

Johannes Gutenberg, the father of the modern printing press, is consistently cited in historical surveys as one of the greatest and most influential figures of the second millennium. Sadly, with every O'Reilly page I turn, he plummets further down the charts. In fact, it was precisely at page 179 of *The O'Reilly Factor*, when Bill put the finishing touches on a chapter about how important it is to have friends, that Johannes Gutenberg actually slipped behind Steve Guttenberg on most historians' lists.

While this is the first nonfiction book O'Reilly wrote, it's the third I've read, and ironically, it's a lot more of the same. Indeed, for someone with nothing to say, he sure repeats himself a lot. Yeah, yeah, Bill, I get it. Clinton got a blow job, the elite media are pinheads, your father was mean and loud, you write like an eleven-year-old. How about something new? For God's sake, you sound like a ninety-four-year-old woman after her second stroke.

I suppose most of us could extend three dull childhood anecdotes and four half-baked observations into eight hundred pages of copy, but we don't have a cable news show to plug it on or a legion of troglodytic followers with more disposable income than they can reasonably spend on Franklin Mint commemorative plates and NASCAR jackets. You win.

I did, however, learn two things from *The O'Reilly Factor: the Good, the Bad and the Completely Ridiculous, etc*: 1) the Founding Fathers wanted regular people, such as poor dirt farmers and carpenters, to sit in the House of Representatives, but today's politicians have corrupted and subverted the egalitarian intentions of those great men (who, by the way, considered women, blacks, and white men without land unworthy of holding office or voting); and 2) O'Reilly's father would have kicked Dr. Spock's ass.

Seriously, this stuff is in print and most likely sitting in your local library. Put another way, a portion of your local taxes were spent to popularize what will no doubt come to be known as the O'Reilly Doctrine: The United States has become much less politically inclusive in the last 230 years, and William O'Reilly, Sr., would have whaled on Benjamin Spock.

Here's the Dr. Spock stuff in all its glory:

"My father had a big chip on his shoulder about people like Dr. Spock who were, in today's parlance, attempting to 'empower' children. Dr. Spock was lucky he never met William O'Reilly Sr. There would have been violence."

O'Reilly didn't elaborate, but I picture a scene like in *West Side Story*—Spock flanked by two rows of stick- and knife-wielding pediatricians, O'Reilly backed by a small phalanx of abusive Irish fathers from the mean streets of Levittown, snapping their fingers and menacing each other with jaunty tunes about appropriate child-rearing practices.

As for the Founding Fathers, O'Reilly completely misrepresents their intentions. They wanted poor carpenters in the House about as much as the pope wants Courtney Love in the College of Cardinals. But he can still dream:

> Their idea changed the world: Regular folks like farmers, carpenters, and bartenders would be elected for a short time, a term of two years, to represent their neighbors in the House of Representatives. This assembly would have the power to check the activities of Senators—the richer, better educated types who had six-year terms—and the president as well. In short, the House was designed to express the true voice of everyday Americans.

Oh, how far we've fallen from this golden age of slavery and indentured servitude.

"But that was then," O'Reilly continues. "Now, American politics has evolved into a position of entitlement, and we've let it happen! No longer does Jared take a coach to D.C. for a couple of years and then return to his plow. Today many politicians are 'lifers.'"

If you think I'm making this up or exaggerating it, I dare you to look for yourself. The Spock lunacy is on page 117 and the bit about the Founding Fathers is on page 144. (On the same page, O'Reilly also tells us, in his usual elegant prose, that after the little dustup with the colonies, King George III was "later diagnosed as insane." Remember, O'Reilly releases his books through major publishers so it takes a crew of copy editors and others vetting his work to make his writing sound like an eleven-year-old's.)

Anyway, go to your local library if you want to verify this stuff for yourself. Get a disguise—maybe a fake mustache and sunglasses or a paper bag with eyeholes cut in it—and check out this book. If you're uncomfortable using your own library card, you could always hire a hooker and get her to grab a copy for you.

Speaking of paying women for sex (believe me, that segue is far less clunky than those at the end of each chapter in his book), there's plenty on O'Reilly's wild sexual exploits here. Indeed, the number of references to O'Reilly's inappropriate sexual conduct in *The O'Reilly Factor* are exceeded only by the number of references to Bill Clinton's inappropriate sexual conduct.

He has two chapters, "The Sex Factor" and "The Dating Factor," which he offers as sage advice but which are actually thinly disguised chronicles of what a player O'Reilly used to be during his leisure-suit, Ron Burgundy disco days as a local TV reporter.

Following is an excerpt. If you happen to be reciting this as part of a reading at a bookstore or a library, you may want to cover the first two rows of your audience in plastic sheeting. They will get sprayed. I myself have lost every lunch from circa 1979 to the present. Here's Bill:

My thing was the music: I was a dancing *machine*. Sock it to me, Donna Summer! Let's shake this place, Gloria Gaynor! Get down!

Now, this was the lad of a quarter century ago, okay? But I make no apologies. I loved the all-out dancing, and quite a few girls loved to dance with me. The dancing got me dates. The dancing said (since you couldn't hear any words in those places under the rotating mirror balls), Hey, let's have some fun and see what happens next. Even Catholic girls had their inhibitions lowered by the howls of the Bee Gees or Sylvester. A few hours at clubs like Septembers or Shenanigans and most of my dates wanted to extend the evening at their place or mine.

Of course, this was written in 2000, four years before O'Reilly was accused by one of his producers of making inappropriate small talk with her over the phone while he masturbated. In fact, reading this kind of stuff now is a little like reading a 1975 John Wayne Gacy article on how to be a clown at children's birthday parties.

To refresh your memory, here's an excerpt from Andrea Mackris's October 2004 complaint against O'Reilly detailing O'Reilly's alleged attempts to charm her:

> Well, if I took you down there then I'd want to take a shower with you right away, that would be the first think [sic] I'd do . . . yeah, we'd check into the room, and we would order up some room service and uh and you'd definitely get two wines into you as quickly as I could get into you I would get 'em into you . . . maybe intravenously, get those glasses of wine into you.

Of course, as we pointed out elsewhere in this book, what's overlooked in the whole O'Reilly sex scandal is not that O'Reilly is a creep (as clear as that is), but that he's really horrible at phone sex.

This is the kind of stuff you say to a woman who has just swallowed too much Xanax, not what you whisper to someone you're trying to seduce.

Indeed, "I would get 'em into you . . . maybe intravenously, get those glasses of wine into you" is not so much sexy phone talk as the definitive *$25,000 Pyramid* clue for "What Ted Bundy Might Say." At best it's about twenty minutes and two double Scotches away from, "It puts the lotion in the basket."

Incidentally, there was rampant speculation, owing to the detailed nature of Mackris's account and the speed with which FOX settled the suit, that Mackris taped their conversations. At the time, O'Reilly called the whole matter the single most evil thing he had ever experienced, and the incident apparently stung him so much that he now says people who secretly audiotape other people are the lowest of the low.

In fact, when author and George W. Bush confidant Doug Wead revealed in February 2005 that he had secretly taped the then-governor, O'Reilly went ape shit. He called Wead "the lowest form of debris in the country" and said, ominously, "I hope Bush gets him. I hope Bush audits him. I hope Bush has guys follow him around and gets him. That's what I would do."

So the lesson is: taping someone else to further your career is wrong, wrong, wrong. Low. Evil, even.

Okay, here's O'Reilly on page 45 of *The O'Reilly Factor*, relating the story of an abusive boss at ABC who was out to get the young O'Reilly by making him needlessly update a story for *Nightline* even though Ted Koppel had already left the studio and no update was possible:

> Ted was long gone, it turned out. More games were being played at my expense. No West Coast update was actually planned.
>
>   This was getting dirty as well as irrational. Pulling a Linda Tripp long before that lovely hit the spotlight, I flicked on my cassette recorder to tape what had become an incredible tirade. The *Nightline* producer was giving new meaning to the word "ballistic."

O'Reilly's gambit worked and got him off the hook with his bosses. He never said whether the producer offered to harden his nipples or asked him if he had a vibrator, but the lesson was that secretly taping your boss is what street-smart Levittown guys who won't get pushed around do. Smart, smart, smart.

By chapter 17, O'Reilly finally gets around to addressing the topic of his book. He includes chapters called "The Ridiculous Factor," "The Bad Factor," and "The Good Factor."

At one point—and forgive me, because I know how society views people who secretly quote verbatim from widely published books—O'Reilly consecutively lists onion-flavored potato chips, Warren Beatty, and abortion as examples of things that are "bad" in America. Boom, boom, boom. Onion chips, Beatty, abortion. No kidding.

I found this extraordinary because I had jotted down my own list of "bad" things in American life before picking up O'Reilly's book and I'd written "Funyuns," "Cary Elwes," and "vivisection."

I asked my coauthor, Joe, for his short list and he said "fried pork rinds," "Corbin Bernsen," and "selling human organs for profit."

Play along at home if you like.

Once again, trying to get all O'Reilly's insanity into a single book review is like pounding 20 kilos of shit into a 5-kilo bag, but, believe me, there's enough weird projection, garden-variety hypocrisy and high-school-essay reasoning to fill up three crazy men's books.

Luckily, however, O'Reilly remains one of a kind.

NOTES

1. Bill O'Reilly, *The O'Reilly Factor: The Good, The Bad and the Completely Ridiculous in American Life* (New York: Broadway Books, 2000).

20

THE NO SPIN ZONE

JUST INSIDE THE front cover of my copy of *The No Spin Zone*,[1] bought used from Amazon.com for $1.43 American (which is $23.52 less than the suggested retail price and $1.35 more than it's worth) is scrawled "Happy Birthday Dad! I'm enjoying this book. I hope you do too! Love, Tom and Cindi."

Tom and Cindi, if your stupidity and hatred of your father are congenital defects, I apologize for mentioning this. If, on the other hand, you've labored full lives to hone these traits, screw you.

Unfortunately, it soon becomes apparent just a few pages into *The No Spin Zone* that Tom and Cindi's Happy Birthday greeting is the most skillfully written part of the book.

Bill, if you'd had the sense to let Tom and Cindi ghostwrite this steaming Egyptian-pyramid-sized pile of offal for you, maybe the *New York Times* wouldn't have treated it like Charles Nelson Reilly at an Alabama tractor pull.

As do his other literary offerings, *The No Spin Zone* amply demonstrates that O'Reilly continues to be locked in an epic struggle with his fans to determine who's dumber.

Not only does Bill come off as a frothing loon again, he also writes like a half-wit.

Consider this sentence, a reference to New York Governor Mario Cuomo's initial reluctance to come on *The Factor*: "But the former governor resisted, even though his son Chris was a correspondent for the FOX News Channel that carries *The O'Reilly Factor*." You mean, as opposed to all the other FOX News Channels that don't carry *The O'Reilly Factor*?

Ironically, by the time O'Reilly writes this painful muddle of a sentence, he has already wailed about the sorry state of our schools.

For instance, on page 114 he claims that "60 percent of poor kids in the fourth grade can barely read." Since he doesn't cite a source or define what he means by "barely," it's difficult to know if this is a credible stat or if he's just mistaking his ass for a bibliography again. But it should be encouraging to O'Reilly that there will continue to be a market for his books for the foreseeable future.

Now, you may be thinking that nitpicking grammatical errors and unsupported statistics[2] are just the sort of things that make most people hate pinheaded liberals and embrace straight talkers like O'Reilly as working-class heroes. Please. After nearly two hundred pages of this crap I'd give anything to be a poor fourth grader who can't read.

That said, I have to grudgingly admit that *The No Spin Zone* is probably O'Reilly's best book, which is a little like being the best Olive Garden in Sicily, but it's something, eh?

Indeed, a couple of times he comes close to making an intelligent point. Unfortunately, he always manages to muck it up for himself.

For instance, at one point he wonders why there isn't more government oversight of federal spending. He's right. Pork-barrel spending is a huge problem, as is systemic waste in federal departments and agencies such as the Pentagon, which, to his credit, O'Reilly calls on the carpet for wasting $40 billion on a helicopter that won't fly right.

So I actually perked up a little when he introduced the transcript of his interview with Comptroller General David M. Walker. O'Reilly interviewed Walker on his show, and I naïvely thought he might have tried to get to the bottom of some of the more extravagant budget items. (Oh, I forgot to mention. This entire book consists of excerpts lifted from Bill's interviews, with his own spin thrown in before and after. Ironic, huh? No, not ironic. What's the word I'm looking for? Moronic. That's it.)

Here's O'Reilly's second question to Walker following a perfunctory puffball about O'Reilly's confusion regarding the GAO's role:

"We have been trying for more than a year to find out how much money Hillary Clinton, Chelsea, and their entourage spent in their two-week jaunt to North Africa. We cannot find out. Can you, Mr. Walker?"

Okay, let's grant O'Reilly his outrage vis-à-vis Hillary. For the sake of argument, let's assume she's incorrigibly corrupt and using federal resources in the most cynical possible fashion.

That said, leading with a question about Hillary's trip abroad, which may have cost a few mill or so, is like securing an exclusive interview with OJ and spending the first thirty minutes grilling him about a fumble that lost a game against the Oilers back in seventy-four. It's like Bill Gates haranguing his wife about her spiraling monthly gum budget. It's just dumb.

Of course O'Reilly acknowledged, at least in print, the *billions upon billions* the Pentagon wastes, so he can't just play the stupid card here. Sure, he may think the Hillary question is illustrative of the endemic prodigality infecting government at the turn of the millennium, but it's actually just illustrative of the number of mildly retarded people watching his show.

If O'Reilly wants to do his little-emasculated-boy dance over what the first lady spent on airfare during his Most Ridiculous Item of the Day (instead of plugging shoddy merchandise for once), that's up to him. But it's really insulting to the public to go to the trouble of securing an interview with a government official who could shed light on a serious problem and then use the opportunity to flog his little high school grudge against the bitchy girl in his class.

It reminds one of the countless segments O'Reilly and FOX devoted to Gary Condit and Chandra Levy instead of covering, say, the news.

I suppose it's a touch disingenuous, though, to express surprise over O'Reilly's idiotic bait and switch. Mere pages earlier he was even more egregious.

Indeed, about a hundred pages into *The No Spin Zone*, O'Reilly started to say something that struck a nerve. Bemoaning the sorry state of television journalism, he said that viewers are subjected to too many prepackaged answers from policy-makers because reporters are generally too predictable or too afraid to ask difficult questions.

O'Reilly declared that he's different. He wants his interview subjects to give genuine answers that require thought and that won't simply rely on Republican or Democratic talking points. He also said he likes to start off with a haymaker to knock the interviewee off his script. Sounds great, right? It's true, a lot of media personalities these days are simply lazy, behaving more like stenographers than real reporters.

To illustrate his point, O'Reilly prints an excerpt from a March 2000 interview with George W. Bush in which he warmed up the then-governor and Republican hopeful with a few general questions before lobbing "a grenade that blasted him into the Zone." (Still no ghostwriter, Bill?)

O'REILLY: So far in this campaign, what stands out in my mind regarding you is the "Jesus Christ political philosopher" remark in one of the New Hampshire debates. Everybody remembers that. [At this point Mr. Bush started to wince.] But when I heard you say that Jesus was your philosopher model, I had no problem with it. I said, "You know, that's a legitimate answer." [Mr. Bush's expression immediately went from a wince to a beam.] Certainly Jesus was a philosopher, certainly he addressed politics—render to Caesar and all that. But somebody might say, "Gee, if Governor Bush is so influenced by Jesus Christ, how can he support the death penalty so avidly, because Jesus would not have?" [Here Mr. Bush's eyes widened just a tad.]

Wow, am I reading this right? Perhaps I've underestimated O'Reilly, the old grizzled beat reporter. Is he really being this impertinent with the Republican presidential front-runner on Rupert Murdoch's own network?

Bill, I'm surprised. You really are looking out for me. Civility be damned. The credibility of the fourth estate is far more important. You are a true tribune of the people. Bravo.

Needless to say, I awaited Bill's next line of questioning with the anticipation of a FOX News associate producer expecting her first settlement check. Bill tantalized me with a promise that the best was yet to come: "That opening salvo forced candidate Bush to depart from his well-rehearsed script. From then on, the interview picked up speed."

Oh, do tell.

O'REILLY: Talking about corruption, Maria Hsia was just found guilty in the Buddhist Temple fund-raising scheme [involving Al Gore]. By all accounts—Charles LaBella's account, Louis Freeh's account—Ms. Reno has not pursued the campaign finance investigation very hard. If you're elected, do you investigate Attorney General Reno?

Whoa, a question about the opposition party's alleged corruption? You've got him on the ropes now, Bill. If the Jesus thing was the jab to the midsection that sent him reeling, this would surely be the knockout punch. How did the Bush campaign ever recover? Rove must have been on damage control for weeks. Let's hope you didn't let him go without a few sharply worded questions about the Teapot Dome Scandal. Nice job, Mike Wallace.

Actually there's a lot of this kind of thing in *The No Spin Zone*. In fact, O'Reilly hoists himself so often, his petard is broken.

For instance, after printing an interview transcript with Dan Rather, he mentions that it created more buzz than almost any other:

Aside from an interview with Michael Kinsley, in which I told the *Slate* editor and liberal commentator to his face (and proved it) that he had attacked my honesty in a cowardly fashion, the Rather appearance sparked more news coverage and editorial comment than any other in the No Spin Zone.

This is a great example, because I remember that interview, and it showed Bill O'Reilly at his Bill O'Reillyest: crazy, obtuse, loud, and puffed up full of ego.

The dustup started when Kinsley wrote a hilarious column in *Slate* in March of 2001 that questioned O'Reilly's frequent pretensions to poverty. In it, Kinsley argued convincingly that O'Reilly's upbringing wasn't nearly as proletarian as he made it out to be.

What O'Reilly seized upon, however, was Kinsley's skepticism over an incident where "socialites and bigwigs" who had been "measuring" him got up to leave at a dinner party.

Wrote Kinsley, "Two people left a Washington dinner party rather than share a table with a prole like Bill O'Reilly? Although I wasn't there, I state baldly: It never happened. That kind of snobbery barely exists in America."

Now, most people of moderate intelligence, without a history of alcoholic blackouts and for whom English is their first, second, or third language would have caught Kinsley's meaning. He clearly wasn't saying that two people didn't get up to leave; he was saying they didn't leave because O'Reilly comes from the working class.

Indeed, Kinsley tried several times to point this out to O'Reilly on his show, but O'Reilly was having none of it.

As the interview went on, and Kinsley gamely tried to drive home his main point—that people weren't leaving because O'Reilly was a prole—it just got more embarrassing.

Now, O'Reilly's exhibit A was a letter from "the woman who invited me to the dinner party" that said, "When so-and-so and so-and-so walked out, I was amazed. You were right, you had warned me."

Here was Kinsley's take on this shocking piece of evidence from a later issue of *Slate:*

Seeking closure, and curious what O'Reilly might have "warned" her of ("I must warn you, ma'am, that people invariably flee the room when I walk in because I'm from Levittown"), on Wednesday I called the hostess of the party, who said she never wrote such a letter. Apparently, "the woman who invited me" refers not to the hostess but to O'Reilly's own date for the evening, whom O'Reilly understandably does not wish to embarrass by naming.

Kinsley also pointed out that this dinner party featured a buffet with seating at random and that the guest list included many other guests with upbringings more humble than O'Reilly's, which may have been piling on, honestly.

But while the incident provides a great example of O'Reilly's stupidity and insanity, it's perhaps more revealing of his absurd ego.

While most people would have slunk away in shame or sputtered a faint apology when it became clear they had misunderstood their guest's finer point, O'Reilly seized on the incident as an example of his moral and rhetorical vigor.

He was so proud of the skirmish, in fact, that he made reference to it in his book in the middle of discussing an unrelated interview. But while he clearly "lost" the scrap with Kinsley, he and his fans think he won because he was louder and more indignant than his guest.

That's our Bill.

Then again, it's clear from reading his books that there's Bill's view of himself, and the world's view of Bill, and never the twain shall meet. You can read only so many times about people who hate him, or producers who froze him out of reporting assignments, or fifteen-year friendships that were terminated over disputes about parking fees, or boys who stood him up for dances in high school, before you're forced to wonder what his problem is.

Of course, Bill's explanation is that he's too blunt and opinionated for most people and thus ruffles feathers everywhere he goes. That's one possible interpretation. Another interpretation is that there's simply a huge gap between how Bill sees himself and how the non-brain-lesioned world sees him. And I don't mean a small gap. I mean the kind of gap you'd encounter in a paranoid schizophrenic or in Jim Carrey's character from *The Truman Show*.

I've read four of Bill's books now, which should earn me some sort of medal. I'm sorry to say, however, that out of four glistening gold mines of insanity, I've brought you mere ingots. For the full experience, you'll have to read the books yourself. You can buy most of them off the Web for less than the price of renting *Glitter*.

I leave you with this Bill quote from *The No Spin Zone*—not because it's the nuttiest or the stupidest, but because it sums up the man's life like few others. It's braggadocio, stupidity, insanity, and obtuseness all rolled into one—in other words, quintessential O'Reilly.

It comes toward the end of his next-to-last chapter—a chapter devoted to all the people who hate him or think he's not a real journalist.

After a section on how the intelligentsia resent him and his success, O'Reilly relates his pride over having finally attained the lofty heights of Scooby-Doo and Joey Lawrence:

"But the popular media are starting to come around. It took a while and we weathered some withering criticism, but in June 2001 I appeared on the cover of *TV Guide*, causing weeping and the gnashing of teeth in many quarters."

Wow, *TV Guide*? Maybe next he can get his old lady into *Hustler*.

Of course, what being on the cover of *TV Guide* has to do with being a good journalist is anyone's guess, but this is O'Reilly's world, and we are all just hapless foils. So, as O'Reilly often does for his own guests, I offer him the last word:

"I have to admit that I am not a humble guy. But that's not my fault, as all of my ancestors were conceited louts."

Thank you, Bill. I'm so glad we had this time together. Please write again.

NOTES

1   Bill O'Reilly, *The No Spin Zone: Confrontations with the Powerful and Famous in America* (New York: Broadway Books, 2001).

2. O'Reilly's stat about the barely-able-to-read fourth-graders appears to buttress his larger point that the public schools are failing.

   Here are some other numbers to ponder, however:

In 1970, 75 percent of youths between ages 25 and 29 had completed high school. By 1990, 86 percent had done so. Minority dropout rates have steadily declined—in 1940, only 12 percent of 25-to-29-year-old blacks had completed high school. In 1950, the black completion rate rose to 24 percent; in 1960, to 39 percent; in 1970, to 58 percent; in 1980, to 77 percent. The rate continued to rise in the 1980s, to 83 percent in 1990. ("The Myth of Public School Failure" by Richard Rothstein, American Prospect, March 21, 1993)

Rothstein throws out a lot of other numbers that debunk conventional wisdom on the subject of public school decline and concludes that since the mid-1960s, "academic performance has improved, especially for minority students."

Of course, 60 percent of O'Reilly's fans will dismiss Rothstein as an East Coast college boy with a Jewish-sounding name who's probably too afraid to come on *The Factor.*[3]

3. My ass.

21

THOSE WHO TRESPASS: A REVIEW OF THE FIRST SIX PAGES, AVAILABLE FOR FREE ON AMAZON.COM

FOLLOWING ARE THE opening three sentences of Bill O'Reilly's *Those Who Trespass*:[1]

As Ron Costello saw it, the nighttime media party in Edgartown provided him a wide-open window of opportunity—one he could make the most of. For he was frustrated and fed up, and what he badly needed was to satisfy a basic human need, the need for some kind of physical release. Chasing the Clintons around the resort island of Martha's Vineyard, looking on as a cracker First Family acted out its vacation in front of millions, was not just tiring for him, but unnecessary.

As you can see, before he even broke the hundred-word mark of his great American novel, O'Reilly had already used the same word three times in the space of one sentence, got in a gratuitous shot at the Clintons, and telegraphed his own sick sexual fantasies through a fictional surrogate who, we would soon discover, just happened to be a reporter for a powerful television news network.

Unfortunately, it doesn't get much better in the next five and three-quarters pages. We'll spare you most of the details, as it's basically just retread from the Andrea Mackris affidavit.

But, for instance, there's this, from paragraph two:

> Already in his sights was a pretty camerawoman lightheaded from too much vodka. Costello felt he had a real chance with this young woman, who was now walking toward the makeshift bar located in the corner of the front porch. Surely this babe was impressed with his résumé. He had been a correspondent with GNN for twenty-six years. The power and prestige of his job brought him big-time perks, like the attention of young women eager to advance in the arbitrary world of television news. That Costello's wife and kids usually stayed in D.C. during his presidential travels heightened his risk-reward ratio considerably.

Wow, Bill. You've got quite an imagination. How'd you ever come up with this stuff? You make J. D. Salinger look like a second-rate typesetter.

Just two things: First, the use of "babe" is a touch sexist and makes you sound just a bit déclassé. And, second, Costello should be spelled O'-R-e-i-l-l-y.

The first six pages of *Those Who Trespass* are an easy read but, unfortunately, this isn't much of a page-turner. It took me the better part of a three-day weekend to finish.

Being a work of fiction, however, it is fair and balanced. Except for that Clinton crack in the first paragraph. But after that it's completely free of petty partisanship. That is, until you get to page 4:

> "He could thoroughly describe the island—from the wilds of Chappaquiddick, where Edward Kennedy had abandoned a trapped and struggling Mary Jo Kopechne in a car filling with sea water, to the stately homes of Chilmark . . . "

Yeah, that does a lot to advance the story. May I also suggest, "Well up the coast was Kennebunkport, where, in his wealthy parents' stately summer home, George W. Bush plotted to bust the budget with upper-class tax cuts, ensuring thousands of children would not get health insurance coverage and would therefore die of easily treatable afflictions, such as they might get from tick bites"?

Toward the end of the first six pages of *Those Who Trespass*, available for free on Amazon.com, an assailant shoves a spoon through the roof of Costello's mouth, penetrating his brain stem. Before this happens, Costello asks, "Why, why are you doing this to me?"

Then the spoon thing happens, after which O'Reilly writes, "Ron Costello was clinically dead in four seconds"—which, I must admit, is as fair and evenhanded a description of a grisly murder as you'll ever find in a tense thriller. Indeed, if they gave out Nobel Prizes for the first six pages of books, O'Reilly would almost certainly be in the top 116,000 or so contenders.

Finally, the attacker says, "For Argentina, that's why." It almost makes you want to track down page 7 and read it. But not quite.

NOTES

1. Bill O'Reilly, *Those Who Trespass: A Novel of Murder and Television* (Baltimore, MD: Bancroft Press, 1998).

ASSESSMENT, INTERVENTION, RECOVERY

▼

HOW THIN IS THAT
SPLOTCHY SKIN?

THERE'S AN UNFORGETTABLE scene in *Fatal Attraction* when Glenn Close's character, who has had a brief but intense affair with Michael Douglas's character, tells him, "I'm not going to be *ignored*."

It's a revealing moment that tells us the protagonist is no longer dealing with a normal woman but with a seriously imbalanced sociopath whose deep insecurities manifest in bizarre acting-out behavior.

Well, *Fatal Attraction* is about a boiled rabbit removed from being a more or less complete psychological profile of Bill O'Reilly.

Rejection is a common human experience. There's really no primer on handling it, so we all have to learn to accept it in our own way. No one can be loved and respected by everyone, and there are few people who command so much respect that others will immediately drop whatever they're doing to accommodate them: the president of the United States, the pope perhaps, maybe the Dalai Lama, extremely wealthy people who are willing to wave enough money around, and, of course, Oprah. That's about it. The rest of us have to live with the occasional indignity—the realization that we think more of someone than they think of us.

Most of us handle it like adults and move on. O'Reilly handles it like a rhesus monkey who's been taken from his mother and put in an electrified wire cage.

YOU SAY YOU WERE WITH SECRETARY OF ENERGY SAM BODMAN, BUT THAT'S NOT HIS SHADE OF LIPSTICK!

ON JUNE 20, 2005, Bill encountered a little production hiccup that anyone who's ever done a talk show has had to deal with: the no-show guest.

O'Reilly had scheduled Congressman Curt Weldon for that evening's program, and when the congressman went MIA, the show quickly tabbed another guest to discuss an overexposed missing-persons story.

As in any professionally run production, the missing guest was seamlessly replaced. O'Reilly, of course, handled the situation with all the grace and dignity of Winnie the Pooh with a honey pot stuck on his head:

> Well, I have some bad news to report. Our guest didn't show up. Congressman Curt Weldon, Republican from Pennsylvania, is supposed to be here, right now, in front of you. He didn't show up. He didn't call. He didn't do anything.

Now a slightly less insane newsman would have said something like, "We hope everything is okay with the congressman and ideally this is just a little mix-up." Oh, but not our Bill. O'Reilly used this opportunity to tell his audience how he would punish the gentleman from the fair state of virtue, liberty, and independence.

"This is grossly irresponsible. So he's banned from *The Factor* forever."

Forever? As Minos sends the wicked to everlasting torment, this, too, is O'Reilly's second circle of Hell.

"And we thought you'd like to know what kind of classy guy the congressman is."

Now, we know that Bill's personality was forged in the crucible of the mean streets of Levittown, so it might be a bit presumptuous for us, who were both brought up in the pastoral splendor of Wisconsin, to question his motives. But where is this coming from, exactly?

Banned from *The Factor* forever? That's the kind of thing you'd say to a guy who's gored your oxen and defiled your virgin daughter, not someone who's missed an appointment.

The next morning we called the congressman's office to get his side. His staff kindly forwarded us this letter, which they said they would also send to O'Reilly:

Bill O'Reilly,

I have now witnessed the ultimate spin—from, of all people, you.

My scheduled taping last evening between 6–6:30 P.M. was preempted by a prolonged 5:15 P.M. meeting with the Secretary of Energy Sam Bodman regarding important National Security issues related to non-proliferation activities in the former Soviet states and by a series of 6 recorded votes on the Floor of the House that started at 6:30 P.M. and lasted until 7:15 P.M.

Contrary to your spin, my staff did give notice to your staff of both conflicts and kept them informed of my status during the scheduled taping. In addition, my staff offered for me to appear as soon as votes ended. Finally, when I tried to personally reach you, your staff was not willing to provide my staff with a suitable number.

As much as I would have enjoyed returning to your show, my job as a Member of Congress and as Vice Chairman of both the House Armed Services Committee and Homeland Security Committee is to cast my recorded vote on issues that affect our nation, in this case, the 2006 Defense Appropriations bill and related amendments which will fund our troops through 2006.

I hope you understand these obligations and I apologize for any inconvenience this unanticipated series of events caused to you and your staff.

Curt Weldon

In his June 22 Talking Points Memo, O'Reilly claimed he had received an e-mail from Weldon's chief of staff shortly before the program started that said Weldon was on his way. Then O'Reilly showed a clip of Weldon on the House floor clearing up O'Reilly's smear attacks from the previous night.

Then Bill said this:

Amazing. What a *colossal waste* of the people's time!

Now look, congressman, man to man, me and you, okay? We have an e-mail that proves your staff didn't tell you the truth. And your own *publisher* apologized to us! Don't embarrass yourself any further, sir.

This, of course, is not important in any way except to demonstrate that the truth has become elusive in America. But folks make mistakes, they should not attack as Weldon did. They should try to correct the mistake. Every human being is fallible. And we should stop the blame game. Let's all own up, all of us, instead of being a country of excuse makers and personal attackers.

So, it's pretty much a case of one man's word against another's. That one of these men spends his evenings working with the secretary of energy on policies to secure sensitive nuclear materials from the former Soviet Union while the other spends his evenings reassuring the families of missing women that their loved ones are probably dead[1] shouldn't really bias the reader one way or the other.

But who's right and who's wrong is really beside the point. The point is that Bill "Folks Make Mistakes" O'Reilly failed to come to the conclusion probably 98 percent of us would have—that his guest was unavoidably detained and that there may have been some kind of unfortunate communication breakdown between their staffs. Instead he concluded, as he reiterated in his Talking Points Memo, that the congressman "stiffed us." And once that conclusion was made, the congressman could be given no quarter.

Now, you may be thinking, "Well, Bill may have been having a bad day. Everyone loses his temper from time to time, and that can make one do things one wouldn't normally do. That they'd likely schedule a CAT scan for any other journalist who behaved this way on the air is not important. This is Bill O'Reilly, who prides himself on rattling cages and sticking it to the pinheads."

Oh, you have much to learn, young apprentice. To quote George W. Bush, "Fool me once . . . shame on . . . shame on you. Fool me . . . you can't get fooled again."

Indeed, judging from his loopy body of work, Bill's banishment of Weldon wasn't just an off-the-cuff, heat-of-the-moment decision. No, he actually writes this kind of stuff down in his books, which means not only are his higher brain centers deeply involved in these decisions, he also thinks this is the sort of example everyone should follow.

Take, for instance, this little morsel of lunacy from his book *The No Spin Zone:*

> Another example is that I have instituted the two-call rule in my personal Zone. If I call a person twice and don't receive a call back, that relationship is over. I leave a short message saying that I will not be calling again.

Now, anyone who's ever, oh, you know, lived can imagine all sorts of legitimate reasons why they might not call back a friend who's called them twice in a row. They might have a family emergency, or be called out of town suddenly on business, or be too emotionally distraught to deal with much of anything, or be near comatose in a helicopter on their way to a hospital after being mauled by a leopard, in which case the first thing they'd want to hear upon their return is an answering machine message from Bill O'Reilly saying he will no longer be complimenting them on their spectacular boobs.

Indeed, considering that Bill appears to run both his personal and his professional lives like he's some sort of demented cross between Ramses II and Mr. T, it's a wonder he has any friends at all. Or maybe he doesn't. Who knows?

If his own stories are to be believed, he dumps friends like a reality show dumps contestants. Remember, he actually writes these petty quarrels down,[2] as if he were a twelve-year-old girl telling her diary about how she's snubbing her best girlfriend because they both like Trevor—the only difference being that Bill's a fifty-six-year-old man with the backing of a major publisher who thinks this stuff is great advice for leading a successful life.

COME ON MY SHOW OR YOU TOTALLY, TOTALLY SUCK

TO BILL, HOLLYWOOD is like a giant clubhouse with a sign outside that says "No Levittowners." Inside they play cool video games and make hot brownies in their deluxe Easy Bake ovens while Bill is on his tiptoes peering in, nerdily resplendent in the unfashionable sweater and brown-and-pink Ben Gay–scented socks his near-sighted grandma knitted him for Christmas.

So it's terribly damaging to Bill's ego when a member of the cool clique declines an invitation to come over to Bill's house to play canasta with him and his mother while enjoying lukewarm Country Time lemonade and stale Nilla Wafers.

It's especially bad if a girl snubs him—particularly a really cute girl. And as we saw in Chapter 12, the cool clique that O'Reilly hates so much he simply has to try infiltrating it is Hollywood.

It was in this spirit that Bill decided one day that someone in the media simply had to get to the bottom of the scandalous Angelina-Jolie-works-tirelessly-for-and-gives-huge-sums-of-her-own-money-to-the-cause-of-alleviating-the-poor's-suffering story.

Finally! A journalist with balls!

From the May 9, 2005, *The O'Reilly Factor*:

"Now we have actress Angelina Jolie in a similar situation. She's the Goodwill Ambassador for the UN Refugee Agency. Question is, what's she doing?"

That is a good question. So we did a grueling eight-second Google search and found out for ourselves. Among the dozens of articles we found was an interview Jolie did with *National Geographic* headlined "Angelina Jolie on Her UN Refugee Role." It detailed her many travels on behalf of the United Nations High Commission for Refugees.

Dumbass.

Now, we've invited Ms. Jolie on this program six times over the course of two and a half years that she's held this UN position. She doesn't come on. In fact, she does very, very little to publicize what she's doing in the UN here in the United States.

Oh, the truth comes out. O'Reilly feels snubbed by another Hollywood starlet.

"She's done a couple of MTV interviews, which is like doing nothing. She's done an ABC morning show that nobody watches, on the weekend. And very minor appearances."

Oh God, is he bringing up ratings again?

Of course, Bill doesn't reserve his contempt for shallow actresses who help the world's most desperate refugees. He also sticks it to pinhead actors who do movies that raise awareness about genocide in Africa.

"This guy, Don Cheadle, we invited him on to talk about Darfur. He had a headache. His elbow hurt. He couldn't do it, you know. And as you said, he's got a movie out now, so he's running around. I think Cheadle's a phony."

You got that, celebs? No matter how many good things you do, if you don't come on *The Factor*, you're a phony.

Now, we don't know for certain, but there have to be dozens of other people who would like to come on a nationally televised cable show and talk about Darfur for two or three segments a night. In fact, that's about the amount of airtime Bill devoted to Natalee Holloway after the Alabama woman disappeared in Aruba in May 2005. Indeed, a November 2005 LexisNexis search of FOX News transcripts from the previous five years using the search terms

"Darfur" and "O'Reilly Factor" returned seven hits, while a search on "Natalee Holloway" and "O'Reilly Factor" returned 213. A closer examination reveals that O'Reilly himself said "Darfur" on exactly three occasions, and fully 33 percent of these involved complaints about Cheadle.

So Bill could have easily done a segment a night on Darfur, even without Cheadle's help, and still had room for two Holloway stories and maybe a plug for a *Factor* tote bag.

Yes, Bill certainly *could* help raise awareness of the continuing crises in Africa, as Cheadle has done. But he won't. Bill only likes stories that expose the suffering of ordinary folks, like suburban girls who leave bars with strangers—not people who are stupid enough to be born in East Africa.

Of course, this was never about helping poor children or people in war zones. It was about Bill's inner child, his battle for ratings, and the greater good of Bill.

That's a fight that will no doubt rage until every last Hollywood hottie has warmed a chair at FOX News.

NOTES

1. "Looks like she's dead because the five people, two arrested, three interviewed, are all shady characters" (O'Reilly commenting on the Natalee Holloway disappearance, June 6, 2005).
   " It's got to be a crime. A woman like that with a long history of responsibility. She had a steady job. . . . She just wouldn't bolt and not tell anybody" (O'Reilly commenting on the Jennifer "Runaway Bride" Wilbanks disappearance, April 29, 2005).

2. In his book *Who's Looking Out for You?*, Bill told a tale about a friend he'd known for fifteen years. You're about to hear a story on the value of holding fast to friendships, right? Not quite.
   O'Reilly wrote that the guy quibbled with him over a parking fee when they were vacationing together and asked to see the bill when O'Reilly told him what the hotel charge was. Needless to say, O'Reilly didn't like this.
   Now, it would be great to track this guy down and get his side of the story. That could be a book in itself. But we have only O'Reilly's account and our ability to read between the lines. O'Reilly said the dispute wasn't really about the money at all, "it was about power. For some reason unbeknownst to me, the guy was asserting himself."

Knowing how O'Reilly pushes people around on his show, the guy's reaction is perhaps not surprising. What may be a little surprising is that O'Reilly abruptly dumped the guy as a friend over this—"just walked away."

Yeah, Looney Tunes.

23

PRESIDENT O'REILLY GOES DOWN HARD IN THE BIG EASY: A HISTORICAL "WHAT IF?"

IT'S A TIME-HONORED nerdly pursuit to speculate on how the course of human history might have changed had one or several pivotal occurrences been replaced by altogether different events.

What if Rome hadn't fallen? What if Hitler's Germany had developed the bomb before the Allies? And, most important, what if Natalee Holloway had gone to Barbados instead?

On rare occasions, however, we're given a precise blueprint for how historical events might have unfolded under different—some might say apocalypse-ish—circumstances.

So it was during the aftermath of Hurricane Katrina, one of the worst natural disasters in American history. Bill had plenty of input, and it's here where our exercise begins.

It's late August 2005. President Bush, after spending four weeks clearing brush and noshing nacho-flavored Slim Jims on his Crawford ranch, is currently flailing about with a hornet's nest stuck on his head after a *Jackass*-style prank by Transportation Secretary Norman Mineta goes horribly wrong.

Dick Cheney remains ensconced in his secret bunker plotting world dominion on a faded Risk board to the rousing strains of Wagner and won't be disturbed.

The name of the current speaker of the House is on the tip of everyone's tongue, but the best they can come up with is a half-audible, "I know it's not Tip O'Neill" from Teddy Kennedy, who's spent the bulk of the afternoon in a Washington Imax theater watching an advance screening of *Magnificent Desolation: Walking on the Moon 3D* while gradually getting paralytic on Stolichnaya and Tang.

Finally, it's discovered that Ted Stevens, president pro tempore of the Senate, who would ordinarily be next in the presidential succession, is just a made-up name congressmen use to order prostitutes.

As Secretary of State Condoleezza Rice prepares to step in as acting president, becoming both the first woman and the first African American to hold the office, she receives an urgent call from Rupert Murdoch, who cites a previously obscure rider inserted into the USA PATRIOT Act by a secretive cabal of Republican lawmakers that says the highest-rated on-air personality at FOX News will be sworn in as commander-in-chief in the event that a) the president, vice president, speaker of the House and president pro tempore are incapacitated or unable to faithfully execute their offices; or b) a skirt is about to be put in charge of the country.

William James O'Reilly, Jr., is granted temporary executive powers, including the near carte blanche authority he insists he needs to deal effectively with the mounting crises on the Gulf Coast.

Thus, two days after Hurricane Katrina makes landfall, flooding New Orleans, touching off rampant looting and lawlessness, and stranding tens of thousands of innocent New Orleans residents without food or clean drinking water, President O'Reilly goes to work.

The following timeline is excerpted from Bob Woodward's exhaustive narrative of that fateful week, *All the President's Pinheads:*

Day 1: Showing the mental toughness of a battle-hardened triage officer, President O'Reilly sets the tone of the relief effort by quickly and decisively arranging his administration's priorities.

While surveying the damage to hundreds of homes and shops that have been razed to rubble by Katrina in Mississippi, he asks his advisors, who seem determined to focus on the widespread destruction, about reports of looting:

"Was there any exploitation of the situation as there has been in New Orleans?" O'Reilly asks.

When told of an incident where looters were seen taking merchandise that had been blown out the back of a Wal-Mart and strewn on the parking lot, O'Reilly asks, "The logical question is why weren't the police there at the Wal-Mart?"[1]

Day 2: Still demonstrating an almost monomaniacal focus on the incidents of lawlessness in the Gulf Coast region, President O'Reilly talks to people on the ground in New Orleans. Hearing of the fear, anger, and panic taking root in the city, O'Reilly wonders aloud, "Now, a lot of people wonder why, if there are no services in New Orleans, no electricity, no fresh water, no food, all of these thugs are hanging around. Did you figure that out?"

When told that a lot of people who chose not to leave ran out of important supplies and the situation then started to boil over, President O'Reilly interrupts with, "Look, I'm trying to figure out whether . . . a criminal element made a calculated decision to stay in town so they could loot."[2]

This becomes a pattern in the early days of the O'Reilly administration, with advisors who seemed intent on discussing the human face of the tragedy frequently interrupted with questions about "thugs" making off with merchandise.

O'Reilly meets with the heads of several domestic retail chains, including Wal-Mart chairman and heir to the multibillion-dollar Wal-Mart fortune, Samuel Robson Walton, who in a backroom meeting reportedly tells President O'Reilly, "Dude, shut the fuck up about the looting already. It's a few shitty televisions and some Hello Kitty crap. It's like twelve seconds of profit. Seriously."

Day 3: Feeling President O'Reilly has been chastened by the ongoing criticism, White House advisors are hopeful he will begin to see the big picture. He does. Unfortunately, it's a limited edition lighthouse print a looter has just swiped from a local Thomas Kinkade Gallery.

Emboldened, President O'Reilly declares martial law and orders law enforcement personnel to "shoot looters on sight."[3] In a heated Cabinet meeting, acting vice president Hannity and acting White House pedicurist Colmes reluctantly side with O'Reilly, while holdovers from the Bush administration for some reason insist that shooting poor, unarmed, black men in the audio section of Circuit City will only make things worse. Further, they stress, such punishment will be seen by 99.9 percent of Americans as cruel and unusual. O'Reilly counters, "But they didn't wanna leave because they sensed there might have been an opportunity to do what they eventually did."[4] He then adds, "A lot of the people who stayed wanted to do this destruction. They figured it out. . . . I'm not surprised."[5]

President O'Reilly orders Hannity to chair a special presidential commission to study roving gangs of looters who follow deadly category 5 hurricanes around the country hoping to score some sweet storm-damaged Iconic Breeze Air Purifiers and *Gilmore Girls* Season 2 DVDs.

Day 4: Frustrated that his martial-law policy has led to open warfare on inner-city streets throughout the country and buffeted by criticism that he's paying too much attention to looters and not enough to helping victims, President O'Reilly returns to his TV show determined to make a difference. He talks to a woman stranded by the flood and promises to get her out of there.[6] He then promises to send a team of rescuers to every victim who arranges an interview on FOX or manages to get past the FOX call screeners. He notes that those interviewed by Keith Olbermann on his comparatively low-rated MSNBC program will just have to suck it up and tread water.

Day 5: President O'Reilly, in a speech he insisted on writing himself, tells a desperate nation hungry for inspiration and reassurance that "thousands of Americans looked the storm reaper in the eye"[7] but inexplicably makes no mention of the Heat

Miser or Snow Miser. *Bartlett's Familiar Quotations* is forced to stop the press run on their latest edition, and FOX itself likens the performance to FDR's "The only thing we have to fear is fear itself" and Winston Churchill's "We will fight them" speeches. Confused elementary school children, on the other hand, note, quite correctly, that there's really no such thing as a storm reaper.

Day 6: In what would later be described as the most retarded initiative of his administration, President O'Reilly urges all U.S. consumers to stop buying gas on the Christian Sabbath:

> Let's buy less gas. In fact, let's buy no gas on Sundays. The USA should have a gas-free Sundays campaign between now and Christmas. None of us should buy gas on our day of rest. The oil companies and OPEC only make money when we buy their stuff. If we cut back even 10 percent on energy buying, they'll get hurt. Let's all do it. If we don't, the national economy will totter, and we'll all be poorer.[8]

Reaction to the speech is mixed. The *Wall Street Journal* calls the no-gas-on-Sundays initiative "stupid as shit," while the *New York Times* hails it as a bold move, writing, "not since Spinal Tap's Nigel Tufnel made all the numbers on his amps go to 11 has a human being proposed so enterprising yet so commonsensical an idea."

The *Weekly World News* reports that Batboy is currently acting as one of the president's chief advisors—a story that gets picked up by all the major networks, dailies, and newswires.

Unfortunately, the campaign merely causes panicked runs on gas on Saturdays and Mondays, forces patriotic old women to sleep in their cars in church parking lots, and screws up inventory control for Slurpees and microwaveable sandwiches at nearly every convenience store in the country.

Day 7: His approval ratings heading south after what the public sees as a series of gaffes, ineffectual policy proposals, and lack of attention to pressing issues, President O'Reilly focuses his energies on spiraling gas prices precipitated by disruptions in refinery capacity. O'Reilly asks oil companies to give up 20 percent of their profits to keep oil prices down.[9]

When the oil company CEOs stop laughing, they agree to attend a special White House conference at which a compromise is hammered out: They'll continue to charge what the market will bear but will give Bill back half the change they took when they picked him up by his ankles in the Oval Office and shook him.

Day 8: Looking to divert criticism from his disastrous post-Katrina strategy, President O'Reilly makes another nationally televised speech to the nation:

> the huge, bureaucratic government will never be able to protect you. If you rely on government for anything, *anything*, you're going to be disappointed, no matter who the president is.
>
> For example, engineers knew for decades the levee system in Louisiana could not withstand a category 5 hurricane, but nobody wanted to pony up the $20 billion to shore it up. That kind of decision happens all day, every day.
>
> Second point, New Orleans is not about race. It's about class. If you're poor, you're powerless, not only in America, but everywhere on earth. If you don't have enough money to protect yourself from danger, danger's going to find you. And all the political gibberish in the world is not going to change that.
>
> The aftermath of Hurricane Katrina should be taught in every American school. If you don't get educated, if you don't develop a skill, and force yourself to work hard, you'll most likely be poor. And sooner or later, you'll be standing on a symbolic rooftop waiting for help.
>
> Chances are that help will not be quick in coming.[10]

What follows is the government's now infamous "Don't Be Poor" campaign. Soon posters are put up throughout the land featuring an imposing picture of O'Reilly pointing authoritatively, framed by big block letters saying, "President O'Reilly wants

YOU to stop being poor."

Slick television ads are produced featuring dramatic images designed to capture the attention of America's youth, accompanied by a stentorian voice-over declaring, "This is you. This is you on a symbolic rooftop. Any questions?"

Day 9: On his last official day in office before President Bush returns to work, President O'Reilly decides to shore up relations with our global allies.

Ignoring the planes, naval ships, hospital ship, and dozens of relief workers and other experts France offered in aid, President O'Reilly mocks their contribution:

> Our great ally France has offered the following in the wake of Katrina: six hundred tents, a thousand cots, some kitchen kits, sixty generators, and twelve experts to advise the American Red Cross. I hope they speak English.
>
> Now I believe the 4-H Club of Bangor, Maine, has topped that offer. The boycott of France remains intact. Get your bumper stickers on billoreilly.com. To not do so would be ridiculous. Why do they even bother? Keep your cots.[11]

Then, like a Roman emperor assessing the tribute received from his subjects in far-flung lands, President O'Reilly ticks off a list of contributions from our allies:

"Japan, now Japan, 1 million dollars. Hey, you know, if I'm Bush I say, hey, keep it."[12]

In the wake of the acting president's comments, career diplomats resign in droves.

Day 10: President Bush returns to work amid cheers from Republicans, Democrats, hurricane victims, global leaders, cherubim, seraphim, tormented souls in both hell and purgatory, and the city of New Orleans, which hails Bush as "a man who can't fuck up any worse."

O'Reilly returns to his show to take on all the smear merchants and ideologues who criticized his presidency, dismissing them as politically motivated left-wing bomb-throwers and character assassins.

For his efforts, O'Reilly is given the Presidential Medal of Freedom. The next day on his radio show, O'Reilly calls it a Congressional Medal of Honor—and all is right with the world.

All O'Reilly quotes above are taken from actual *O'Reilly Factor* broadcasts in the days following Hurricane Katrina.

No kidding.

NOTES

1. *The O'Reilly Factor,* August 31, 2005.
2. Ibid.
3. *The O'Reilly Factor,* September 1, 2005.
4. Ibid.
5. Ibid.
6. *The O'Reilly Factor,* August 31, 2005, in interview with stranded hurricane victim Shirley Mae Washington, O'Reilly promised, "All right, Miss Washington, we'll get you out of there and we thank you for the call."
7. *The O'Reilly Factor,* August 31, 2005.
8. *The O'Reilly Factor,* September 1, 2005.
9. *The O'Reilly Factor,* August 31, 2005.
10. *The O'Reilly Factor,* September 5, 2005.
11. Ibid.
12. *The O'Reilly Factor,* September 6, 2005.

24

BILL:
PORTRAIT OF A SOCIOPATH

WE HAVE TO admit we've been pretty glib throughout some of this book. For instance, in Chapter 17, we wrote that Bill's *The O'Reilly Factor for Kids* was the worst book in the history of publishing.

Now, that may or may not be true. We have yet to read much of Danielle Steel's work, or that quickie book about the Brad Pitt/Jennifer Aniston breakup. Indeed, it's possible that Paris Hilton's book was more intellectually shallow and that ancient Sumerian cuneiform tablets used to record monthly wheat apportionments were more tedious. We simply don't know. If you need a more authoritative take on what is in fact the boringest piece of shit in the history of literature, consult the Library of Congress.

To be fair, then, it's more accurate to say *The O'Reilly Factor for Kids* is the worst book either of us has ever read. Which it is. By a long shot. And we've both slogged through *The Autobiography of Charles Nelson Reilly*.[1]

Here's another example. Throughout this book we've referred

to O'Reilly as being splotchy, or rife with splotch, or splotchtastic. Now, not only are we shamelessly cribbing from Al Franken, who put the notorious oreilly.splotch.jpg image on his last book's cover, we can't even verify for ourselves that O'Reilly's glorious mug is truly as befouled as Franken claims it is. It's possible that Franken, as O'Reilly himself seems to think, took an unretouched pic of Bill and spent an hour or so in Photoshop—making liberal use of the liver spot tool—to produce the gargoylish spectacle that's long since etched itself indelibly into our horror-struck temporal lobes.

The point (which we concede may by now seem as forlorn as a lone lucid synapse flicker in the electrical storm of bullshit that is Bill's head) is that a book of this scope and magnitude must at some point be brought to heel by the rigors of scientific inquiry to make its case fully.

It's one thing to offer reams of white-hospital-gown, feces-hurling insanity from the man himself, but it's quite another to present a considered diagnosis of "crazy" that can actually stand up to peer review.

Now, it's a given that we're hardly qualified to make a professional assessment of a fellow human being's mental health, even if he is a colossal nutburger. It would have been nice to get a Harvard Ph.D., or a celebrity headshrinker like Dr. Phil, or even someone who has merely played a psychologist, like Bob Newhart or Dr. Laura, to make a more thorough assessment.

But we can look shit up as well as anyone. What we've discovered through our exhaustive research, which consisted of about 10 minutes on Google and 87 minutes discussing the series finale of *Frasier*, is that sociopathic disorders are generally assessed with the Hare Psychopathy Checklist–Revised.

We've presented the categories from the checklist below with room for your own notes, giving you, the reader, a chance to interact with and mark up this book, making resale problematic and thus ensuring a marginally higher sell-through at bookstores and other retail outlets.

In your assessment, consider the evidence we've put forth as well as any independent study you may have done.

For each of the following categories, you should score 0 for no O'Reillyness, 1 for partial O'Reillyness, and 2 for quintessential O'Reillyness.

Remember, this is just for fun. We make no claims as to the actual soundness of Bill's mind, and neither should you. Calling Bill "crazy" is just silly, idle chatter, like calling the ACLU fascist or saying Michael Savage is entertaining.

Have fun. Our answers will appear at the end of the chapter.

1. GLIB and SUPERFICIAL CHARM
   SCORE _____

2. GRANDIOSE SELF-WORTH
   SCORE _____

3. NEED FOR STIMULATION
   SCORE _____

4. PATHOLOGICAL LYING
   SCORE _____

5. CONNING AND MANIPULATIVENESS
   SCORE _____

6. LACK OF REMORSE OR GUILT
   SCORE _____

7. SHALLOW AFFECT
   SCORE _____

8. CALLOUSNESS and LACK OF EMPATHY
   SCORE _____

9. PARASITIC LIFESTYLE
   SCORE _____

10. POOR BEHAVIORAL CONTROLS
    SCORE _____

11. PROMISCUOUS SEXUAL BEHAVIOR
    SCORE _____

12. EARLY BEHAVIOR PROBLEMS
SCORE _____

13. LACK OF REALISTIC, LONG-TERM GOALS
SCORE _____

14. IMPULSIVITY
SCORE _____

15. IRRESPONSIBILTY
SCORE _____

16. FAILURE TO ACCEPT RESPONSIBILITY
FOR OWN ACTIONS
SCORE _____

17. MANY SHORT-TERM MARITAL RELATIONSHIPS
SCORE _____

18. JUVENILE DELINQUENCY
SCORE _____

19. REVOCATION OF CONDITIONAL RELEASE
SCORE _____

20. CRIMINAL VERSATILITY
SCORE _____

TOTAL ALL SCORES

ANSWERS

1. GLIB and SUPERFICIAL CHARM
O'Reilly takes great pride in his verbal sparring abilities. Whether it be his BookTV confrontation with Al Franken or his CNBC *Tim Russert* debate with Paul Krugman, Bill loves to show he can argue with the best of them. He spars verbally so often that he refers to these incidents as fights and asks his audience members to give feedback as to who won.

2 POINTS. Definitely.

2. GRANDIOSE SELF-WORTH

Well, for anyone who thinks O'Reilly's britches are still fitting rather loosely, we have one thing to say: *Factor*-led boycott. We've seen Bill threaten to bring down foreign economies single-handedly. We saw him talk to people on the telephone during the aftermath of Hurricane Katrina and tell them he would personally have them rescued amid thousands of refugees trapped in the city.

I think we're safe in saying 2 POINTS on this one.

3. NEED FOR STIMULATION

Bill loves to be on the cutting edge of an issue—particularly where one doesn't exist. He exhibits an obsessive need to feed his sense of outrage. But like any dog with a bone, his obsessive gnawing eventually turns to boredom, and he moves on to the next cause. Whether it's an unknown lunatic professor speaking at a small college or a suburban girl who goes off with strangers in Aruba, Bill is angry and he wants you to be angry too.

We're giving him 2 on this one.

4. PATHOLOGICAL LYING

Bill is at his best when he's lying . . . particularly to himself. We've documented lies throughout this book. For more lies, check out sweetjesusihatebilloreilly.com, mediamatters.org, and newshounds.us.

2 POINTS. Without a doubt.

5. CONNING and MANIPULATIVENESS

Spin. This is what O'Reilly is about. Like an evangelist preacher banging his secretary on the side, Bill fights valiantly against the very evil he practices. The man spins everything from government statistics to Jesus Christ, our Lord and Savior (aka philosopher).

2 POINTS

6. LACK OF REMORSE OR GUILT

With clever bons mots like "let them eat sand," Bill feels entitled to make the vilest of comments without showing the least inclination for remorse. When he does apologize, he does so grudgingly and is more likely to continue flailing at his target than to show any genuine humility.

2 POINTS.

7. SHALLOW AFFECT

Bill has the emotional maturity of a two-year-old. His self-centeredness is reflected in the way he approaches stories. Whether complaining about the traffic he must endure on the way to the office or the time it takes to get through security at the airport, his reportage continually reflects a Billocentric universe. His compassion for others is limited to their ability to act as props in pathetic stage plays in which he casts himself as a tireless advocate for their well-being.

2 POINTS.

8. CALLOUSNESS and LACK OF EMPATHY

Perhaps Bill's lowest moment was during Hurricane Katrina when he suggested that looters should be shot on sight. Yes, Bill felt strongly that anyone taking nonessential items should be fragged. How this would have affected the rapidly deteriorating situation in New Orleans is anyone's guess.

Perhaps it would have ushered in a veritable Age of Aquarius in the Big Easy, wherein "the folks" rallied around their benevolent overlords in a show of solidarity against neighbors and relatives who had been shot in the head for pinching clock radios, touching off a hundred-year golden age of peace and prosperity highlighted by the frequent sight of young garland-festooned lasses dancing about the maypole with their beaming, peasant-dress-clad mothers. But more likely it would have been kinda like the ending of *Gangs of New York*.

2 POINTS.

9. PARASITIC LIFESTYLE

Bill makes a living by preying on people's fears. He seeks to divide at every turn. He exaggerates the poverty of his childhood to ingratiate himself with the masses. And perhaps worst of all, he is constantly peddling crap with the name of his show emblazoned on it. Constantly. However, he is no slackass.

So only 1 POINT.

10. POOR BEHAVIORAL CONTROLS

Bill exhibits little or no ability to manage his temper. His irritability, impatience, threats, aggressive impulses, and penchant for verbal abuse are not just symptoms but practically trademarkable features.

2 POINTS. If we could give him a 5, we would.

11. PROMISCUOUS SEXUAL BEHAVIOR

The guy forces phone sex on underlings. Allegedly.

2 POINTS.

12. EARLY BEHAVIOR PROBLEMS

Bill has hinted at being something of a scamp and running with a wild bunch through the mean streets of Levittown during his younger days. But he has left few overt clues about his past, so we've had to piece them together like paleontologists sifting through layers of sediment. So if his books are the Afar Region of Ethiopia, the story about O'Reilly harassing funeral mourners with a sacred incense pot to send a message to funeral directors about his altar-boy tips (as recounted, incredibly enough, in his book *Who's Looking Out for You?*) is our Lucy.

As befits this category, that youthful indiscretion is not exactly the same as killing neighborhood pets and using them in clumsy preadolescent Satanic rituals, but it's not your typical prank either. Either way, it's the kind of thing most people would keep quiet about, not include in widely circulated books.

1 POINT.

13. LACK OF REALISTIC, LONG-TERM GOALS

Well, Bill's long-term plan is an extended career of crazy talk. If there's one thing you can say about the man, it's that he has direction. He just happens to be going the wrong way.

0 POINTS.

14. IMPULSIVITY

Okay, back to Mackris. O'Reilly goes to dinner with this woman and one of her friends, whom he's never met. He subsequently brags about his sexual exploits and invites this stranger into his sexual harem.

2 POINTS

15. IRRESPONSIBILITY

Well, we have no idea about this one. Bill is highly irresponsible when it comes to his job and telling the truth, but he does appear to follow through on his commitments.

0 POINTS.

16. FAILURE TO ACCEPT RESPONSIBILITY FOR OWN ACTIONS

Bill is the Queen of Denial. He denies statements he's made minutes earlier. He denies his beliefs and biases. He takes no responsibility for his sexual peccadilloes and lets his employer make cash settlements so he can announce that both sides have agreed there was "no wrongdoing."

2 POINTS.

17. MANY SHORT-TERM MARITAL RELATIONSHIPS

Well, Bill waited until he was in his forties to get married.

We gonna give him 1 POINT.

18. JUVENILE DELIQUENCY

Again, we mostly have to speculate based on vague hints

such as, "Now, I don't want you to think that I sat around when I was your age and carefully chose my companions because of their virtues." (*The O'Reilly Factor for Kids*.) Then there was the time he got into a physical altercation with his dad and threatened him, though, to be fair, he may have just been defending himself.[2] But as far as we know, he didn't participate in any drive-bys. So . . .

1 POINT.

19. REVOCATION OF CONDITIONAL RELEASE
Nope. Bill has never done time.

0 POINTS.

20. CRIMINAL VERSATILITY
Again, "there was no wrongdoing." Whether Bill believes he did anything wrong is another story. The man has a Michael Jackson self-denial quality that's eerie.

2 POINTS.

We score him a 30. Bill's damn close to being a certifiable sociopath. Okay, so we can't say that really, but damn. Seriously.

NOTES

1. See? More creative license. We don't even know if such a work exists. Though it should. It so should.
2. In his infamous NPR *Fresh Air* interview with Terry Gross, Bill was asked about the "mini-brawl" he had with his father when he was a teenager. Here's an excerpt:

   > When I was seventeen my father and I got in some argument and he gave me a shot in the arm and I gave him a shot back, and I said from now on this is the way it's going to be. You know, I'm bigger than you now and I'm six foot four and, you know, at that point probably around 210, and he's six foot three, about two, so I said you want to put the gloves on, let's go, and that's how Irish people settle things sometimes.

25

THE FUTURE OF SWEET JESUS, I HATE BILL O'REILLY INTL.

AT **SWEET JESUS,** I Hate Bill O'Reilly headquarters, we're nothing if not enterprising. Just as Abraham launched a nation, and *Diff'rent Strokes* begat *The Facts of Life* and *Hello, Larry,* this book is just a beginning.

Indeed, we've gazed into the future, and potential O'Reilly-hating projects abound. Following are just a few sundries we've managed to slap together with the help of *Sylvia Browne's Book of Dreams,*[1] half a pack of Tarot cards, and several late nights spent watching *In Search Of . . .* on cable while looped on Diet Fanta Grape and overripened Camembert.

Of course, we firmly believe that the children are our future. But even more to the point, endless royalty checks from several vertically integrated revenue streams—all based on Bill O'Reilly's limitless arrogance and stupidity—are our future.

Among the million-dollar ideas the auguries have shown us are an O'Reilly musical, movie, several television projects, and a Caribbean cruise.

Welcome to our gold mine, and enjoy . . .

TV GUIDE PAGE

8 P.M.

NBC *Bill O'Reilly Special Victims Unit* Detectives Ailes and Murdoch must silence another female accuser before she falls into the hands of the notorious Krugman.

BRV *Queer Eye for the O'Reilly Guy* Five gay men—experts in fashion, interior decorating, cuisine, grooming, and Old Spice Superfund toxic waste removal—must try their best to turn square suburbanite Bill O'Reilly into a hip metrosexual. In the show's touching conclusion, Bill thanks the guys for their help but counsels Carson to shut up about his sexuality, saying "no one needs to know."

MTV *Real World Levittown* Amaya and Colin hook up. Rachel has a personal crisis. Bill unloads a pallet of Jergens lotion, and the roommates confront him over their $875 phone bill.

LIF *Not Without My Loofah: The Andrea Mackris Story* (2006) NC-17. Tracey Gold, Red Buttons. A beautiful, talented FOX News producer is totally weirded out by her skeevy middle-aged spaz of a boss.

OXY *Oprah after the Show* My boss sucks at phone sex.

FOOD *Bill O'Reilly: The Really Naked Chef* More ways to get wine into your date intravenously.

FNC *The O'Reilly Factor* Interviews with Rick Santorum, Natalee Holloway's dental hygienist's ex-boyfriend's pedicurist's alpaca trainer, and a Spin Stops Here toaster cozy.

CNN *Paula Zahn Now* Paula and her guests get totally crushed by *The Factor*, okay? Why is this even on?

ABC *Bill O'Reilly and Dawn* Guests include Flip Wilson, Dinah Shore, Ann Coulter, and the Ward Churchill Dancers.

8:30

MTV *Punk'd* Newsman Bill O'Reilly stabs Ashton Kutcher in the eye with a lobster fork and banishes him from *The Factor* forever.

FOX *Daddy Needs a New Producer, So She Might as Well Have a Honkin' Big Rack, All Right?* Bill O'Reilly, Clarence Thomas, and Russ Meyer, Jr., select from a field of twenty-five hopefuls vying for a chance at a cable news producer job and a prize package worth $60 million.

NBC *Bill & Grace* Sparks fly when Bill and Jack become infatuated with the same woman, until Bill finds out she's really a drag queen and banishes her from *The Factor* forever. When Grace confronts Bill over their $875 phone bill, he banishes her from *The Factor* forever. Karen writes a smear book, and Bill banishes her from *The Factor* forever. Special guests Madonna and Dick Morris.

CAR *Captain Bill and the Cataract Crusaders* Captain Bill frees another nine-year-old from the clutches of the evil Fun 'n' Sun.

9 P.M.

10 *Elimidate* An attractive young bartender must choose between Bill O'Reilly, Robert Novak, Sean Hannity, and George Will. Bill awkwardly removes his shirt on the dance floor.

PBS *Nova* An investigation into the fascist movement to include only science in high school science curricula.

A&E *Sexual Harassment, She Wrote* Jessica finally relents and leases a studio apartment in Manhattan outside FOX News headquarters.

DOCUMENTARY

"Let Them Eat Sand: A National Geographic Special"

In the first of a fascinating three-part series, popular FOX

News television host Bill O'Reilly explores the history of the Afghan people. Through exhaustive interviews with ordinary Afghanis, experts on Central Asia, members of the United States diplomatic corps, relief agencies such as Oxfam, and international human rights organizations such as Amnesty International and Human Rights Watch, O'Reilly concludes that the Afghan people's inability to overthrow the repressive Taliban prior to the 2001 U.S. invasion was their own fucking fault.
9 p.m. National Geographic Channel

Memo

TO: Louis B. Mayer or current occupant, Metro-Goldwyn-Mayer
FROM: Joseph Amann and Tom Breuer
RE: *Sweet Jesus, I Hate Bill O'Reilly* major motion picture

Dear Mr. Mayer,

With the tremendous success of our book and Web site, our many O'Reilly-related television projects, and the seventy-four-week sold-out run of *Sweet Jesus, I Hate Bill O'Reilly: The Musical*, we feel the time is ripe to produce a feature-length motion picture.

Our efforts thus far have proven that Mr. O'Reilly can be hated in a wide variety of media, and we believe the silver screen is no exception. We would like to make this one a "talkie" as we feel it opens up many exciting possibilities.

Our film is *Broadcast News* meets *Nixon* meets *Medea* meets *A Clockwork Orange* meets *The Silence of the Lambs* meets *Nosferatu*, but with a heart. O'Reilly is batshit crazy, but we plan on making him a more sympathetic character by giving him a puppy, which he eventually eats, but then also a kitten, which he does not.

Here's a thumbnail sketch of the plot: When his Caribbean cruise is canceled due to complete, utter, abject lack of interest, O'Reilly decides to go anyway. When young, attractive girls and wealthy dowagers start disappearing from the ship, O'Reilly, the straight-shooting, by-the-book investigative journalist must try to solve the crimes with the help of his loose-cannon wisecracking sidekick, Drudge, and Rasta, the lovable newest addition to the Radio Jamaica K-9 unit—which, as we mentioned, O'Reilly butchers and eats in the first act.

With the help of Drudge and O'Reilly's love interest, a beautiful young psychologist (played by Dr. Joyce Brothers, we hope), O'Reilly gradually unravels an intricate web of evidence, only to discover that all clues point to him as the killer.

O'Reilly then must fight to clear his name, but he can't because, of course, he's guilty. When he can no longer deny his own guilt, he denounces himself as a smear merchant, banishes himself from *The Factor* forever, buys a Jazzercise franchise in Vancouver and spends his evenings in seamy dives insisting to inquisitive patrons that the only reason they recognize him is because he was once a Breck Girl.

The movie will recall classic film noir of the early 1940s, only this time with Corey Feldman, Jo Anne Worley, and Bruce Jenner, who tragically hasn't worked since *Can't Stop the Music*.

We're confident the success of this film will spawn a series of equally successful sequels, including *Sweet Jesus, I Still Hate Bill O'Reilly*, *Sweet Jesus, I Hate Bill O'Reilly Academy: Back in Training*, *Eternal Sunshine of the Spotless Face*, and, of course, the ecumenically titled *Sweet L. Ron Hubbard, I Hate Bill O'Reilly*.

We hope to contact your flunkies soon regarding this very exciting project. Thank you for your attention.

Messrs. Amann and Breuer

SWEET JESUS, I HATE BILL O'REILLY: THE MUSICAL

WHILE IT'S EVERY humble scribbler's secret wish to stand before the footlights on the Great White Way, most of us have to live our lives safely moored within the dull, uninspiring glow of our word processors.

Alas, the actor's life is not for us. Amann's knees would scarcely withstand the nightly rigors of a real Broadway musical, and at best Breuer's dancing resembles the faltering, frenetic steps of an elderly man being remote-controlled by a pair of drunk wolverines.

Which isn't to say we can't still dream. Indeed, our dreams are splattered in lurid detail all over one of this book's appendices. Sorry.

Check out *Sweet Jesus: I Hate Bill O'Reilly: The Musical* at the back of the book.

SWEET JESUS, I HATE BILL O'REILLY: THE CARIBBEAN CRUISE

WHEN BILL O'REILLY announced he would be cruising the Caribbean in a trip sponsored by the conservative Thomas More Law Center, we had just two questions: Where do we buy tickets, and are drinks included?

Sadly, not all dreams come true.

Of course, we had every intention of going on The Battle for American Values cruise with Bill. On June 6, 2005, we called Corporate Travel Service to secure our reservations. We imagined how much fun we'd have with O'Reilly on the open seas. We planned to buddy up with FOX's humble correspondent and use the stories of our antics to help promote this book. Alas, on that fateful day we were greeted not by a travel agent but by this disheartening automated message:

> Hello and thank you for your interest in the Thomas More Law Center Cruise with Bill O'Reilly. Unfortunately, the cruise did not have the participation that all parties anticipated. Although the guest appearance by Mr. O'Reilly and the other speakers have been canceled, the ship will still sail . . .

When we contacted Corporate Travel Service, they told us that the goal was to get eight hundred people onboard for the Caribbean fantasy week with O'Reilly. Even though the cruise was promoted on *The O'Reilly Factor* and O'Reilly's Web site, they sold only a fraction of the tickets available.

We couldn't believe it, so we contacted the Thomas More Law Center. A representative told us that the response was "surprisingly poor." The organization ultimately renegotiated with Holland America Cruise Line in an attempt to pare down the expected guest list but still hold the event as scheduled. Sales continued to trickle in, and finally, after two more negotiations with Holland America to reduce the group size, the event was finally scrapped.

We were crestfallen. How would O'Reilly ever win The Battle for American Values if he couldn't manage to launch a single ship? So the date passed. Our Caribbean fantasies of a floral-shirted O'Reilly, intoxicated by the scent of his own Hai Karate, making awkward passes at shipboard staff, languished beneath the hoarfrost of another bitter Midwestern winter.

As we were putting the finishing touches on this book, we tried to think of ways we could reclaim our shattered dreams.

Yes, if there were only a way . . .

NOTES

1. Sylvia Browne with Lindsay Harrison, *Sylvia Browne's Book of Dreams* (New York: Dutton, 2002).

SWEET JESUS, I HATE BILL O'REILLY: THE MUSICAL

NARRATOR: Throughout history, great men have risen to glory, living epic lives, until the fell winds of tragedy brought low the tall cedars of righteousness onto their kickass empires of goodness. Caesar. Richard III. Seminal eighties Christian metal band Stryper. William James O'Reilly, Jr.

The fates of two of these grand figures were captured lyrically and immortally by the great Bard. Stryper got back together a couple of years ago and recently released an album. Their saga goes on. I shit you not.

But, alas, O'Reilly's story has yet to be told. And so, tonight, we gather to right a great injustice.

For O'Reilly's is a compelling tale: a rags-to-riches fable ripped from the pages of antiquity.

Raised in the Dickensian squalor of 1950s-era Levittown, New York, O'Reilly once proclaimed, "You don't come from any lower than I came from on an economic scale."

But perhaps his modesty prevented him from elaborating further on the pitiless poverty that shaped his grim worldview. For when it came time to dress for his lessons, the other children at his private school, as recounted in a heartrending December 2000 story in the *Washington Post*, "scorned him for his 'two sports coats,' bought at the unfashionable Modell's."

Then there were the used cars, the summer vacations on a Greyhound to Miami, and the father with the hair-trigger temper who struggled to make ends meet as a currency accountant for a successful multinational oil company.

And when London called for a year of study abroad, O'Reilly answered. And though his family was dirt-poor, his parents somehow managed to send him overseas without financial aid.

After college, Bill would go on to teach high school, eventually landing a job in broadcasting.

From his disco days at local network affiliates, to a job as a correspondent for the big boys, to the rise of his own media empire, to his legacy as the nation's highest-rated cable news personality who's asked an employee if she had a vibrator, he stayed true to the simple, wholesome values of his hometown.

And so this is where our story begins—the story of the greatest man to ever rise from the mean streets and crumbling corridors of Levittown, New York, not counting Bill Griffith, creator of Zippy the Pinhead.

It begins, fittingly enough, on a dusty front stoop as the sun sets on another sultry New York summer's day.

CURTAIN

"Levittown"
(To the tune of "Summertime" from *Porgy and Bess*)

MRS. O'REILLY:
Levittown, and the livin' is easy
Though money's scarce
And the smokestacks are high
I can dream
Of a future for my son

Oh baby Billy, don't, oh don't you cry
Though we're poor
We're gonna get ya some learnin'
Grow you up
all smart and spry
The best we can do
is two semesters in London
Oh baby Billy, don't, oh don't you cry

MR. O'REILLY:

Billy Boy
You best listen to Daddy
Or I swear
I'll punch you square in the eye
You best never
Become a liberal pussy
Oh baby Billy, don't, oh don't
(becomes angry)
Don't you fuckin' cry

MRS. O'REILLY:

Levittown, and the livin' is easy
But we got nothin'
And the smokestacks are high
Dad's mean and loud
But your mama's real lovin'
So hush, little Billy, don't
Don't you cry

FADE TO BLACK

SETTING: A high school playground. **O'REILLY** is surrounded by a group of boys who have begun taunting him.

BOY #1: Hey, O'Reilly. Nice sports coat. Get that at Modell's?
BOY #2: Yeah, it's almost as snazzy as the other one. Can only afford two, huh?

O'REILLY: C'mon guys, cut it out. Enough with the raspberries, okay? My pa's a poor oil company currency accountant. Why don'tcha lay off?

BOY #3: Where ya goin' to college, O'Reilly? The University of London? Hope ya like cleanin' floors, 'cause that's what yer gonna be doin'.

BOY #1: Yeah, either that or flippin' burgers in a diner. If you're lucky!

BOY #2: Have fun at your loser private schools, loser.

O'REILLY (whimpering): Knock it off, guys.

"It's a Hard-Luck Life"
(To the tune of "It's the Hard-Knock Life" from *Annie*)

O'REILLY:
It's a hard-luck life for me
It's a hard-luck life, you see
Papa thinks that
BOYS: You're a lass
O'REILLY: He would kick ol'
BOYS: Doc Spock's ass

ALL:
It's a hard-luck life
Got no clothes to speak of, hell
Just two sports coats from Modell's
O'REILLY: Old used cars
BOYS: Instead of new
O'REILLY: Bused to Florida
BOYS: 'Steada flew
ALL: It's a hard-luck life

O'REILLY: Don't it feel like everybody has a trust fund
BOYS #1&2: Don't it look like you can't dress anyhow
BOYS #3&4: Every day from smelly Levittown you're bused in
BOYS #1&2: Every day it's iceberg lettuce with your chow

O'REILLY:
No one's there when your clothes cannot be salvaged
No one cares when your college fund is less
U of London's all I'll likely ever manage
BOYS: And your dad thinks you'd look better in a dress, ohhhh!

ALL: Empty-trust-fund life
Dirty-sports-coats life
Crappy-mid'-class life
No-tomorrow life
BOY #1: Vanderbilts you never see
O'REILLY: Vanderbilt, what's that, who's he?
ALL: No one cares for you, no how
When you come from Levittown
It's a hard-luck life!
BOY #2 ([spoken] imitating O'Reilly's dad): You're gonna clean your room
Or you can forget about that year studying abroad in Europe
O'REILLY: Slap him so he cannot see
Jab him like a killer bee
Bash his skull into a tree
I love you, Papa O'Reilly
BOY #2 ([spoken] imitating O'Reilly's dad): Get to work!
You're a sissy! If I ever meet Dr. Spock, there's gonna be violence!
O'REILLY:
It's a hard-luck life for me
It's a hard-luck life you see
No one cares for you, no how
When you come from Levittown
It's a hard-luck life
It's a hard-luck life
It's a hard-luck life!

FADE TO BLACK

SETTING: A disco club in Anytown, USA. The seventies are in full swing, and the dance floor is a heaving mass of sweaty hard bodies and hormones. Suddenly, a sea of polyester and platform shoes parts, and a young, mutton-chopped **O'REILLY** saunters onto the dance floor with his local news team, catching the eye of several foxy ladies.

SPORTSCASTER: Whoa, Bill, looks like you could score more'n Dr. J here tonight, if ya catch my drift.

WEATHERMAN: I feel a warm front comin' in. Hot, humid, with a 90 percent chance of *disco inferno*.

O'REILLY: All right, all right, boys. Now here's the news. I do my interviews one on one, okay? I've got my eye on a very special lady. She looks foxier than Audrey and Judy Landers combined. Take a hike, okay?

(**O'REILLY** walks away and approaches **DISCO LADY**.)

WEATHERMAN: Whoa, Bill's the king. He gets more lovin' than Captain Stubing.

SPORTSCASTER: Yeah, and you get less than Gopher.

WEATHERMAN: Sit on it, Bob.

"Hey O'Reilly"
(To the tune of "Big Spender")

DISCO LADY:
The minute he walked in the club
You could see that disco music was his thing
A dancing machine
Gloria Gaynor!
Yeah, get down
Even Catholic girl 'hibitions lowered by the howls

So let me ask what say you
Let's extend this date to your place or mine

Hey O'Reilly
Sock it to me all the night
Hey, let's have some fun, fun, fun
And see what happens next, next
I can show you my pad
You're a hot hoofin' lad

The minute he walked in the club
You could see that disco music was his thing
A dancing machine
Gloria Gaynor!
Yeah, get down
Even Catholic girl 'hibitions lowered by the
howls

So let me get right to the point
I'd like some tasty wine, maybe intravenously
Hey O'Reilly
Hey O'Reilly
Hey O'Reilly
Use that loofah thing on me

FADE TO BLACK

SETTING: It's the mid-nineties. **O'REILLY** is at a large conference table surrounded by several lawyers and various other suits. With him is **MURDOCH. O'REILLY** is signing a contract.

O'REILLY: Well, that's that. Signed my life away. Hope you know what you're doin', Murdoch.

MURDOCH: Oy, we're gonna take it to 'em, Billy. Fair and balanced, all the way. The left-wing press is dead as a dingo now.

O'REILLY: Hope you're right, Murdoch. I'm puttin' a lot on the line here. Where did you and your suits come up with this big idea, anyhow?

MURDOCH: Well, let me just tell you like this . . .

"Springtime for Rupert"
(To the tune of "Springtime for Hitler" from *The Producers*)

CHORUS:
Republicans were having trouble
Thanks to Hill and Billy
Needed a new news channel to make the Dems look silly
Where oh where was it?
Our slick new crock of shit?
We looked around and then we found
Reporters who'd counterfeit

MURDOCH:
And now it's springtime for Rupert and O'Reilly
Wingnuts are happy and gay
We're marching with the GOP
Colmes still don't have no washroom key

Springtime for Rupert and O'Reilly
America hates liberals again
Springtime for Rupert and O'Reilly
Massachusetts, don't marry those men
Springtime for Rupert and O'Reilly
Winter for Franken and France
Springtime for Rupert and O'Reilly

CHORUS: Springtime, springtime, springtime, springtime
Springtime, springtime, springtime
MURDOCH: Gay bashers go into your dance
COULTER: I have no soul, may be a man, last name Coulter, first
name Ann
HANNITY: Don't be a liberal, be a real American, Hillary's a
lesbo, Bill likes heroin

GUESTS: O'Reilly is coming, O'Reilly is coming, O'Reilly is
coming

GUEST #1 (spoken): I'm a lefty!

GUEST #2 (spoken): I'm secular!

GUEST #3 (spoken): I'm with the ACLU!

O'REILLY: Springtime for Rupert and O'Reilly

ALL GUESTS: We're liberals!

O'REILLY: Cut their mics, don't you see

They've had their time, and that's a crime

Last word's for me

Cut their mics, I'm on the fence

But these liberal bomb-throwers make no sense

Everything I do is for the folks

I'm a balanced, independent kinda bloke

Cut his mic, shut his hole

FOX is very fair and balanced . . . that's our goal

CHORUS: FOX is very fair and balanced

O'REILLY: Cut his mic!

CHORUS: FOX is very fair and balanced

O'REILLY: Cut his mic!

CHORUS: FOX is very fair and balanced

O'REILLY: . . . that's our goal

CHORUS:

Ol' Billy, he's no wiltin' lily

He scares young children and his guests

He's got them hiding under desks

Ol' Billy, oh he's quite a dilly

They're freaking out at CNN

Oh *Crossfire,* he is crushing them

And Paul Begala's just a fem

Ol' Billy, he's no wiltin' lily

O'REILLY:

I was on a tabloid show, replaced by Deborah Norville

Wanted a new venue where they'd let me spout some more swill

FOX, it was brand new
You'd have done it too
I said "me like"
And grabbed a mic
Now Murdoch's making do

O'REILLY (spoken): But it wasn't always so easy
It was the go-go eighties
I was shakin' my booty in the dance clubs
And working at a local TV station
Then I got a call from the networks and, would you believe it?
They made me a correspondent. A correspondent!

O'REILLY (singing):
If it's a slow news day
I'll just grandstand my way
The thing you gotta know is
Journalism's show biz
Look at me
Watch the show
I'm the Irish Lillian Gish, don'tcha know?
We've got marching orders
From money hoarders, it's clear
Liberals take a hike
Or I'll cut your mic, you'll see
It's all about me!
And now it's . . .

CHORUS:
Springtime for Rupert and O'Reilly
Right wing's the right wing today
Pigs flying in the skies again
Bushies are on the rise again
Springtime for Rupert and O'Reilly
Big yachts are sailing once more
Springtime for Rupert and O'Reilly

O'REILLY: Means that . . .

CHORUS: Soon we'll be knowing . . .

O'REILLY: We've got to be knowing . . .

CHORUS: You know we'll be knowing . . .

O'REILLY: You bet we'll be knowing . . .

O'REILLY & CHORUS: We'll know that ol' Hillary's a whore!

FADE TO BLACK

SETTING: The newsroom at FOX. There's lots of activity—people milling around working on stories and chattering.

O'REILLY is rushing to a meeting when he gets stopped in the hall by **AILES.**

AILES: Whoa, Bill. Where's the fire, pal? Hey, I need just a minute of your time.

O'REILLY (agitated): Better make it quick, Roger. This Hillary story's about to blow wide open.

AILES: Well, it can wait. I swear, I get dizzy just watchin' ya.

O'REILLY (smiling and shaking his head): Sorry, Roger. I get so caught up sometimes. You know how it is.

AILES: I do. Now, see here, let me introduce you to your new producer. Name's Andrea Mackris. She's a real pistol. I think you two'll hit it off.

O'REILLY (clearly smitten): N-n-n-nice to meet ya, An-An-An-Andrea.

MACKRIS (shaking his hand): Likewise, I'm sure.

O'REILLY (still shaking her hand): If there's anything I c-c-c-can do for ya, j-j-j-just gimme a call.

MACKRIS (now feeling uncomfortable): Sure. I'll do that. Thanks, Mr. O'Reilly.

AILES (rolling his eyes): I can see things are gonna get pretty intra'sting 'round here.

O'REILLY drifts back, alone, to his office.

"Andrea"
(To the tune of "Maria" from *West Side Story*)

O'REILLY:
An-DREE-a
It's the hottest name I've ever heard
An-DREE-a, An-DREE-a, An-DREE-a, An-DREE-a
The most spectacular boobs in the world in a single
word . . .
An-DREE-a, An-DREE-a, An-DREE-a, An-DREE-a,
An-DREE-a, An-DREE-a . . .
An-DREE-a. Just leered at a girl named An-DREE-a
and suddenly the office will never be so safe for she
An-DREE-a. I will pleasure myself to An-DREE-a.
And suddenly I've found how truly skanky Ann
Coulter can be
An-DREE-a, say it loud and there's disco playing
Say it too much and I'll soon be paying
An-DREE-a, I'll never stop ogling An-DREE-a.
An-DREE-a, An-DREE-a, An-DREE-a, An-DREE-a,
An-DREE-a, An-DREE-a . . .

FADE TO BLACK

SETTING: **O'REILLY**'s desk at FOX. He's on the air, discussing immigration with two guests, a **CONSERVATIVE** and a **LIBERAL**.

O'REILLY: What say you, professor? Thousands of illegals come
over the border every year and the government's doing nothin'
about it.

LIBERAL: Bill . . .

O'REILLY: It's a national emergency. We can't keep track of 'em,
professor.

LIBERAL: Bill . . .

O'REILLY: Why shouldn't we use the military to patrol the borders?

CONSERVATIVE: I agree with you completely, Bill. Thousands pouring over the border every year, and we have no way to monitor this. How many are potential terrorists? How many are criminals? How many are hiding in your basement or attic right now, planning on giving your daughter an STD?

LIBERAL: Bill . . .

O'REILLY: Let him speak, professor.

CONSERVATIVE: I was done.

O'REILLY: Well, it's a disgrace. A national disgrace. Let me tell ya . . .

"525,600 Immigrants"
(To the tune of "525,600 Minutes," from *Rent*)

O'REILLY:
525,600 immigrants, 525,000 illegals live here
525,600 immigrants. How do you measure, measure
your fear?
In Mexicans, Guatemalans, Hondurans in Nicaraguans
In green cards, in gangstas, in murder and strife
In 525,600 immigrants, how do you measure this
American life?
How about druuuuugs? How about drugs? How about drugs?
Measure in drugs. Vans full of drugs. Shipments of drugs.

CONSERVATIVE:
525,600 immigrants. 525,000 foreigner scares.
525,600 immigrants. How can you stop them without
the military there?

LIBERAL: So why can't we help and why do we sigh?
Our flag should be burned, and no more soldiers should die.

O'REILLY (spoken): Shut up! Shut up! Cut his mic! Now!

O'REILLY: It's another Talking Points, for this story never ends
What say you professor on this disturbing trend?
Remember the thugs. Remember the thugs. Remember the

thugs. Measure in thugs. Measure, measure this trend in thugs. Trucks full of thugs.

FADE TO BLACK

SETTING: Mexican restaurant in Manhattan. **O'REILLY** is discussing current events with his FOX News cronies when the conversation takes an unexpected turn.

O'REILLY: You know, Hannity, I realize it's Halloween and everything, but I'm thinkin' colorful fifties-era Latin dresses may have been a bad idea after all.

SEAN HANNITY: You are so gay, O'Reilly.

JOHN GIBSON: Shit, it's Franken! And he's got his Air America pals with him.

HANNITY: They got a lotta nerve comin' here. They know this is our turf.

O'REILLY: Hold on, boys. I'll handle this.

"Air America"
(Sung to the tune of "America" from *West Side Story*)

O'REILLY:

Oh Al Franken, my competition
Looks more Judeo than Christian
Always the lawsuits I'm filing
Always the judge and jury smiling
And producers dialing
And the bile I'm spewing
And my ass he's chewing
I love the ol' FOX News Channel
What do you say, my right-wing panel?

O'REILLY AND GANG:

I can't abide Air America
Pinheads lied on Air America

Pussies cried on Air America
Socialists on Air America

FRANKEN: Liberals backing the right horse
O'REILLY: Go back to Russia and eat borscht
FRANKEN: We want democracy to soar
O'REILLY: I went to Thailand and watched whore

FRANKEN AND GANG: Freedom blooms on Air America
Ratings zoom on Air America
Bush is doomed on Air America

O'REILLY: Clintons loom on Air America
FRANKEN: Hosts tell the truth and have no splotch
O'REILLY: I have a burning in my crotch
FRANKEN: We have to take on the right wing
O'REILLY: I'll take that little loofah thing . . .

O'REILLY:
Millionaires fund Air America
Billionaires spun Air America
Trust fund heirs on Air America
FRANKEN: Death tax fine on Air America

INTERLUDE

FRANKEN: We keep it real and we have pride
O'REILLY (points to self): Ratings so big that I can't hide
FRANKEN: We cover all the news we know
O'REILLY: White woman's missing, I must go . . .

O'REILLY:
Still have to hate Air America
Nobody likes Air America
I've never heard Air America
But Smalley is on Air America

FADE TO BLACK

SETTING: FOX News/CNN mixer. The theme is a fifties-style sock hop. Some of the **FOX GUYS** have stepped outside for a smoke. They're sitting on bleachers near a softball field. The **FOX GALS** are chatting near a dance floor.

HANNITY: So, Bill. Heard ya called Mackris last night. How'd it go?

O'REILLY (cockily): You don't wanna know!

FOX GAL #1: So, Andrea. Hannity tells me Bill called you.

MACKRIS: Don't remind me.

FOX GAL #2: He's cute. You know, not Fabian cute. More like Richard Nixon after the stroke cute. But cute.

MACKRIS: Listen, I'm gonna throw up. Seriously. You've really just got to stop talking now.

GIBSON: You gonna get in her pants, O'Reilly?

O'REILLY: Come on, guys. You know I don't kiss and tell.

HANNITY: What are you talking about? You wrote two chapters in your last book about getting laid.

O'REILLY: Well, let me just put it this way . . .

"Summer Callin'"
(To the tune of "Summer Nights" from *Grease*)

O'REILLY: Summer callin', had me a blast

MACKRIS: Summer callin', boy was he crass

O'REILLY: Phoned a girl, crazy for me

MACKRIS: Took a call, gross as can be

BOTH: Workin' days, driftin' away, to uh-oh, those workday nights

FOX GUYS: Well-a well-a well-a, huh
Is there more, is there more
Oh, this can't be a joke

FOX GALS: Please no more, please no more
Did he show you his Polk?

O'REILLY: She was soapin' up in the tub

MACKRIS: Said that he could help with my scrub

O'REILLY: She said no finger without a ring

MACKRIS: He'd reach low with that falafel thing

BOTH: Workin' days driftin' away, to uh-oh a producer's plight

FOX GALS: Well-a well-a well-a, huh

Please no more, please no more

Oh you really must stop

FOX GUYS: Is there more, is there more?

Did she call up a cop?

MACKRIS: I was sitting home and alone

O'REILLY: Then I made a call on the phone

MACKRIS: It was Bill, strokin' his wand

O'REILLY: Told her 'twas an anal jihad

MACKRIS: Said he'd give orgasms so fine

O'REILLY: And fill her up with an IV of wine

FOX GALS: Please no more, please no more

Oh, our stomachs will churn

FOX GUYS: Is there more, is there more?

Tell us what did she learn?

MACKRIS: Got too friendly, please let it end

O'REILLY: Said vibrators could be her friend

MACKRIS: Oh it really was quite a fright

O'REILLY: Kept her tuned for Mr. Right

BOTH: Lawsuits are well on the way, but uh-oh those summer days

FOX GUYS: Is there more, is there more

Did you get her alone?

FOX GALS: Please no more, please no more

Did you discard your phone?

O'REILLY: I turned colder, finished the deed

MACKRIS: Then my ears started to bleed

O'REILLY: I just thanked her, then took a bow

MACKRIS: Oh, but FOX is a cash cow

BOTH: Summer calls, oh it takes balls, but oh, what a legal fight

FOX GALS: Please no more! Please no more!

FADE TO BLACK

SETTING: O'Reilly's office. News of the Andrea Mackris lawsuit has just hit the media and **O'REILLY** is getting an earful from **AILES**.

AILES: You've gotta fix this, Bill. This could sink your show. Didn't you ever think of that?

O'REILLY (flustered): But, but, but . . .

AILES: Just make it go away. We've got too much invested in you.

AILES exits. Outside there's a clamor. *Factor* fans have gathered, hoping to hear from Bill. They're shouting things like "say it ain't so," "tell us the truth" and "we believe you, Bill!"

O'REILLY opens his window . . .

"Don't Cry for Me *Factor* Viewers"
(To the tune of "Don't Cry for Me Argentina" from *Evita*)

O'REILLY:

It wasn't so sleazy, not so deranged

But let me explain this ordeal

And I still need my audience when it's all said and done

They won't believe me

The elites will now say I'm in quite a stew

And claim I'm caught up in these crimes

But the folks will stand by me, stay true

I had to challenge this extortion,
though you'll think it strange
Couldn't spend sixty million, oh no
And what could I tell my wife and my son?

So I chose lawsuits
Running 'round, telling everyone I knew
But no one believed me at all
What's in that complaint just isn't true

Don't cry for me, *Factor* viewers
The truth is I never called her
Well, she did not answer
Though I left a message
She did not call back
There was no wrongdoing

And as for my fortune and as for fame
They never mattered to me
Though it seemed to the world that low ratings might
sting

Those are just numbers
They are the encumbrances they always looked to be
But please don't switch to Larry King
I love the folks, and hope they tune in

Don't cry for me, *Factor* viewers
The truth is I never called her
Well, she did not answer
Though I left a message
She did not call back
There was no wrongdoing

Have I said enough?

This is the most evil thing to ever happen to me

I'll never speak of it again, and despite the detailed transcripts

I promise every word I say is true

FADE TO BLACK

SETTING: News reports are coming in on the lack of an operational link between Iraq and al-Qaeda as well as the failure to find WMD in Iraq.

Sitting alone in his office, **O'REILLY** hears the FOX News team launch into a cacophony of backpedaling and analysis.

O'REILLY clutches a newspaper. On one side the headline is "O'Reilly hit with Sex Lawsuit," on the other, "No WMD in Iraq." **O'REILLY** picks up a trade magazine: "After Sex Scandal, Can *Factor* Stay on Top?"

O'REILLY: It's not fair. It's just not fair. I did everything right.

AILES enters.

AILES: Yes you did, Bill. Yes you did. No regrets, okay, fella? We're still a team. And our boy's still in the White House. We got the liberals on the run, all right?

O'REILLY (wiping a tear from his face with his sleeve): Yeah, you're right. No regrets, Roger.

AILES: All right, big guy. Let's go. Chin up. Who ever heard of a mopey O'Reilly?

O'REILLY: You said it, Roger. Got a show to do. I'm still the ratings champ, huh?

AILES: That's more like it.

AILES exits. **O'REILLY** starts to leave, but suddenly the lights dim, and a spotlight hits him . . .

"What I Did for Rove"
(To the tune of "What I Did for Love" from *A Chorus Line*)

O'REILLY:
Kiss Iraq goodbye,
And forget about Osama
Kept my ratings up, Hannity's too
And I can't regret what I did for Rove
What I did for Rove

Look, the stockpiles are dry
There's more al-Qaeda in Alabama
It's as if we always knew
But I won't forget what I did for Rove,
What I did for Rove.

Wrong?
No, George is never wrong.
As liberals prattle on
The spin's what we'll remember

Kiss today goodbye,
It's a clusterfuck tomorrow,
But we did what we had to do
Won't forget, can't regret
What I did for Rove.

CHORUS (Hannity, Colmes, Gibson, Brit Hume, et al.):
What I did for Rove.

O'REILLY: What I did for

ALL:
Rove
Karl is never wrong.
As critics jabber on

The spin's what we'll remember.
Kiss Iraq goodbye.

O'REILLY: And point me toward the next war

CHORUS: Point me toward the next war.
We did what we had to do.
Won't forget, can't regret
What I did for Rove
What I did for Rove

O'REILLY: What I did for

ALL: Rove!
Curtain

THE BILL O'REILLY FUND

IN BILL'S WORLD, it's not just pinhead people that could use a good smearin', but pinhead organizations as well. These range from media watchdog groups that point out his lies, to civil rights organizations that fight to protect our country's founding principles, to local high schools that produce plays he doesn't like.

They form a motley patchwork of groups held together by one common thread—a big fuzzy Irish bundle of rage with a bad cable TV show.

You can help fight back. Please take a close look at the information on the following worthy organizations. We've provided URLs and contact info. If, after checking them out, you'd like to make a donation in Bill's name, who are we to stop you?

Media Matters for America

www.mediamatters.org

Media Matters is a Web-based, not-for-profit media watchdog group that monitors O'Reilly and other conservative media personalities and news outlets. Bill despises them. They were, of course, an invaluable resource for this book.

Go to the group's home page and click on the Donate link at

the top. Make sure to write "The Bill O'Reilly Fund" in the donation form's comments field.

News Hounds

www.newshounds.us

With the slogan "We watch FOX so you don't have to," this group of bloggers provides a steady source of information on the network's conservative bias and spin. You can support them by going to their Web site and clicking on Make A Donation.

National Public Radio

www.npr.org

Ever since his famous interview with *Fresh Air*'s Terry Gross, O'Reilly has been on a rampage against NPR. Bill came off like a paranoid lunatic in the interview. What better reason to give them money?

> Make checks payable to: National Public Radio
> Mail to:
> NPR-Development Office
> Attn: The Bill O'Reilly Fund
> 635 Massachusetts Avenue N.W.
> Washington, DC 20001

American Civil Liberties Union

www.aclu.org

We hear Bill doesn't care for this fine group of patriots. Check out their Web site and read about all they do.

> Make checks payable to: ACLU
> Mail to:
> ACLU
> Attn: The Bill O'Reilly Fund
> 125 Broad Street

18th Floor
New York, NY 10004

National Endowment for the Arts

arts.endow.gov

With such provocative segment titles as "Should Taxpayer Dollars Fund Offensive Art?," O'Reilly has joined the small army of conservative spinmeisters doing everything they can to gut this country's already pathetically meager federal arts funding.

Make checks payable to: National Endowment for the Arts
Mail to:
    National Endowment for the Arts
    Development Office
    Attn: The Bill O'Reilly Fund
    1100 Pennsylvania Avenue NW, Suite 525
    Washington, DC 20506

Amherst Regional High School

In 2004, Amherst Regional High School put on a production of *The Vagina Monologues*. Everyone loved it, except for Bill and one local loon. Of course, Bill trashed them. They received so much hate mail from *Factor* viewers that we thought we should try to generate for them some anti–hate mail.

Make checks payable to: Amherst Regional High School
Mail to:
    ARHS
    Attn: Aware Program
    21 Mattoon Street
    Amherst, MA 01002

Acknowledgments

▼

AL FRANKEN HAS been a great inspiration and helped introduce the world to sweetjesusihatebilloreilly.com through his show on Air America Radio. His generosity is appreciated more than he'll ever know.

Henry Quinn is a brilliant, hilarious, sharp-tongued blogger who coined the phrase "Sweet Jesus, I Hate Bill O'Reilly." Although he is currently retired from O'Reilly bashing, his daily rants were both an inspiration and a resource.

Media Matters for America. O'Reilly hates them. We love them. Their tireless efforts in documenting O'Reilly spin and lies made this book a lot more fun to research. They were an invaluable resource.

News Hounds is a small group of citizens who are the best FOX News watchdogs out there. We'll pick their brains even more for our next book.

Tim Amann was our manuscript's first critic. His notes invariably consisted of either "that's hilarious" or "make this funnier."

James Norton is editor of flakmag.com. He was an amazing sounding board in the early going, and is probably the only person who will get the Gord the Rogue reference in Chapter 4.

Jim Gilliam and Robert Greenwald of Brave New Films are the producers of the documentaries *Outfoxed* and *Wal-Mart: The High Cost of Low Price*. They were the first to lend their support and guidance into the publishing world.

Matthew Carnicelli is our extraordinary literary agent and believed in this project from the get-go. We will never be able to repay him. Well, technically we have to.

Carl Bromley at Nation Books. It's hard to imagine a better editor. When we submitted our first manuscript, it was a bit stressing waiting for feedback. We got back notes like, "As I have to tell my wife, the F-word is far more effective if you are selective in its use."

JOSEPH WOULD LIKE TO ADD:

I've learned quite a few things from my parents over the years. My father is a true conservative who taught me that the gradual erosion of our civil liberties is far more insidious than any foreign threat. My mother instilled in me the core belief that all people are equal—not just Americans, but every citizen of the world, black or white, Christian or Muslim, rich or poor. I hold no more or less value than a child in Botswana. I like it that way.

Joe Merkes has been the most kind and supportive person in my life for the past fifteen years. Without him, this book would not have happened.

Finally, and in all seriousness, I'd like to thank Eric Burns, Jim Pinkerton, Jane Hall, Neal Gabler, and, yes, Cal Thomas. I look forward to the half-hour every week that they enter my living room. Sweet Jesus, I love *FOX News Watch*. Not only is it the best show on FOX News, it's one of the best panel shows on television. Bill O'Reilly could learn a great deal from their civilized and well-informed debates. They are a joy to watch, and I recommend the show wholeheartedly.

TOM WOULD LIKE TO ADD:

I'd like to thank the entire Breuer clan, particularly my parents, two of the kindest and most intelligent people I know, who in countless ways made this book possible—except for the vulgar parts.

Many friends have contributed their support and good humor over the years, happily derailing my chosen career path of bitter seclusion highlighted by compulsive hoarding of Susan B. Anthony dollars and maundering, late-night rants directed at Jack Van Impe. In particular, I'd like to thank Daniele Burich, Colleen Walsh, and Dave Piechowski, whose emotional support and refusal to openly mock me when I told them about this project helped me immeasurably in the past year.

Finally, I'd like to thank David Horst, who inspired as well as taught and without whom I might very well have pursued a far more respectable yet far less rewarding career. In deference to Dave, I promise to not split too many more infinitives.

Index

▼